The Fate of Russia

Nicholas Berdyaev

(Kl. № 15)

Translated by Fr. S. Janos

frsj Publications

The Fate of Russia

Printed in the United States of America

Printed on acid-free paper.

For information address:

frsj Publications
Fr. Stephen J. Janos
P.O. Box 210
Mohrsville, PA 19541

Contents

IV. THE PSYCHOLOGY OF WAR
AND THE MEANING OF WAR

V. THE PSYCHOLOGY OF POLITICS
AND OF THE SOCIETAL ASPECT

****

A WORLD IMPERILED

(In Place of a Preface)

With bitter a feeling I have reread the pages of a collection of my articles, written from the time of the War up to the Revolution. GreatRussia is no longer, and there no longer stand before it the world-wide tasks, which I attempted to make sense of for myself. The War inwardly has collapsed and lost its meaning. Everything takes on completely different a measure. Those values, which I assumed in my essays, I regard inwardly correct, but already inapplicable to current events. All has been turned around in the world, and necessary still are the new reactions of a living spirit towards everything that is happening. These new reactions are needed also for the spirit, remaining true to its faith, to its ideas. It is not faith, not the idea that has changed, but rather that the world and people have changed in regard to this faith and this idea. And from this they change in their judgements about the worldly correlations. None of the purposes of the World War can be positively decided, and first of all there cannot be decided the Eastern Question. Russia's falling out of the War -- is a fateful fact for the course of the War. And the fateful meaning of this collapse I see furthermore not in this, that it tips the scale in favour of the side hostile to us. The meaning of this event lies deeper. Russia's downfall and misfortune has contributed to the military successes of Germany. But these successes are not so real, in them there is much of the illusory. German victories have not increased the German peril for the world. I am even inclined to think, that the danger of this is lessened. The military and outwardly mighty visage of Germany evokes almost pity, if one look deeper into the expression of the German face. Germany is to the point of perfection organised and disciplined, but incapable. It has exhausted and worn itself down, and it is compelled to hide its fright at its own victories. Its dominion over the enormous and mysterious chaotic element, in the past named Great Russia, cannot but frighten it. It lacks the powers to deal with the great and fallen colossus. It will have to retreat before it, having exhausted all its strength. The powers of the German people have become exhausted, all more and more, just like the powers

1

also of all the peoples of Europe. And at present the European world faces far greater dangers, than those, which I beheld in this war. The future of all the Christian culture of Old Europe is subject to the greatest of peril. If the World War continues still much longer, then all the peoples of Europe with their old cultures will be plunged into darkness and gloom. From the East, not Aryan and not Christian, comes a threat to all Europe. The results of the war will be of no use to those, who count on this. No one will be victorious. The victor will be in no condition to make use of his victory. All alike will be beaten. Soon there will be reached the point, that it will be all the same, whoever is victorious. The world is entering into such an altering of its historical existence, that these old categories will no longer still apply.

The whole time of the war I stood for the war to its victorious finish. And so the sort of sacrifice frightened me. Now however I cannot but wish, that the World War will soon be ended. I have to wish this both from the point of view for the fate of Russia, and from the point of view for the fate of all Europe. If the war is to drag on still, then Russia, having ceased to be a subject and transformed into an object, Russia, having become an arena of clashing peoples, will continue to rot, and this decay will have gone too far until the day of the finish of the war. The dark destructive powers, killing our native land, base all their hopes on this, that throughout all the world there will occur a terrible cataclysm and the foundations of Christian culture will be destroyed. These powers speculate on the outcome of the World War, and their expectations may not be so very mistaken. The whole of Europe is threatened by an inner explosion and catastrophe, similar to ours. The life of the peoples of Europe will be thrown back to the elemental level, and barbarisation threaten it. And then the chastisement will come from Asia. Upon the charred ruins of old Christian Europe, exhausted, shaken to its very foundations by its own barbaric chaotic elements, there will result the desire to occupy a governing position by a different race, foreign to us, with a different faith, with a civilisation foreign to us. In comparison with this perspective the whole World War is but a family squabble. In the results of the World War now already there profits, and really can be victorious only the Far East, Japan and China, a race not having exhausted itself, and moreover indeed the Far West, America. After the enfeeblement and disintegration of Europe and Russia there will rule Chineseism and Americanism, two powers, which can find points of proximity between them. Then will be realised a Chinese-American realm of equality, in which will be impossible still any sorts of ascent and uplift.

The Russian people did not hold up under the great trial of war. But the whole of Europe also might not hold up under this tribulation. And there then might ensue the end of Europe, not in that sense in what I wrote about it in one of the articles of this book, but in a far more terrible and exceptionally negative sense of the word. I thought, that the World War would lead the European peoples out beyond the bounds of Europe, that it would overcome the isolation of European culture and enable unification of West and East. I thought, that the world would be brought closer together by way of the terrible sacrifices and sufferings towards a resolution of the world historical problem of East and West, and that to Russia would fall the lot to have a central role in this resolution. But I did not think, that Asia could ultimately prevail over Europe, that the bringing together of East and West would instead be a victory for the Far East, and that the light of Christian Europe would be extinguished. But this at present does threaten us. The Russian people has lost the desire to fulfill its own mission in the world, it has not found within itself the strength for its fulfillment, it has committed an inner betrayal. Does this mean, that the idea of Russia and the mission of Russia, as I thought it to be in this book, has proven false? No, for I continue to think, that I have correctly understood this mission. The idea of Russia remains true, even after the people altered its idea and fell low. Russia, as a thought of God, remains great, within it is an ineradicable ontological core, but the people has made a betrayal, has been tempted by a lie. In the essays regarding the psychology of the Russian people, gathered within this book, might be found much, explaining the catastrophe that has happened in Russia. I had a feeling from the very first days of the war, that in Russia and in all of Europe they were entering into some great inevitability, into a new historical dimension. But I believed and I hoped that, in the resolution of the mysterious fates of mankind, Great Russia would assume an active and creative role. I knew, that in the Russian people and in the Russian intelligentsia were hidden principles of self-destruction. But it was difficult to admit, that these active principles should have progressed on so far. The blame lies not upon the extreme revolutionary-socialist currents alone. These currents but brought to a finish the dissolution of the Russian army and the Russian state. This dissolution was initiated already by the more moderate liberal currents. We have all set our hand to this. It was impossible but to shake loose of the historical foundations of the Russian state during the time of the terrible World War, it was impossible but to poison the armed people with the suspicion, that the authorities were betraying and treasonous to it. This was the madness, undermining the possibility of carrying on the war.

Now already a different task stands before us, and indeed before all the world. The Russian Revolution is not a phenomenon political and social, this first of all is a phenomenon of spiritual and religious an order. And it is impossible to heal and restore Russia to health by political means alone. It is necessary to resort to greater a depth. The Russian people is faced with a spiritual downturn. But the Russian people ought not to remain in the isolation, into which it is consigned by the catastrophe happening to it. Throughout all the world, throughout all Christian mankind there ought to begin the uniting of all the positive spiritual and Christian powers against the anti-Christian and destructive powers. I believe, that sooner or later there has to arise in the world a "sacred union" of all the creative Christian powers, of everything truly and eternally holy. It will begin, however, with repentance and with atonement of the sins, for which the terrible tribulations have been sent us. All camps and classes are guilty. The exclusive immersion of Europe in social questions, to be resolved by malice and hatred, is the downfall of mankind. The resolution of social questions, the surmounting of social injustice and misery, presupposes the spiritual regeneration of mankind. For an entire century the Russian intelligentsia lived by negation and it undermined the foundations of the existence of Russia. Now instead it has to turn to positive principles, to absolute sanctities, in order to regenerate Russia. But this presupposes a reworking of the Russian character. We have to adapt for ourself certain Western virtues, whilst remaining Russians. We ought to sense also in Western Europe that same universal sanctity, by which we ourself should be spiritually alive, and seek unity with it. The world is entering into a period of prolonged disconcerting and immense upheavals. But the great values have to be carried forth through all the tribulations. For this the human spirit has to be clothed in armour, has to be armed in knightly a manner.

In these articles I have lived with the war and have written of unsettling events in life. And I preserve the sequence of my vital reactions. But at present to my thoughts about the fate of Russia is added my bitter pessimism and deep grief over the rift of my native land from its past.

I. THE PSYCHOLOGY
OF THE RUSSIAN PEOPLE

The Soul of Russia[1]

I.

The world war sets in sharp relief the question concerning the Russian national self-consciousness. Russian national thought senses the need and obligation to solve the enigma of Russia, to comprehend the idea of Russia, to define its purpose and place in the world. Everyone tends to sense in the present day world, that great worldwide tasks face Russia. But this profound feeling is accompanied by a consciousness of the vagueness, almost the indefinableness of these tasks. In times past there was a presentiment, that Russia is destined for something great, that Russia -- is some special land, not like any other land in the world. Russian national thought grew up with the sense of Russian as God-chosen and God-bearing. This courses its way from the old idea of Moscow as the Third Rome, through Slavophilism -- to Dostoevsky, Vladimir Solov'ev and the contemporary Neo-Slavophils. To ideas of this sort had fastened an accretion of falsehood and lie, but there is reflected in these ideas something also genuinely of the people, something genuinely Russian. A man cannot all his life have an idea of some special and great vocation and be keenly aware of it during the periods of greatest spiritual ascent, if this man have neither the calling nor be foreordained to anything remarkable. This is biologically impossible. This is impossible likewise in the life of an entire people.

Russia has not as yet played a defining role within world life, it has not as yet genuinely entered into the life of European mankind. GreatRussia has still entirely remained an isolated province within European and world life, its spiritual life has been aloof and closed. Russia still all entirely does not know the world, it distortedly perceives its image and falsely and superficially makes judgements about it. The spiritual powers of Russia have not yet become innate to the cultural life of European mankind. For Western cultural mankind, Russia all still remains completely transcendent, some sort of an alien East, which attracts by its

---

[1] DUSHA ROSSII. Originally published separately as a pamphlet, Moscow, I. D. Sytin, 1915, 42 p. (Klepinina № 7).

mystery, whilst repelling by its barbarity. Even Tolstoy and Dostoevsky attract Western cultural man, as some sort of an exotic fare, unwontedly acute for him. The mysterious depths of the Russian East attracts to itself many in the West. But all the same there has not ensued a time with the acknowledging of the spiritual life of the Christian East on an equal par with the spiritual life of the West. In the West they have still not sensed, that the spiritual strengths of Russia can redefine and transform the spiritual life of the West, that Tolstoy and Dostoevsky can make for a change in the prevailing mindsets of the West both for the West itself and that within it. The light from the East has been seen only but by a few select individuals. The Russian state long since already is acknowledged a great power, with which all the states of the world have to reckon, and which plays a visible role in international politics. But the spiritual culture of Russia, that core of life, in regards to which the statecraft itself is but a superficial externality and implement, still does not occupy a great-power position in the world. The spirit of Russia cannot yet dictate to peoples those conditions, which Russian diplomacy can dictate. The Slavic race has not yet occupied that position, which the Latin or the German races have occupied. Here at root is what ought to change after the present day Great War, which presents a completely unprecedented inter-connection and enmeshing of Eastern and Western mankind. The great strife of the war ought to lead to a great unification of East and West. Russia occupies, certainly, a great-power position within the spiritual world concert. That which has transpired within the bosom of the Russian spirit, ceases to be something still provincial, isolated and closed-in, has become of the world and in common for mankind, not Eastern only, but Western also. And for this, long since already have ripened the potentials of the spiritual powers of Russia. The War of 1914 is more intensely and more deeply plunging Russia into the whirlwinds of world life and it melds together the European East with the European West, moreso than had the War of 1812. It is already possible to foresee, that in the results of this war Russia will ultimately become European in the same measure, in which Europe acknowledges the spiritual influence of Russia upon its own inner life. Thus strikes an hour of world history, when the Slavic race with Russia at its head will be summoned to a defining role within the life of mankind. The forefront Germanic race is exhausting itself in militaristic imperialism. Many keen people in the West have had a presentiment of the vocation of the Slavs. But the realisation of the world tasks of Russia cannot be left to the caprice of the elemental powers of history. Creative efforts are necessary in the national mindset and the national will. And if the peoples of the West be compelled, finally, to catch sight of the unique visage of Russia and admit its calling, it then remains all still unclear, how do we perceive ourself, what is Russia and to what is it called? Russia remains for us ourself an enormous mystery. Russia -- is full of contradictions, antinomies. The soul of Russia is not veiled over by any sort of doctrines. Tiutchev said for his Russia:

> Russia by mind comprehended cannot be
> Nor by wide arshins measured:
> Its uniqueness be that --
> In Russia is possible only but to believe.

And truly it can be said, that Russia is incomprehensible for the mind and immeasurable by any sort of arshins of doctrines and teachings. For each believes in Russia in his own way, and each finds in the complete contradictions of Russian life facts supporting his faith. To get at the riddle of the mystery, hidden within the soul of Russia, is possibly at the same time to admit the antinomic aspect of Russia, its keen contradictions. Therein will the Russian self-consciousness be set free from lie-ridden and false idealisations, from repulsive boasting, and equally also from the characterless cosmopolitan negativity and fawning on the foreign.

The contradictions in the Russian lifestyle have always found reflection within Russian literature and Russian philosophic thought. The creativity of the Russian spirit is twofold and the same, as in Russian historical life. This is seen clearest of all within our most characteristic national ideology -- in Slavophilism, and in our greatest national genius -- in Dostoevsky -- a Russian's Russian. Everything paradoxical and antinomic within Russian history has left its imprint upon the Slavophils and Dostoevsky. The visage of Dostoevsky is twofold and the same, as is the visage of Russia itself, and it evokes a sense of contradictions. Unfathomable depth and unbounded loftiness is combined with such degradation, ignobility, the absence of worth, slavery. The infinite love for people, in truth the love of Christ, is combined with human hatred and cruelty. The thirst for absolute freedom in Christ (Grand Inquisitor) is countered with the submissiveness of the slave. Is not Russia itself such?

Nicholas Berdyaev

Russia -- is the least statelike, the most anarchistic land in the world. And the Russian people -- is the most apolitical of peoples, never having managed to set its land right. All the genuinely Russian, our national writers, thinkers, publicists -- all were non-statists, all were uniquely anarchists. Anarchism -- is a phenomenon of the Russian spirit, and it has variously been present both in our extreme left, and in our extreme right. The Slavophils and Dostoevsky -- were anarchists essentially the same, as were Mikhail Bakunin or Kropotkin. And this anarchistic Russian nature also found itself typical expression in the religious anarchism of Lev Tolstoy. The Russian intelligentsia, though infected with a superficial positivism, has been purely Russian in its non-statism. In its best, its heroic part, it struggled for an absolute freedom and truth, unrestricted by any sort of state aspects. Our Populism -- is a characteristically Russian phenomenon, with its like unknown to Western Europe, -- the manifestation of a non-statist spirit. And the Russian liberals have always been moreso humanists, than statists. No one has wanted the power to rule, all were afraid of the power to rule, as something impure. Our Orthodox ideology concerning autocracy -- is a manifestation the same of a non-state spirit, it is a refusal of the people and society to construct a state life. The Slavophils recognised, that their teaching about autocracy was unique a form of a denial of the state. Everything about the state represents something positivistic and rationalistic. The Russian soul desires a sacred societal aspect, a God-chosen power. The nature of the Russian people conceives itself, as something ascetical, shunning earthly deeds and earthly blessings. Our leftist revolutionary currents are not so deeply different in their attitude to the state in contrast to the rightist currents and the Slavophils, -- within them is a remarkable dose of the Slavophil and ascetic spirit. Such ideologies of the state, as with Katkov or Chicherin, always have seemed non-Russian, something foreign on Russian soil, just as foreign and non-Russian always has seemed the bureaucracy, being occupied with state matters -- a non-Russian occupation. At the wellsprings of Russian history rests a remarkable legend about the summoning of the Varangian foreigners for administering the Russian Land, since "our land be great and abundant, but order in it there is not". How characteristic this is for the fateful incapacity and lack of desire of the Russian people itself to arrange order in its own land! The Russian people as it were desires not so much a free state, freedom within a state, as rather freedom from the state, freedom from concerns about worldly arrangements. The Russian people does not want to be a masculine builder, its nature defines itself as feminine, passive and submissive in matters of state, it always awaits a bridegroom, a man, a ruler. Russia -- is a land submissive and feminine. The passive, the receptive femininity in regard to the state power -- is so characteristic for both the Russian people and for Russian history.[1] There are no limits to the humble endurance of the much-suffering Russian people. The state ruling authority always was an external, and not an inward principle for the non-statist Russian people; it was not created by it, but the rather came as it were from the outside, like a bridegroom to the bride. And so often therefore the ruling power has provided the impression of being foreign, something on the order of a German domination. Russian radicals and Russian conservatives alike have thought, that the state -- is "they" and not "we". It is very characteristic, that in Russian history there was no period of knightly chivalry, there was not this masculine principle. And with this is bound up the insufficient developement of the personal principle in Russian life. The Russian people has always loved to live in the warmth of the collective, a sort of dissolving back into the element of earth, into the bosom of the mother. Knightly chivalry forges a sense of personal worth and honour, it creates the tempering of the person. This personal tempering has not been created over the span of Russian history. In Russian man there is a softness, in the Russian face there is no sharply distinct profile. Tolstoy's Platon Karataev -- is rounded in features. Russian anarchism -- is feminine, and not masculine, is passive, not active. And the rebelliousness of Bakunin is a plunging into the chaotic Russian element. The Russian non-statism -- is not a conquering of freedom for oneself, but the rather a surrendering of oneself, a freedom from activity. The Russian people desires to be of the earth, like a bride awaiting a man. All these traits of Russia were set down at the basis of the Slavophil philosophy of history and the Slavophil societal ideals. But the Slavophil philosophy of history seeks to avoid knowing the antinomic aspect of Russia, it reckons only with one thesis of Russian life. But within it also is the antithesis. And Russia would not be so mysterious, if within it were only that, about which

---

[1] This is fully confirmed also by the Russian Revolution, in which the people has remained spiritually passive and submissive to a new revolutionary tradition, but in the condition of a wicked obsession. [trans. note: footnote apparently added, when the 1915 "Soul of Russia" pamphlet was incorporated into the 1918 book, "The Fate of Russia".]

we at present have spoken. The Slavophil philosophy of Russian history does not explain the riddle of Russia's transformation into the greatest empire in the world, or it explains it too simply. And the most deeply innate sin of Slavophilism was in this, that they mistook the natural-historical features of the Russian element to be Christian virtues.

Russia -- is the most bureaucratic statelike land in the world, everything in Russia has been transformed into a tool of politics. The Russian people has created the mightiest state in the world, the largest empire. From the time of Ivan Kalita successively and persistently there have been reached dimensions, mind-boggling for all the peoples of the world. The powers of the people, about which it is not without basis to be striving towards inner spiritual life, is surrendered to the colossus of the state, transforming everything into its tool. The interests of building, supporting and guarding the state occupy a completely exceptional and stifling place within Russian history. The Russian people has almost no strength left for the free creative life, all its blood has gone for the strengthening and defense of the state. Social classes and orders are but weakly developed and have not played the role, which they have played within the history of Western lands. The person has been smothered by the vast dimensions of the state, presenting insuperable demands. The bureaucracy developed to monstrous proportions. Russian statecraft assumed a position sentry-like and of safeguarding. It came about in the struggle against the Tatar-Mongols, in the Time of Troubles, with the invasion of foreigners. But it then transformed itself into a self-sufficing abstract principle; it lives its own particular life, a law unto itself, not wanting to assume its subordinate function to the life of the people. This peculiarity of Russian history has imposed upon Russian life an imprint of joylessness and smothering. The free play of the creative powers of man has been impossible. The grip of power of the bureaucracy in Russian life was an inner assault unperceived. And somehow unperceived it entered organically into the Russian state and took hold upon the feminine and passive Russian element. The Russian land did not accept this as its own destined, it had mistaken its suitor. Great sacrifices were imposed upon the Russian people for the building up of the Russian state, much its blood was shed, but it remained itself powerless within its vast state. Imperialism is foreign to the Russian people in the Western and bourgeois sense of the world, but it submissively surrendered its powers to the building up of imperialism, in which its heart was disinterested. Herein is hidden a mystery of Russian history and the Russian soul. No sort of philosophy of history, whether Slavophil or Westerniser, has yet solved the enigma, why a most unstatelike people has created such an immense and mighty state, why so anarchistic a people is so submissive to bureaucracy, why a people free in spirit as it were does not desire a free life? This mystery is bound up with the relationship of the feminine and masculine principles in the character of the Russian people. This antinomic aspect occurs throughout all Russian life.

There is a mysterious contradiction between the relationship of Russia and the Russian awareness towards nationality. This -- is a second antinomy, no less in significance, than that of the relationship to the state. Russia -- is the most unchauvenistic land in the world. With us nationalism always produces an impression of something non-Russian, imposed, something unperceived. The Germans, the English, the French -- are chauvinists and nationalists in the masses of their people, they are filled with national self-conviction and self-smugness. Russians almost seem ashamed, that they are Russians; foreign to them is national pride and often even -- alas -- foreign is a national sense of worth. An aggressive nationalism is altogether uncharacteristic for the Russian people, any tendency towards a forceful Russification. The Russian does not shove, does not put on airs, does not despise others. In the Russian element there is something truly lacking in avarice, there is a sense of sacrifice, unknown to Western peoples. The Russian intelligentsia always reacted with disgust towards nationalism and loathed it as something impure. It confessed supra-national ideals exclusively. And howsoever superficial, howsoever banal have been the cosmopolitan doctrines of the intelligentsia, in them nonetheless though distortedly, was reflected the supra-national, the all-mankind sense of spirit of the Russian people. The intelligentsia-rebels were in a certain sense nationalists moreso, than our bourgeois nationalists, who in their expression of outlook are similar to the bourgeois nationalists of all the lands. But a man of a different and non-intelligentsia spirit -- the national genius Lev Tolstoy -- was truly Russian in his religious thirst to surmount all national boundaries, all the burden of a national flesh. And the Slavophils were not nationalists in the usual sense of the word. They wanted to believe, that in the Russian people lives an all-humanity Christian spirit, and they exalted the Russian people for its humility. Dostoevsky outright proclaimed, that Russian man -- is everyman, that the spirit of Russia -- is an universal spirit, and the mission of Russia he understood otherwise, than nationalists tend to understand it. The nationalism of the most recent forms is an indubitable Europeanisation of Russia, a conservative Westernism upon Russian soil. And Katkov, that ideologue of nationalism, was a Westerniser, he never was an expresser of the spirit of the Russian people. Katkov was an apologist and slave to a sort of foreign sense of the state, as a sort of "abstract principle". Supra-nationalism, universalism -- are uniquely innate the same to the Russian national spirit, just like is the non-statism, the anarchism. What is national namely in Russia is its supra-nationalism, its freedom from nationalism; in this is the unique essence of Russia, differing from every other land in the world. Russia is called to be a liberator of peoples. This mission is lodged within its unique spirit. And the justice for the world tasks of Russia is already presupposed by the spiritual powers of history. This mission of Russia is apparent within the present day war. Russia has no greedy aspirations.

Suchlike is one of the theses concerning Russia, which rightly might be expressed. But there is also the antithesis, which no less is without basis. Russia -- is the most nationalistic land in the world, a land of unseen excesses of nationalism, of the pressuring of subject nationalities by Russification, a land of national boasting, a land, in which everything is nationalised right up to the universal Church of Christ, a land, esteeming itself as of a singular vocation and spurning all Europe, as rot and the devil's brood, consigned to perdition. The reverse side of Russian humility manifests itself as an extraordinary Russian self-conceit. The most humble is also the greatest, the mightiest, solely called in vocation. "Russian" is also that which is right, good, true, godly. Russia -- is "Holy Rus'". Russia is sinful, but in its sinfulness it remains an holy land -- a land of saints, living by the ideals of sanctity. Vl. Solov'ev joked at the assuredness of the Russian national self-conceit in imagining this, that all the saints spoke in Russian. That selfsame Dostoevsky, who preached the everyman and appealed to an universal spirit, preached also a most fanatical nationalism, he raged against the Polish and the Jews, he denied that the West has any right to be considered a Christian world. The Russian self-conceit always finds expression in this, that Russia esteems itself not only the most Christian, but also the sole Christian land in the world. Catholicism is not acknowledged at all as Christian. And in this always has been one of the spiritual sources of a false attitude to the Polish Question. Russia, in its spirit called to be a liberator of peoples, too often has become an oppressor, and therefore it evokes towards itself hostility and suspicion, which we now have to surmount.

Russian history presents quite exceptional a spectacle -- with the quite total nationalisation of the Church of Christ, which defines itself, as universal. Churchly nationalism -- is characteristically a Russian phenomenon. Our [Old Believer] Old Ritualism is steeped in it. But the same nationalism reigns also within the ruling church. And the same nationalism pervades also the Slavophil ideology, which always has substituted the Russian for the universal. The universal spirit of Christ, the masculine universal Logos has been made captive by the feminine national element, by the Russian earth of its pagan lineage. There was thus formed a religion of dissolving away into mother-earth, into the collective national element, into the living warmth. Russian religiosity -- is a feminine religiosity -- a religiosity of collective biological warmth, experienced as a mystical warmth. Weakly developed within it is the personal religious principle; it is afraid to emerge from out of the collective warmth into the cold and fire of personal religiosity. Such a religiosity refuses the masculine and active spiritual path. This is not so much the religion of Christ, as rather the religion of the Mother of God, a religion of mother-earth, feminine divinity, a sanctification of the fleshly way of life. And V. V. Rozanov in his own manner with genius gave expression to this Russian religion of natal flesh, a religion of multiplication and comfort. Mother-earth for the Russian people is Russia. Russia is transformed into the Mother of God. Russia -- is a land God-bearing. Such a feminine, national-elemental religiosity has to impose itself upon men, who take upon themselves the burden of spiritual activity, they bear the cross, they lead spiritually. And the Russian people in its spiritual life imposes itself upon the saints, upon the startsi-elders, upon men, in regard to whom it seems proper only to bow down to, as before an icon. The Russian people does not dare even to think, that it is possible to imitate and be like the saints, that sanctity is an inward path of spirit, -- this would be as it were too masculinely bold. The Russian people wants not so much the sanctity, just like it does not want power, as rather a surrendering of itself to power, the transferring to the power of all its burdens. The Russian people in its masses is lazy in its religious ascent, its religiosity is of the plains, and not of the heights; the collective humility comes to it easier, than the religious tempering of the person, than the sacrificing of the warmth and comfort of the national-elemental lifestyle. For its humility the Russian people receives in reward this comfort and warmth of the collective life. Suchlike is the basis amongst the people for the nationalisation of the church in Russia. There is in this a tremendous admixture of religious nationalism, as it were preliminary to the Christian religion of spirit, the religion of person and freedom. Christian love itself, which is essentially spiritual and opposed to the bonds of flesh and blood, was naturalised within this religiosity, was turned into a love for "one's own sort" of man. Thus was strengthened the religion of flesh, and not of spirit, thus was safeguarded the bastions of religious materialism. Upon the boundless Russian plains are erected churches, saints and startsi-elders are acclaimed, but the soil of the plains, the steppes, is still something naturalistic, the lifestyle is still pagan.

The great deed, wrought by Vladimir Solov'ev for the Russian consciousness, mustneeds first of all be seen in his merciless criticism of churchly nationalism, in his eternal appeal for the universal spirit of Christ, for the liberation of the spirit of Christ from its captivity to the national element, the naturalistic element. Vl. Solov'ev in his reaction against churchly nationalism too readily tended towards Catholicism, but the great truth of his fundamental strivings and motives is indisputable, and yet to be acknowledged by Russia. Vl. Solov'ev is a true antidote against the nationalistic antithesis in Russian life. His Christian truth in resolution of the question of the Polish and the Jews ought always to be set in opposition to the untruth of Dostoevsky. Churchly nationalism has led to the state enslavement of the church. The Church, which is a spiritual, a mystical organism, passively has surrendered itself to synodal power on the German model. The enigmatic antinomy of Russia in regard to nationality is bound up all the same with the incorrect correlation of the masculine and the feminine principle, with a lack of developement and of the revealing of the person, born in Christ and called to be a bridegroom for his earth, to be a light-bearing man for the feminine national element, and not its slave.

The same enigmatic antinomy can be traced throughout everything in Russia. There can be established innumerable a quantity of theses and antitheses concerning the Russian national character, to uncover many a contradiction within the Russian soul. Russia -- is a land of boundless freedom of spirit, a land of wandering and search for the truth of God. Russia -- is the most non-bourgeois land in the world; there is in it not that same philistinism, which so repulses and repels Russians in the West. Dostoevsky, from whom one can learn much of the soul of Russia, in his disconcerting Legend about the Grand Inquisitor, was a proponent of so bold and boundless freedom in Christ, such as no one ever yet in the world was impelled to affirm. The affirmation of freedom of spirit, as something characteristically Russian, always was an essential trait of Slavophilism. The Slavophils and Dostoevsky always set in opposition the inward freedom of the Russian people, its organic religious freedom, which it will not give up for any worldly blessing, -- in contrast to the inward non-freedom of the Western peoples, their enslavement to the external. Within the Russian people truly there is freedom of spirit, which obtains only with one who is not absorbed in the thirst for earthly gain or worldly felicity. Russia -- is a land of essential freedom, unknown to the advanced peoples of the West, with their reinforced philistine norms. Only within Russia is there not that grip of bourgeois conventions, the despotism of the philistine family. Russian man with great ease surmounts all the bourgeois aspect, he can depart every lifestyle, can depart every normalisation of life. The wanderer type is so characteristic of Russia and is so beautiful. The wanderer -- is the most free man in the world. He walks about the world, but his element is the air, he has no roots into the earth, in him there is no earth-hold. The wanderer -- is freed of the "world" and all the burden of the world, and for him earthly life is reduced to a not-large knapsack upon the shoulders. The grandeur of the Russian people and its vocation towards an higher life is concentrated within the wanderer type. The Russian wanderer type has found its expression not only in the life of the people, but also within cultural life, within the life of the finest part of the intelligentsia. Here too we know of wanderers, free in spirit, attached to nothing, eternal pilgrims, seeking after the unseen city. The account about them can be perused in the Russian great literature. The wanderers in cultural and intelligentsia life are termed at one point vagabonds of the Russian earth, at another as rebels. They exist already in Pushkin and Lermontov, and later in Tolstoy and Dostoevsky. Spiritual wanderers they are, all these Raskol'nikovs, Myshkins, Stavrogins, Versilovs and Prince Andrei and P'er Bezukov. The wanderers have not their own city, they seek the city to come. Vl. Solov'ev always sensed himself not an inhabitant and citizen of this world, but only a stranger and wanderer, not having his own home. Thus also was Skovoroda -- a wandering seer from among the people in the XVIII Century. The spiritual wandering and restlessness is there in Lermontov, in Gogol, it is there in L. Tolstoy and Dostoevsky, and on the other side -- it is there in the Russian anarchists and revolutionaries, aspiring variously towards the absolute, going out beyond the borders of all the positive and visible life. The same thing is there also in Russian sectarianism, in the mystical thirst of the people, in that ecstasy of desire, in order that "the Spirit should glow". Russia -- is a fantastic land of spiritual intoxication, a land of the Klysty, of the self-immolators, of the Dubokhors, the land of Kondratii Selivanov and Grigorii Rasputin, the land of pretenders and Pugachevism. The Russian soul sits not in one spot, this is no small-place soul, no locale-bounded soul. In Russia, in the soul of the people there is a sort of endless searching, a searching for the invisible city of Kitezh, an home unseen. Distances open up before the Russian soul, and no traces of an horizon are there before its spiritual eyes. The Russian soul is ablaze in its fiery search for truth, for the absolute and Divine truth and for the salvation of all the world and the universal resurrection unto new life. It grieves eternally over the sorrow and suffering of the people and all the world, and its torment knows no solace. This soul is absorbed in finding resolution to the ultimate and accursedly difficult questions concerning the meaning of life. There is a rebellious and unsubmissive aspect within the Russian soul, not to be appeased nor satisfied by anything temporal, relative or conditional. All farther and farther along it has to go, to the very end, to the limit, to the exit point from "this world", from this earth, from everything merely local, narrow, attached to it. More than once already it has been demonstrated, that Russian atheism is itself religious. The heroically disposed intelligentsia has gone to death in the name of materialistic ideas. This strange contradiction becomes conceivable, if one sees, that beneathe the materialistic trappings it aspires towards the absolute. The Slavic revolt -- is something fiery, a fiery element, unknown to other races. And Bakunin in his fiery thirst for a world conflagration, in which everything old would be burnt up, was a Russian, a Slav, messianic. Suchlike is one of the theses concerning the soul of Russia. The life of the Russian people with its mystical sects, and Russian literature, and Russian thought, and the sad lot of Russian writers, and the lot of the Russian intelligentsia, torn off from the soil and at the same time so characteristically national, all this, all this gives us the right to assert this thesis, that Russia -- is a land of endless freedom and of spiritual distances, a land of wanderers, solitaries and seekers, a land rebellious and harsh in its elementalness, in its Dionysianism amongst the people, with no wish to know forms.

And here also is an antithesis. Russia -- is a land of unprecedented servility and horrid abasement, a land, lacking in the awareness of the rights of the person and not defending the dignity of the person, a land of inert conservatism, of the enslavement of religious life by the state, a land of strong manners and hard on the flesh. Russia -- is a land of merchants, immersed in fleshly burdens, acquisitive, conservative to the point of immobility, a land officials, forever transgressing the bounds of their reclusive and morbid bureaucratic kingdom, a land of peasants, wanting nothing more than the land, and having assimilated Christianity in a totally external and avaricious manner, a land of clergy, immersed in a material lifestyle, a land of ritualism, a land of the intelligentsia, inert and conservative in its thought, and infected with the most superficial of materialist ideas. Russia does not love beauty, it fears beauty, as a splendour, it wants no sort of a plenteous abundance. It is almost impossible to move Russia along from a spot, since it is so ponderous, so inert, so lackadaisical, so immersed in the material, so submissively reconciled with its life. All our societal classes, all our segments of the soil: nobility, merchants, peasants, clergy, officialdom, -- all neither want nor do they love ascent; all prefer to remain in the lowlands, the flat-lands, to be "like everything". The person everywhere is subjected to the organic collective. Our landed strata are bereft of the sense of rights and even of dignity, they want no self-initiative or activity, and they always trust that others after them will do the same. And our political revolutionism is just as lacking in freedom, a sterile and inert thought. The Russian radical-democratic intelligentsia, as a crystalised stratum, is spiritually conservative and alien to true freedom; it would sooner deal with ideas of a mechanical equality, than those of freedom. To some it would seem, that Russia is doomed to slavery and that there is no way out for it into free life. It is possible to suppose, that the person has been asleep still, not only in the conservative Russia, but also in the revolutionary Russia, that Russia remains still a land of the impersonal collective. But it mustneeds be understood, that the age-old Russian collectivism is but a passing phenomenon of a primitive stage of natural evolution, and not an eternal manifestation of spirit.

How does one make sense of this enigmatic contradiction with Russia, this alike veracity of mutually-exclusive theses concerning it? Here also, just like everywhere, with the question about the freedom and slavery of the soul of Russia, about its wanderlust and its immobility, we come up against the secret correlation of the masculine and the feminine. The root of these deep contradictions -- is in the disunitedness of the masculine and the feminine within the Russian soul and the Russian character. The unbounded freedom is countermanded by a boundless slavery, the eternal wont for wandering -- by an eternal stagnancy, and therefore the masculine freedom does not imbue the feminine national element in Russia from within, from the depths. The masculine principle is always awaited from the outside, the personal principle does not reveal itself within the Russian people. Hence the eternal dependence upon the foreigner. In philosophic terms this signifies, that Russia always senses the masculine principle for itself as something transcendent, and not immanent, something incidental from the outside. With this is connected the fact, that everything masculine, liberating and formative in Russia has been as it were not Russian, foreign, Western European, French or German, of Greek in the past. Russia on its own is incapable as it were to form itself into a free lifestyle, incapable to form of itself the person. The turning towards its own soil, towards its own national element in Russia so readily assumes a character of enslavement, leads to immobility, turns into reaction. Russia is like an eligible girl, awaiting a bridegroom, who ought to scale whatever the heights, but there arrives not the intended, instead only a German official to dominate her. And in the life of spirit they do dominate her: now Marx, now Kant, now Steiner, now some other foreigner of a man. Russia, so unique, a land of so extraordinary a spirit, has found itself constantly in a relation of servitude to Western Europe. It has not learned from Europe, what is needful and good, has not partaken of European culture what might prove salvific for it, but like a slave it has been made subject to the West or else in a wild nationalistic reaction it has threatened the West, threatening the culture. The god Apollo, the god of masculine form, has nowise alighted into Dionysiac Russia. Russian Dionysianism -- is barbaric, and not Hellenic. And though in other lands there might be found all the contradictoriness, but it is only in Russia that the thesis is countermanded by the antithesis, the bureaucratic state is begotten of anarchism, servility is begotten of freedom, extreme nationalism from supra-nationalism. From this vicious circle there is only one exit: the revealing within Russia itself, in its spiritual depths of a masculine, personal, formative principle, mastering its own national element, the immanent awakening of a masculine and light-bearing consciousness. And I want to believe, that the present-day world war will lead Russia out of this vicious circle, will awaken in it the masculine spirit, will show the world the manly face of Russia, will establish the inwardly needed correlation of the European East and the European West.

II.

There has broken out now, finally, the long anticipated world struggle of the Slavic and the German races. Germanism long since already has penetrated into the bosom of Russia, imperceptibly it has Germanised the Russian state and Russian culture, it has governed the body and the soul of Russia. And now the Germanism comes out into the open in war against the Slavic world. The Germanic race -- is masculine, self-assuredly and narrowly masculine. The Germanic world tends to sense the femininity of the Slavic race and it thinks, that it has to dominate this race and its lands, that it only has the power to render this land cultural. Germanism long since already has sent out its match-makers, it had its agents and it sensed Russia as predestined for it. The whole Peterburg period of Russian history stood beneathe the standard of the inward and outward influence of the Germans. The Russian people was almost prepared to become reconciled to this, that only the Germans could govern and civilise it. And it took quite exceptional a world catastrophe, it took the demented acts of Germanism with its pride and self-conceit, wherein Russia should become conscious of itself, should shake off from itself its passivity, should rouse in itself its masculine powers and sense itself called to great deeds in the world. In the world struggle against the Germanic race it is impossible to oppose it with only femininity and the submissiveness of the Slavs. It is necessary to reveal a manly face against the threat of being swallowed up by Germanism. The war of the Slavic world with the Germanic world is not only the clash of armed forces upon the fields of battle; it goes deeper, this -- is a spiritual war, a struggle for the dominance of a different spirit in the world, the clash and the interweaving of the Eastern and the Western Christian world. In this great, truly worldwide struggle Russia cannot but become conscious of itself. But its self-consciousness ought also to be its self-purgation. Self-consciousness presupposes self-criticism and self-accusation. Boasting has never come about through self-consciousness, it comes about through a full obscuring of it. A brilliant example of the full loss of true self-consciousness and full darkness through boasting and self-conceit is Germany at present. The masculine, the light-bearing consciousness of a people -- always involves criticism, always is liberative from its own darkness and enslavement, always is a mastering of the chaotic elements within it. And the self-consciousness of Russia ought first of all to be liberative from the domination and enslavement of its own national element. And this means, that the Russian people as regards its own Russian earth ought to be manly and light-bearing, ought to rule its earth and give form to its chaotic elements, and not be enslaved by it, not passively surrender itself to it. This means likewise, that man is called to govern over nature, and not nature over man. Russia has lived too natural, too insufficiently human a life, too racial and insufficiently personal a life. The personal human principle has not all still gained mastery over the impersonal natural elements of the earth. Russia has experienced this its age-old natal biology as being its age-old collective mysticism, and in the person of some of its ideologues it has seen this to be its superiority over Western Europe. Russia in the masses of its people has confessed a religion of natal flesh, and not a religion of spirit, it has confused a natal and natural collectivism with a collectivism that is spiritual and super-natural. But as a mysterious land of contradictions, Russia has concealed within itself a prophetic spirit and the presentiments of new life and new revelations.

In this decisive hour for the Russian consciousness it is necessary clearly and bravely to be aware of the dangers facing us. The war can bring Russia great good, not material only, but also spiritual good. It awakens a deep sense of the people and of national unity, it surmounts the inner discord and hostility, the petty connivings of parties, it manifests the face of Russia and forges a masculine spirit. The war exposes the falsities of life, snatches away the veils, disdains the false sanctities. It -- is a great enabling for opportunity. But it bears also danger with it. Russia can fall to the level of a false nationalism and a truly German-like chauvinism. It can get caught up with ideals of a world domination non-Russian in spirit, and alien to the Slavic race. The war bears with it a danger of callousness. And Russia ought most of all be free of hatred towards Germany, from the slave-like feelings of malice and revenge, from that denial of value in the spiritual culture of the enemy, which as such would be merely another form of slavery. One would want to believe, that all this will not be so, but it would be a bad thing to shut one's eyes to the possibility. In the Russian national element there is a sort of eternal danger of winding up in captivity, of being submissive to that external to it. And a true renewal of Russia can only be in a radical liberation from every captivity, from every stranglehold and enslavement to the external, the outside, the foreign, i.e. the revealing within of an inner manliness, an inner light, a spirit self-governing and creative. The war ought to free us, as Russians, from the servile and submissive attitude towards Germany, from the unhealthy and over-strained attitude towards Western Europe, as towards something remote and external, at times the object of passionate love and dreams, and at other times of tremendous hate and fear. Western Europe and Western culture should become immanent for Russia; Russia should become ultimately European, and it is namely then that it will become spiritually unique and spiritually independent. Europe is ceasing to hold a monopoly on culture. The world war, in the bloody cycle of which there has been dragged in already every part of the orb and every race, in its bloody torments has to give birth to a firm awareness of the oneness of all mankind. Culture ceases to become something exclusively European and becomes instead world-wide and universal in scope. And Russia, occupying a place in the middle betwixt East and West, is called to play a great role in the leading of mankind towards unity. The world war brings us critically to the problem of Russian messianism.

The messianic consciousness is not a nationalistic consciousness; it is profoundly contrary to nationalism; this -- is universal a consciousness. The messianic consciousness has its roots in the religious consciousness of the Hebrew people, in the experiencing by Israel of its God-chosenness and uniqueness. The messianic consciousness is the consciousness of a chosen people of God, a people, in which would appear the Messiah and through which the world would be saved. A God-chosen people -- is as a messiah amongst the peoples, the sole nation with a messianic consciousness and destiny. All the other nations -- are lower nations, not chosen ones, nations with an ordinary and non-mystical a fate. All the nations have their own vocation, their own destiny in the world, but only one nation can be the chosen one for messianic aims. The people of a messianic consciousness and destiny are likewise but one, just as there is one Messiah. The messianic consciousness -- is world-wide in scope and supra-national. In this there is an analogy with the idea of the Roman empire, which likewise is universal and supra-national, just as is the ancient Hebrew messianism. This messianic consciousness of the Jews, encompassing all the world in its scope, had justification in this, that the Messiah had appeared in the bosom of this people, and was spurned by them. But after the appearance of Christ, messianism in the ancient Hebrew sense was already become impossible for the Christian world. For the Christian there is neither Greek nor Jew. In the Christian world there is no solely-select nation of God. Christ came for all peoples, and every people, in the face of the Christian consciousness, has its own destiny and its own allotted fate. Christianity does not permit of a national exclusiveness nor national pride, it condemns any such consciousness, whereby my nation should be above all nations and the solely religious nation. Christianity is an ultimate affirmation of the oneness of mankind, a spirit encompassing all humanity and all the world. And this was fully conceived of by Catholicism, although tied in with relativistic historical-body aspects (papism). The messianic consciousness is a consciousness prophetic, and the messianic self-awareness -- is a prophetic self-awareness. In it -- is the salt of religious life, and this salt has been received from the Hebrew people. This prophetic messianic consciousness does not vanish away in the Christian world, but the rather is transmuted and transformed. And within the Christian world there is possible a prophetic messianism, the consciousness of an exceptional religious calling of some particular nation, a faith is possible, that through this nation will be told the world the words of a new revelation. But the Christian messianism has to be cleansed of everything not Christian, deriving from national pride and self-conceit, from reducing it back onto the path of the old Hebrew messianism, on the one hand, or a new exclusionary nationalism -- on the other hand. The Christian messianic consciousness cannot be an assertion, that only alone does the Russian people possess a great religious calling, that it alone -- is a Christian nation, that it alone is chosen for a Christian destiny and a Christian allotted fate, and that all the other remaining nations -- are lower, non-Christian and bereft of religious vocation. Within such a conceit there is nothing Christian. There was nothing Christian in the endless refrain of the Slavophils about the rottenness of the West and the absence within it of a Christian life. Such a Judaisation of Christianity turns us back from the New Testament towards the Old Testament. Judaism within Christianity is a potentially entrapping danger, from which it is needful to stay clear of. And every exclusionary religious nationalism, every religio-national conceit is a Judaism within Christianity. The extreme nationalising of church is also a Judaism within Christianity. And in Russian Christianity there is much of the Judaistic element, much that is Old Testament in character.

THE FATE OF RUSSIA

The Christian messianic consciousness can only be a consciousness whereby that in the ensuing world epoch, Russia is called to says its own word to the world, just as the Latin world and the Germanic world have said it. The Slavic race, at the head of which stands Russia, ought to reveal its spiritual potential, to manifest its prophetic spirit. The Slavic race has to go as replacement for other races, already having played their role, already tending towards a decline; this -- is a future-looking race. All the great nations pass through a messianic consciousness. This coincides with periods of especial spiritual uplift, when by the fates of history a given people is called to accomplish something great and new for the world. Such a messianic consciousness was there in Germany at the beginning of the XIX Century. But now we see an end of German messianism, the complete vanishing of its spiritual powers. Within Christian history there is no one chosen nation of God, but rather various nations at various times are chosen for a great mission, for a revealing of spirit. Long since already in Russia has been born the prophetic feeling, that there has begun the hour of history, when it would be called for great revelations of spirit, when the centre of world spiritual life would be within it. This is not a Jewish messianism. Such a prophetic feeling does not exclude a great chosenness and destiny of other peoples; it is but a continuation and advancement of deeds, wrought by all the peoples of the Christian world. This Russian messianic consciousness was muddled and held captive by the pagan national element and distorted by survivals of the Judaistic consciousness. The Russian consciousness has to be cleansed and set free from this pagan and Judaistic captivity. And this means, that Russian thought and Russian life ought to he radically freed from the morbid and mortifying sides of Slavophilism, not only the official, but also the national. Within Slavophilism there was its own truth, which always was good to set in contrast to Westernism. It sought to preserve. But there was many a falsehood and lie, much slavery within the material lifestyle, many "lofty deceits" and idealisations, impeding the life of spirit.

Russia cannot define itself, as East, and thus oppose itself to the West. Russia ought to conceive of itself as also West, as an East-West, an uniter of the two worlds, and not a divider. Vladimir Solov'ev broke spiritually with the old Slavophilism, with its false nationalism and its exclusionary Easternism. And after the action of Vl. Solov'ev, Christian universalism had ultimately to be regarded as confirmed within the consciousness. Every particularism essentially is not of a Christian nature.

The exclusive dominance of the Eastern element in Russia was always a slavery of the feminine natural principle and it ended in a realm of chaos, now reactionary, now revolutionary. Russia, as a self-declared East, Russia nationally self-sufficing and exclusive -- signifies a non-openness, signifies a non-revealedness of the masculine principle, the human and personal slavery of a principle naturo-elemental, of a national affinity and traditional lifestyle. Within the religious consciousness this signifies the absolutisation and apotheosis of the corporeal-relative, a contentedness with the animal-like warmth of the national flesh. Within this -- is an eternal temptation and great danger for Russia. The feminine aspect of the Slavs makes them mystically sensitive, capable of hearkening to the inner voices. But the exceptional dominance by the feminine element hinders them from fulfilling their calling in the world. Russian messianism has need of a masculine spirit, without which ever again and again there will be a stumbling back into this alluring and constraining primordial element of the Russian earth, which awaits its own enlightenment and form. But the end of Slavophilism is likewise an end also of the Westernism, the end of the very opposition of East and West. In the Westernism too there was particularism and provincialism, there was not an universal spirit. Westernism signified a sort of unhealthy and unmanly attitude towards the West, a particular lack of freedom and powerlessness to sense of Russia itself as an effective power. The Russian self-awareness cannot be that of either the Slavophils, or of the Westernisers, since both these forms signify an immaturity of the Russian people, its lack of maturity for world life, for a world role. In the West there cannot be a Westernism, this visionary dream about the West there is impossible, since it is about some higher condition. The higher condition is not the West, just as it is also not the East; it is nothing geographically or materially delimited. The world war should overcome Russia's existence of being exclusively the East, and Europe too, as exclusively the West. Mankind will emerge beyond these boundaries. Russia will emerge into world life a determining power. But the world role of Russia presupposes a conviction, of the creative activeness of man within it, and an escape from the condition of passivity and dissolution. Already within Dostoevsky, eternally twofold, there is a prophecy about a revelation of man, about an exceptionally acute anthropological awareness. The true Russian messianism presupposes the liberation of religious life, of the life of the spirit from the exclusive attachment to natural and state principles, from every fettering down to the material lifestyle. Russia has to pass through a religious emancipation of the person. Russian messianism is grounded first of all upon the Russian wont for wandering, the roaming and searching, upon the Russian rebelliousness and unappeased spirit, upon the prophetic Russia, upon Russians -- not having their own city, and seeking after the city to come. Russian messianism cannot be connected with the Russia of its lifestyle, inertly-stagnant, the Russia, heavy laden with its natural flesh, with Russia, merely guarding a ritual-belief, with Russians -- satisfied with their city, a pagan city, and fearful of the city to come.

Everything uniquely original in the Slavic and Russian mysticism -- is in the search for the city of God, the city to come, in the awaiting of the descent to earth of the Heavenly Jerusalem, in the thirst for universal salvation and universal good, in an apocalyptic disposition. These apocalyptic, prophetic expectations stand in contrast to that feeling, that the Russians already have their own city and that this city -- is "Holy Rus'". Upon this lifestyle of a contented feeling was based Slavophilism to a remarkable degree, and upon it is based all our rightist religio-national ideology. The religion of the sacred -- is a guarding of that which is, and in the spirit of Russia it clashes with the religion of prophecy, -- the exaction of the rightfulness to come. Here is one of the innate contradictions of Russia. And if there might be much to adduce in defense of this thesis, that Russia -- is a land of the guarding of its holy things primarily and that in this be its religious mission, then no less can there be adduced the defense of this antithesis, that Russia primarily is a land of religious craving, of spiritual thirst, of prophetic presentiments and expectations. In the figure of Dostoevsky was embodied this religious antinomy of Russia. He had two faces: the one oriented towards the guarding, towards attachment to the national religious lifestyle, of being caught up in the genuine lifestyle, -- an image of spiritual repleteness, and the other face -- prophetic, oriented towards the city to come, -- an image of spiritual hunger. The contradiction and the conflict between spiritual satiety and spiritual hunger -- is fundamental for Russia, and from it can be explained many an other contradiction of Russia. Spiritual satiety provides for the passive surrender of oneself to the feminine national element. This is not still a being full with the food of God, this is all but a natural being full. Spiritual hunger, unsatisfied by the nationalistic national fare, is a sign of the liberation of the masculine principle of the person. The same contradiction, which we see in the national genius of Dostoevsky, we see also in Russian popular life, in which always there are two faces seen. The spiritual satiety, the safe-guarding of the old, the lifestyle and the external-ritualistic understanding of Christianity, -- is one image of the religious life of the people. The spiritual hunger, prophetic presentiments, mystical absorption at the summits of Orthodoxy among some sides of our sectarianism and schismatics, in the wont for wandering -- is another image of the religious life of the people. The Russian mysticism, the Russian messianism is connected with the second image of Russia, with its spiritual hunger and thirst for God's truth on earth, just as in Heaven. An apocalyptic mindset profoundly distinguishes Russian mysticism from the German mysticism, which is but an immersion into the depths of the spirit and which never was a striving towards the city of God, towards the end-time, towards the transfiguration of the world. But the Russian apocalyptic mindset has a strong tendency towards passivity, towards waiting it out, towards femininity. In this is expressed a characteristic trait of the Russian spirit. The prophetic Russian soul senses itself pervaded by mystical currents. In the life of the people this assumes the form of a fear of the Anti-Christ. In recent times these authentic religious experiences of the people have penetrated into our cultural religio-philosophic currents, though but in a mirrored and too stylised, artificial form. There was even formed an aesthetic cult of religious frights and terrors, as a true sign of a mystical disposition. And in this again there is no masculine, active and creative spirit, which Russia has need of most of all for the fulfillment of the world tasks, to which it is called. The prophetic Russia has to pass over from expectation to creation, from acute terror over to spiritual boldness. It is all too clear, that Russia is not called to felicity, to bodily and spiritual well-being, to attachment to the old flesh of the world. Within it there is no gift for the building of an average culture, and in this it is deeply distinct from the lands of the West, it is distinct not only in its backwardness, but also by its spirit.

Herein is a mystery of the Russian spirit. This spirit tends to strive towards the final and ultimate, towards the absolute in everything; towards absolute freedom and absolute love. But within the naturo-historical process reigns the relative and the average. And therefore the Russian thirst for absolute freedom in practice too often leads to slavery in matters relative and average, and the Russian thirst for absolute love -- to hostility and hate.[1] Characteristic to Russians is some lack of ability, lack of talent in all matters relative and ordinary. And the history of culture and the social is indeed all involved with the ordinary and the relative; it is neither absolute nor final. Since the Kingdom of God is a kingdom absolute and final, Russians then tend to yield away everything relative and ordinary over into the domain of the kingdom of the devil. This is a feature very nationally Russian. To gain oneself relative societal freedom is difficult for Russians not only because, that in the Russian nature is passivity and oppression, but also because, that the Russian spirit thirsts for God's absolute freedom. Therefore it is difficult for Russians to construct a relative culture, which always is a matter preliminary, but not final. Russians constantly find themselves in slavery regarding matters of the ordinary and the relative, and they justify this by that in matters of the ultimate and absolute they are free. Herein lies concealed one of the deepest motifs of Slavophilism. The Slavophils wanted to leave to the Russian people the religious freedom of conscience, the freedom of thought, the freedom of spirit, and yield all the rest of life over to the ruling powers, unlimitedly governing the Russian people. Dostoevsky in his legend about the "Grand Inquisitor" proclaimed an unprecedented freedom of spirit, an absolute religious freedom in Christ. And Dostoevsky was ready indeed not only submissively to be reconciled, but even to defend the social slavery. And even otherwise, the same Russian feature was expressed also in our revolutionary-maximalists, demanding the absolute in everything of the relative societal aspect and yet incapable of creating a free sociability. Here we approach from a new side the basic contradictions of Russia. All this devolves into the same exposure of the masculine and feminine principles in the bosom of the Russian element and the Russian spirit. The Russian spirit, striving for the absolute in everything, is lacking of a masculine mastery within the sphere of the relative and the middle, it yields to the power of external forces. And thus in the average culture it is always ready to yield to the power of Germanism, to German philosophy and science. It is the same also in matters of statecraft, essentially in matters relative and average. The Russian spirit desires a sacred state in the absolute and it is ready to reconcile itself with a beastly state in the relative. It desires holiness in life absolute, and only holiness captivates it,

---

[1] The Russian Revolution has graphically demonstrated the whole danger of Russian absoluteness.

29

but all the same it is ready to reconcile itself with filth and the cringing in life relative. And therefore Holy Rus' always had as its reverse side the beastly Rus'. Russia as it were has always only desired either the angelic or the beastly, and has insufficiently revealed within itself the human. Angelic holiness and beastly lowliness -- here are the eternal swayings of the Russian people, unknown to the more average Western peoples. Russian man is enraptured of holiness, and he is enraptured also by sin, by lowliness. Humble sinfulness, not daring to raise oneself too far, is so characteristic of the Russian religiosity. In this is the sense of rapture from being immersed in the warm national flesh, in the lower earthly element. And thus even the prophetic and the messianic itself in the Russian spirit, the thirst for transfiguration, transforms itself into a sort of slavery. I have attempted to characterise all the contradictions of Russia and find in them the points of unity. This is a path towards self-consciousness, towards the awareness of what is necessary for Russia to reveal its great spiritual potentials, for the realising of its world tasks.

How ought a man to relate to his earth, Russian man to the Russian earth? Here is our problem. The image of natal earth is not only the image of mother, it is likewise -- an image of bride and wife, which man makes fruitful by his logos, his masculine and light-bearing and form-giving principle, and the image of the child. Man ought first of all to love his earth, to love it in all its contradictions, with its sins and deficiencies. Without love for his earth man remains powerless to create something, is powerless to master the earth. Without the element of earth the masculine spirit is powerless. But the love of man for the earth is not the slavery of man by the earth, it is not passive in the immersion and dissolving in its elements. The love of man for the earth ought to be masculine. Masculine love is an egress from the naturalistic dependency, from the natal immersion into the elemental primordial collectivism. In Russia everything is still too governed not only by a natural economy in its material life, but also a natural economy in its spiritual life. From this period of a natural economy the Russian people is emerging amidst torments, and this process is injurious and tormentive. Russian rebelliousness and wanderlust is connected with the sundering off from the natal naturalistic dependency, assumed as an higher condition. This sundering is not a sundering from the natal earth. And the Russian rebels and roamers remain Russians, characteristically national nonetheless. Our love for the Russian earth, with many a suffering and sacrifice, abides in all epochs, all relationships and all the ideological constructs. The soul of Russia -- is not a bourgeois soul, -- a soul, not swayed afront a dream of gold, and even for this alone one can love it endlessly. Russia is dear and beloved even in its most monstrous contradictions, in its enigmatic antinomy, in its mysterious elements. And everyone sensed this, when the war began.

But the Russian element demands the formative and light-bearing logos. The insufficiency of a masculine character and that tempering of the person, which in the West was wrought by chivalry, -- is a very dangerous insufficiency of Russians, both for the Russian people and for the Russian intelligentsia. The love itself of Russian man for his native earth has assumed a form, hindering the developement of the masculine personal spirit. In the name of this love, in the name of falling into the bosom of the mother, there has been spurned in Russia the knight-chivalrant principle. The Russian spirit was enveloped by the protecting flesh of its national mother, it fell back into the warm moist flesh. The Russian temperament, so well known to everyone, is connected with this warmth and moistness; in it there is much still of the flesh and insufficient of the spirit. But flesh and blood do not inherit eternity, and eternal only can be the spirit of Russia. The Russian spirit can only be revealed by way of manly sacrifice in life amidst the animate warmth of the collective natal flesh. The mystery of Russia can be unriddled only by its liberation from the distortive slavery of the dark elements. In the cleansing fire of the world conflagration much will be burnt, and the old material trappings of the world and man will drop away. And the rebirth of Russia therein for new life can only be bound up with manly, active and creative paths of spirit, with the revealing of Christ within man and the people, and not with the naturalistic natal element, eternally attracting and enslaving. This -- will be a victory of the fire of spirit over the moist and warm soul and flesh. In Russia by virtue of its religious character, always striving towards the absolute and the end, the human principle cannot reveal itself in the form of humanism, i.e. of the irreligious. And in the West even, humanism has vanished, has outlived itself, has gone into a crisis, from which Western mankind tormentedly seeks a way out. To but belatedly repeat the Western humanism, Russia cannot. In Russia the revelation of man can only be a religious revelation, only a revealing of the inner, and not the outer man, a revealing of Christ within. For suchlike is the absolute spirit of Russia, in which everything has to transpire from within, and not externally. Suchlike is the appeal of Slavophilism. In it one can only believe, it is impossible to prove it. The

Russian people needs foremost to appeal to a religious manliness not in war only, but also in the life of peace, where it ought to hold mastery over its earth. The masculinity of the Russian people is not something abstract, sundered off from the feminine, as it is with the Germans. There is the secret of an unique fate in this, that Russia with its ascetic soul ought to become great and mighty. Not weak and puny, but strong and great it will conquer the temptation of the kingdom of this world. Only a great and strong sacrifice, only its free annihilation in this world will save and redeem. The Russian national self-consciousness ought fully to encompass within itself this antinomy: the Russian people in its spirit and vocation is a supra-state and a supra-national people, as regards its idea neither loving the "world" nor that which is in the "world", but to it is given the mightiest national state for this, that its sacrifice and denial should be voluntary, from a position of strength, and not weakness. But the antinomy of the Russian lifestyle has to be carried over inwardly by the Russian soul, which would become masculinely sacrificial, within itself living out its own mysterious destiny. The revealing of a masculine spirit in Russia cannot be through the grafting onto it of the average Western culture. Russian culture can only be an end-point, only an emergence beyond the bounds of culture. The masculine spirit has the potential to include in Russia the prophetic, the Russian wont for wandering and the Russian search for truth. And inwardly it would unite with the feminineness of the Russian earth.

Concerning the "Eternal Baba" in the Russian Soul[1]

I.

There has appeared a book by V. V. Rozanov, "The War of 1914 and the Russian Renaissance". The book -- is brilliant and disturbing. Rozanov here is foremost a Russian stylist, a writer with genuine flashes of genius. In Rozanov there is a special and mysterious life of words, a magic word-collection, an attractive feel for words. In him there are no words that are abstract, or dead or bookish. All the words -- are alive, biological, full of blood in their veins. The reading of Rozanov -- is a sensuous delight. It is difficult to convey in one's own words the thoughts of Rozanov. For him indeed there are no sort of thoughts. Everything is locked up within the organic life of words and cannot be torn away from them. His words are not symbols of thought, but the rather flesh and blood. Rozanov -- is an extraordinary artist with the word, but in what he writes, there is no Apollonian transmutation nor giving of form. In the dazzling life of words he gives forth with the raw cheese of his soul, at random, without any processing. And he does this with a talent that is unique and unrepeatable. He scorns every "idea", every logos, every activity and resistance of the spirit in regards to the soul and the processes of life. Writing for him is a biological function of his organism. And he is never opposed to his biological processes, he puts them directly down on paper, he transfers to paper the vital currents. And Rozanov does this quite exceptionally, an unprecedented thing, which it is difficult to approach with the usual criteria. The ingenious physiology of Rozanov's writings is engendered by his lack of ideas, his lack of principles, his indifference towards good and evil, his lack of belief, by the complete absence of moral character and

---

[1] O "BECHNO BAB'EM" V RUSSKOI DUSHE. First published in the newspaper "Birzhevye vedomosti", 14-15 Jan. 1915, № 14610-14612[?]. (Klepinina № 287).

33

spiritual support. Everything written by Rozanov, a writer of rich talent and great vital significance, is a tremendous biological flooding, to which it is impossible to deal with by any sort of criteria or measures of value.

Rozanov -- is something from primordial biology, surviving as a mystic. Rozanov is not afraid of contradiction, since biology is not afraid of contradiction, indeed only logic is afraid. He is ready to deny on subsequent pages, that which he said on the preceding pages, and remains completely within the vital and not logical process. Rozanov cannot and does not want to withstand the influx and force of living impressions, of sensual feelings. He is completely lacking in any manliness of spirit, any active power of withstanding the elements blowing in the wind, any inward freedom. Every vital breath and feeling transforms him into a reservoir, receiving into him their flow, the flood of which with an extraordinary rapidity flows onto paper. Such a stock of nature compels Rozanov always to bow down before the fact, the force or history. For him even God in His might is a vital current. He could not withstand the flood of the nationalistic reaction of the decade of the 80's, he could not withstand the flood of decadence of the beginning XX Century, he could not withstand the revolutionary flood of 1905, nor then the new reactionary flood, the impetus of Anti-Semitism in the epoch of Beilis, and finally, he is unable to withstand the mighty flood of war, the hoisting of an heroic patriotism and the perilousness of chauvinism.

Many are captivated in Rozanov by that which is in his writings, in the unique life of his words there is the sense as though of Mother Nature, of Mother earth herself and her vital processes. They tend to love Rozanov because they have grown so tired of abstraction, of bookish-pedantry, of disenchantment. They sense in his books, as it were, a greater life. And they are prepared to forgive Rozanov his monstrous cynicism, his vileness as an author, his falseness and betrayal. Orthodox Christians, often very intolerant and exclusionary, have forgiven Rozanov everything, they have forgotten, how for many years he blasphemed Christ, how he scoffed at and suggested a turning away from Christian sanctity. Yet all the same Rozanov is his own man, kindred and close to the biological, an uncle of sorts, elated with the Orthodox lifestyle.

Essentially, he has always loved an Orthodoxy without Christ and has always remained faithful to such a pagan Orthodoxy, which indeed is much dearer and closer, than the austhere and tragic spirit of Christ. In Rozanov there is so much that is characteristically Russian, truly Russian.

He -- is an ingenious expression of a certain side of the Russian nature, of the Russian element. He is possible only in Russia. He was begotten in the imagination of Dostoevsky and even surpassed through his improbability everything, that this ingenious imagination had to offer. And indeed the imagination of Dostoevsky was purely Russian, and down to the very depths the Russian was begotten. And if it be pleasing to have a writer, so ultimately Russian, and if it be instructive to see in him the revealing of the Russian element, then also it becomes frightful for Russia, it becomes terrible for the fate of Russia. In the very innards of the Russian character there is discovered the "eternal baba", not the "eternal feminine", but rather the eternal baba. Rozanov -- is himself an ingenious Russian baba, a mystical baba. And this "baba" is to be sensed also in Russia itself.

II.

The book of Rozanov concerning the war finishes with a description of the flood of feelings, which gushes forth within him, when at one time he went along the street of Petrograd and encountered a regiment of cavalry. "I all atremble gazed at this endlessly moving column of imposing horsemen, of which was so huge compared with me!... The slightest wrong move -- and I would be done for... A sense of depression more and more came upon me. I sensed myself in the grip of a strange power, -- by this hugeness, that my "I" was as it were carried off as a speck into the whirlwind of this hugeness and this multitude... when I suddenly began to sense, that not only "I was afraid", but also -- I was fascinated by it, -- I was overcome by a strange enchantment, -- which only this one time -- this one here -- that I had experienced it in life. A strange thing happened: the overwhelming masculinity of that which was in front of me, -- it as it were transformed the structure of my makeup and flung it back, it turned this makeup upside down -- into the feminine. I sensed an extraordinary tenderness, an exhaustion and drowsiness throughout all my being... My heart raced within me -- with love... I wished as though, that they should be all the more huge, that they should be all the more... This colossus of physiology, this colossus of life ought also to be a source of life -- it evoked in me a purely feminine feeling of lack of will-power, of submissiveness and the insatiable wish "to stay near", to see, to not lower the eyes... Definitely, this was the start of a girlish infatuation" (p. 230-232). And Rozanov exclaims: "Strength -- here is the one beauty in the world... Strength -- it subdues, before it they fall down, indeed ultimately, -- they implore... The altogether "weak" -- "we" implore, here "I" am on the pavement... In strength lies the mystery of the world... Huge, strong... My head was clear, but my heart was churning... like a woman's. The point of the army, is that it transforms us all into trembling women, taking in the air..." (p. 233-234). This remarkable description gives the feel of touching upon, if not for "the mystery of the world and history", as Rozanov makes pretense, then rather for a particular mystery of Russian history and the Russian soul. The feminineness of Rozanov, so artistically rendered, is likewise a feminineness of the soul of the Russian nation. The history of the formation of the Russian state, the most immense state in the world, so inconceivable in contrast to the life of the stateless Russian people, can be derived from this mystery. The Russian people has a stately gift for submissiveness, of the humbling of the person before the collective. The Russian people does not sense itself a man, it is all ready to be a bride, it senses itself a woman afront the colossus of the state, "strength" makes it submissive, it senses itself in Rozanov's "I am down upon the pavement" at the moment of the passing of the cavalry. Rozanov himself through the extent of the whole book stays with this trembling "I am down on the pavement". For Rozanov not only the point of the army, but also the point of the state power is in this, that it "transforms us all into women, weak, trembling, taking in the air...". And he wants to show, that the whole of the Russian people is thus in relation to the state might. In the book of Rozanov there are astonishing and contrived pages with an unprecedented apology for the selfly smug power of the state might, transformed into a genuine idolatry. Such a worship of state power, as a mystical fact of history, there has not been yet in Russian literature. And herein is hidden a very interesting coinciding of Rozanov with the Slavophils.

III.

The book of Rozanov witnesses to a rebirth of Slavophilism. It shows, that Slavophilism has engendered the war, and in this -- is the basic meaning of the war. Rozanov decisively hails forth for Slavophilism. And he himself repeats timeworn Slavophil matters, long already since repudiated not by the "Westerniser" thought, but instead by the thought continuing amongst Slavophils. After Vl. Solovi'ev there can be no longer a return to the old Slavophilism. But even moreso than the thought itself, it is the Slavophilic turning back with life that has been repudiated. For Rozanov it would seem, that it is a patriotic and national issue calling for war, and as such it is a revival of Slavophilism. I think however, that the historical present day topples over both the Slavophil as well as the Westerniser platforms, and it obliges us to the creativity of a new self-consciousness and a new life. And it is vexing to see, that we are instead looking backwards, looking back to outlived forms of consciousness and life. The world war, ultimately, leads to a surmounting of the old settings of the question concerning Russia and Europe, about the East and the West. It puts an end to the inward split between the Slavophils and the Westernisers, annulling both Slavophilism and Westernism as being both but provincial ideologies, set within limited horizons.

Is it indeed possible that world events, unprecedented in world history, can teach us nothing, can fail to lead us to the birth of a new consciousness, and instead leave us set still within the old categories, those from which we wanted to tear away before the war? A Russian rebirth cannot be a rebirth of Slavophilism, it will be an end both to the old Slavophilism, and to the old Westernism, it will be the beginning of a new life and a new consciousness. For Rozanov, however, the war has inspired but the thousand times repeated old words, now having become stale and tasteless: "the whole of Russian history is tranquil, unstormy; the whole Russian condition -- is peaceful, unstormy. The Russian people -- are tranquil. In good circumstances and a favourable setting they invariably mature into friendly and courteous, good people. The Russian people -- are indeed "dandy" (p. 51). But on no less grounds it would be possible to affirm, that the Russian soul -- is rebellious, searching, a soul wandering, wanting the New City, never satisfied with anything half-fast or relative. From this famed and often falsely resounding "tranquility, unstorminess and dandiness" is begotten the inertia, which is dear to the eternal-baba heart of Rozanov, and never does it beget a new and better life. In Rozanov's verses there is that eternal pitfall, that eternal temptation of the Russian people, that source of its inability to become a people manly and free, mature for its independent life in the world. And it is terrible, that not only Rozanov, but others also, called to be expressers of our national consciousness, should pull us backwards and inwards, that they should surrender us over to the temptation of passivity, of submissiveness, of slavery to our national element, with a womanish religiosity. S. Bulgakov, V. Ivanov, V. Ern want to revive not only the eternal, but also the too temporal, the old and the outmoded in Slavophilism. And thus with its tremendous power, with the power of the national element, of the earth, there ought not to stand forth the manly, the light-bearing and steadfast spirit, which is called to mastery by the elements. Herein is begotten the pitfall of chauvinism, of outward bragging and the inner slave's humility. And as for the world inside Russia, Rozanov namely and those like him make impossible the overcoming of hostility and malice. These people have a strange understanding of the mutual reconciliation and re-unification of hostile parties and currents, they tend to understand it thus, as the Catholics understand the re-unification of the Church, i.e. as exclusively an annexation to the one side, to which is imputed all the fullness of the truth. This old method does not heal the historical split between the "right" and the "left" camps. Repentance ought to be mutual, and the amnesty ought to be mutual, the accord on the self-delimitations and yielding ought to be mutual. They believe both, that the war will lead up to this, but not this, that our nationalist ideologies hinder this. Rozanov's mindset serves the cause of harm, and not peace.

Having started with a toast to the health of the Slavophils, Rozanov finishes it off with another for their demise. He betrays a decided preference for the official and state Russia in place of a Russia populist and social, for the official Slavophilism over the social Slavophilism. The Slavophils considered the Russian people -- to be a non-statist people, and they built upon this quite much. Rozanov, on the contrary, considers the Russian people to be a statist people, predominantly so. In the statist outlook of Rozanov, which for him is something quite unexpected, since in him statism and citizenship were in quite low regard, -- he indeed was always a singer of the praises of the private lifestyle, of the familial kinship setting, -- there is the sense of a proclivity to the spirit of the times, a baba incapable of withstanding the flood of impressions of the present day. The opinions of the Slavophils about the non-statism of the Russian people demands great correctives, since it is too much out of kilter with the actual Russian history, with the fact of the creation of the Russian immense state.

But the methods, by which Rozanov affirms statism and bows in worship to its power, -- are altogether not statist, altogether not of the citizen, altogether not manly. Rozanov's attitude towards the state's might is the attitude of a non-statist, womanish people, for whom this might is always a principle outside them and over them, and foreign to them. Rozanov, just like our radicals, hopelessly confuses the state with the government, and he thinks that the state -- is always "they" and not "we". What a slavery there is in the words of Rozanov about the state, what an eternal estrangement there is from a manly might. This is some form of swooning, unworthy of a people, called to a mature existence, a manly maturity. In his servile and baba-like swooning before the power of the state, so imposing by its remoteness and strangeness, Rozanov even reaches the point, where he praises the official government power for its persecution against the Slavophils. A new flood of impressions has gushed forth within Rozanov. The Slavophils, who at the beginning of his book spoke for Russia and the Russian people, at the end of his book have become but a small coterie of literateurs, full of self-conceit and cut off from life. The true expresser of Russia and the Russian people was instead the official governance, to which the Slavophils made bold to show opposition. ""Slavophilism" died out, since that it shew itself unnecessary and in vain, only but mixing itself up in the parallel thought of that "official governance", which alone was able to act... They (the Slavophils) in particular were cowardly concerning Russian history, repeating about it, but only abstractly, that it is holy... Holy Rus' seemed less rational and less credible, than their literary and social party. And herein was where the persecution against them, was "sufficiently understandable"" (p. 122). The revival of Slavophilism appears totally unnecessary. The state power was also the true Slavophilism, alongside of which was the pitiful and unnecessary literary and ideological Slavophilism. Slavophilism will resurrect only on this condition, that it repent itself afront the official governance and tag along behind it. Idolatry afront the empowered fact would attain the result.

The Slavophils were not capable of idolatry and therefore they were powerless. "The blemish in Slavophilism was this, that they did not see behind officialdom the heart, which still always was beating. The uniform was pulled open, -- and we beheld the heart, which had always ached. And it had ached on its own, imitating no one, it had ached of itself" (p. 127). "Woefully, the mistake and the defect of the Slavophils in particular consisted in their as it were aethereal history, their as it were immaterial history" (p. 125). Slavophilism showed itself to be no better than the Westernism, it -- was thus indeed abstract, literary, ideological, cut off from genuine life, which is the "official" Russia. The Slavophils, actually, tended to bow down moreso before the Russian "idea", than before its power and fact. The scorn of Rozanov for ideas, for thoughts and literature, has no bounds. The official for him stands higher than the writer. The official's service -- is a serious matter, but literature -- is a mere diversion. The Russian people -- are a statist and a serious people. "It was pleased with the state even in the very executions, -- since in executing, the state saw in it both the soul and the man, and not some mere pasttime, with which to amuse itself. Whereas alas, literature is but an "amusing diversion" concerning man" (p. 135). Rozanov wants with an artistic polish to express an obligatory point of view on the world, that viewpoint of the old aunts and uncles, according to which the state service is a serious matter, but literature, ideas etc -- are trifles, mere diversions. But as regards all this matter of literature there is Rozanov himself. He is himself right through and through a literateur, a literary prattler. Rozanov was once some sort of official in a controller's department. But he scarcely wants to go down in history in such a capacity. He wants to go down in history as a noted literary figure and that not a single line, written by him, be rejected. However much of literature as Rozanov may have in the actual feeling for the people's life, he is still yet remote from the people's life and how little there is that he knows of it.

The people and the state in the blindly talented literature of Rozanov is as different from the people and the state in actual life, as his book's finely spirited army differs from the tragic army, which marches to the banks of the Vistula and in the Carpathians. The organicity, the populism, the objective cosmism of Rozanov bear only a semblance of existence. He is completely subjective and impersonal, he knows nothing and wants to know nothing, besides the gushing flood of his own impressions and feelings. The very prostration of Rozanov before the fact of power is merely the gushing forth onto paper of the flood of his old-womanish baba experiences, almost sexual in character. He himself exposed his psychology in his ingenious book, "Solitude", which should have been the final book of his life and which always would have its place in Russian literature. In vain does Rozanov cry out for seriousness against amusements and diversions. He himself is lacking in serious moral character, and everything, which he writes about the seriousness of the official power, remains for it an irresponsible plaything and diversion of literature. He will never take responsibility upon himself for everything said by him in his book about the war.

IV.

There is something unseemly and troubling in a too light, too complaisant and literary ideological attitude towards the war. Merezhkovsky rightfully comes out against the "nightingales over the blood". It is possible to see a deep meaning in the present war, and it is impossible not to see in it a deep spiritual meaning. Everything, done at present in the war materially and externally, -- is but a sign of that, which transpires upon another, a deeper spiritual reality. It is possible to feel, that the fire of war is cleansing. But war -- is a manifestation of the deeply tragic, the antinomic and the terrible, and the present war -- is moreso, than any other war in world history. "Blood -- is a liquid altogether peculiar", -- writes Goethe in "Faust". And one mustneeds have communion with the mystery of blood, in order to have a right ultimately to see in it any joy, any good, any cleansing or salvation. The closet-study, the ideological apotheosis of the elements of war and the literary glorification of war, as the saving-means from all things bad and evil, is morally unacceptable and religiously inadmissible. The war is an inner tragedy for every being, it is infinitely serious. And it seems to me, that with too great a levity and happiness Rozanov experiences the springtime of the war, sitting himself down in his closet-study. He writes about the heroic approach, though heroism is foreign to him ultimately and he denies it with his every squeak. But thus he cannot be opposed to the influx of heroism, just as he cannot be opposed to the destroying of the German embassy, which he attempts to defend. One must remember, that the nature of war is negative, and not positive, it -- is a great revealer and exposer. But the war itself by itself cannot create a new life, it -- is but the end of the old, a reflection upon the evil. The apotheosis of war is indeed as improper, as would be the apotheosis of revolution or of the state.

V.

In the book of Rozanov there is yet another disagreeable and ticklish matter. Rozanov comes off wholeheartedly for Christianity, for Orthodoxy, for the Church, everywhere he presents himself as a faithful son of the Orthodox Church. He believes that the Slavophils did not love because they were not Christians. He repeats in a whole series of

41

generalised spots about a betrayal of Christianity, about a falling-away from the faith of the fathers, he mentions even about "Buchner and Moleschott", concerning which nothing particularly clever is remembered now, to the effect that they went off into the nowhere. But I think, that the Christian religion has had quite more dangerous, more profound an antagonist, than "Buchner and Moleschott", than the naïve Russian nihilists, and this antagonist has been -- V. V. Rozanov. Who was it that wrote the ingenious blasphemy against Christ entitled, "About Jesus MostSweet and the Bitter Fruits of the World", who was it that sensed a dark principle in Christ, as the source of death and non-being, the eradicating of life, and who was it that opposed to the "demonic" Christian religion a bright religion of birth, a divine paganism, an affirmation of life and existence?[1]

Oh, how innocent, how uninteresting and unremarkable are the attitudes towards Christianity of Chernyshevsky and Pisarev, of Buchner and Moleschott in comparison with the negativity of Rozanov. The opposition of Rozanov to Christianity can be compared only with the opposition of Nietzsche, but with this difference, that in the depths of his spirit Nietzsche was closer to Christ, than is Rozanov, even in suchlike an instance, when he comes out in defense of Orthodoxy. Better, more vivid and ingenious are the pages of Rozanov written against Christ and Christianity. Rozanov, as a manifestation of being, is in a most profound, polar opposition to everything regarding Christ. With Rozanov, certainly, there can occur a spiritual turnaround, in him there can occur a new birth, from being a pagan he can become a Christian. And it is indecent to reproach a man, for earlier having been something else. But with Rozanov the question is not in this. Each line in Rozanov witnesses to this, that within him there has not occurred the turnaround, that he has remained the same pagan, defenseless before death, that he always was, and just as polarly opposed to everything regarding Christ. There are those documents of his soul: "Solitude" and "Fallen Leaves", which he himself published for the world. But Rozanov has experienced a fright before the terror of life and death. About death he earlier did not even bother to think, since he was exclusively concerned with birth and in it he sought salvation from everything. And Rozanov out of fear did accept Orthodoxy, but an Orthodoxy without Christ, -- the Orthodox lifestyle, the whole animate

---

[1] Vide the book of Rozanov, "Temnyi lik" ("Dark Countenance").

warmth of the Orthodox flesh, everything that is pagan within Orthodoxy. But he indeed always loved this in Orthodoxy and he always lived in this collective animate warmth -- the only thing he did not love nor was able to accept was but Christ. There is not a single squeak, that would testify, that Rozanov had accepted Christ and in Him had begun to seek salvation. Rozanov herein cleaves to Christianity, cleaves to the Orthodox Church as regards the sidelines, not with a religious conformity and interests, but as regards motifs national, of lifestyle and of the publicist. It thus is impossible ultimately to be a Russian and not have connections with Orthodoxy! Orthodoxy thus is necessary for Rozanov for the Russian style, like a samovar and bliny. And indeed with the "leftists", with the intelligentsia elements and the nihilists it would be easier to meld in, having in hand the instruments of Orthodoxy. But I think, that some of the atheistic intelligentsia at a certain depth are closer to Christ, than is Rozanov. The Russian intelligentsia, at best, are heroic on their part, very national in their anti-nationalism, in their apostasy and austerity, and even in their denial of Russia. This -- is a manifestation of the Russian soul, more Russian, than the nationalism of the Western German form. Rozanov himself sees within Russian Westernism a purely Russian self-denial and humility (p. 53). And it is impossible to relate everything in the life of the Russian intelligentsia to "Buchner and Moleschott", or "Marx and Engels". Neither Marx, nor Buchner, ever sat deeply within the Russian soul, they engaged only the superficial consciousness.

The great misfortune of the Russian soul is indeed this, it is the same misfortune within Rozanov himself, -- it is in a womanish passivity, transformed into a "baba-ism", in an insufficiency of manliness, in an headlong rush towards marriage with a stranger, a foreigner at that. The Russian nation lives too much in a popular-element collectivism, and within it there has not yet solidified the consciousness of the person, of its worth and its rights. This is to be explained in that the Russian state was so saturated by the unremarkable and often so assumed the guise of a foreign domain. The "Rozanovian", the baba and the slave, the national-pagan, the pre-Christian all is still very strong in the Russian popular element. This "Rozanovschina" is ruining Russia, it pulls it inward, sucks it inward, and the deliverance from it would be a salvation for Russia. In regard to the winged words of Rozanov, "the Russian soul is scared of sin", I would also add, that it is also bruised and stifled by it. This primordial fright impedes the brave creating of life, it controls it by the land and the popular element.

And if there is an intended reason for this war, then it is directly opposite that reason, which Rozanov wants to ascribe to it. This meaning can but be in the forging of a masculine and active spirit in the Russian people, in an egress from the feminine passivity. The Russian nation will defeat Germanism, and its spirit will assume a great-power position in the world, only by having conquered the "Rozanovschina" within itself. We have at length already spoken about the Russian national culture, about the national consciousness, about the great vocation of the Russian nation. But our hopes are deeply contrary to everything "Rozanovish", to the "eternal baba-ish", to the chauvinism and bragging, and to this spiritually vampire-like regard for the blood, being poured out by the Russian armies. And one might think, that for the great mission for the Russian nation in the world there would remain essential that great Christian truth, that the human soul stands greater, than all the kingdoms and all the world...

War and the Crisis of the Intelligentsia Consciousness[1]

I.

Across the wide masses of the Russian Intelligentsia, the war ought to generate a deep crisis of consciousness, a broadening of horizons, an altering of the basic values of life. The customary categories of the thought of the Russian Intelligentsia have proven completely unsuitable for judging about such large-scale events, as happen now in the present-day world war. The consciousness of our Intelligentsia has not been oriented towards the historically concrete and it is lacking in the proper organs for judgement and appraisal in this area. This consciousness makes a fatal use of its judgement and evaluations, taken from areas altogether different, and more customary for it. The traditional Intelligentsia consciousness was totally focused upon questions of internal politics and it was oriented exclusively towards social interests. The world war inevitably refocuses the awareness upon international politics and it evokes an exceptional interest on the role of Russia in world life. The horizon of the consciousness is rendered worldwide. There is a surmounting of the provincialism of awareness, the provincialism of interests. By the caprice of fate, we are being led forth into the expanse of world history. Many of the traditionally minded Intelligentsia, accustomed to evaluate everything in accord with their abstract-sociological and abstract-moral categories, have felt a sense of confusion, when there is demanded of them a live reaction to world happenings of such magnitude. The customary doctrines and theories are rendered irrelevant before the threatening face of world-historical fate. The provincial perspective of Russian radicalism, of Russian Populism and Russian Social-Democratism did not account for such world events. The traditional consciousness was accustomed to scorn everything

[1] VOINA I KRIZIS INTELLIGENTSKOGO SOZNANIYA. First published in the newspaper "Birzhevye vedomosti", 25 July 1915, № 14986. (Klepinina № 201).

45

"international" and wholly consign it under the heading "bourgeois". But after the world war started, no one still with contempt can turn away from the "international", since it now affects the internal life of the land. Among the Russian Intelligentsia there have awaken instincts, which were not accounted for in the doctrines and which indeed were stifled by the doctrines, instincts of outright love for native-land, and the principle underlying them of a vital impulse to revive an awareness. For many this change of consciousness is experienced as tragic and it is accompanied by a sense of being cast adrift by history. It failed to transpire with the world, what they were accustomed to foresee would happen, what was supposed to happen according to the traditional doctrines and theories. Demolished was not only their "world-outlook", but even their customary feelings. The forceful refocusing by world history towards international interests, towards the historical fate of peoples and their mutual interactions focuses also likewise inside the life of each suchlike people, and it elevates and strengthens the national feeling and self-awareness. The focus upon the international and the world-historical sharpens the feeling of the value of one's own nationality and the consciousness of its tasks in the world. But absorption within the struggle of parties and classes weakens the sense of nationality. For wide circles amongst the Intelligentsia, the war bears an awareness of the value of their nationality, the value of every nationality, a value which the Intelligentsia has had almost completely lacking. For the traditional Intelligentsia consciousness there existed the value of the good, of justice, the welfare of the people, the brotherhood of peoples, but there did not exist the value of nationality, occupying a quite unique place in the hierarchy of world values. Nationality was presented not as of value in itself, but as something subordinated to other abstract values of the good. And what explained this first of all was this, that the traditional consciousness of the Intelligentsia was never focused upon the historically concrete, it always lived by abstract categories and values. The historical instincts and historical awareness amongst the Russian Intelligentsia was almost as weak as obtains with women, it was almost completely bereft of the possibility of assuming an historical perspective and acknowledging historical values. And this signifies always the prevailing of perspectives of welfare over perspectives of value.

Consequently, indeed, to have as a governing point of view -- the welfare of the people, leads to a denial of the meaning of history and historical values, since historical values presuppose the sacrificing of the people's welfare with its worship of the people, a sacrificing in the name of that which is higher than the welfare and happiness of the people and their empirical life. History, such as creates values, is essentially tragic and it does not permit of any sort of delays for the benefit of people. The value of nationality within history, as with every value, tends to assert a sacrifice, as something higher than the mere welfare of people, and it clashes with the exclusive assertion of the welfare of the people, as an higher criterion. The worth of the nation stands higher than the benefiting of people. From the point of view of the present-day generation it might be possible to consent to a shameful peace, but this is impossible from the perspective of the value of nationality and its historical destiny.

II.

The crux of the crisis, occurring for us under the influence of the war, can be formulated thus: a new consciousness has been born, turned towards the historical, towards the concrete, with a surmounting of the abstract and doctrinaire consciousness, the exclusive sociologism and moralism of our thought and values. The consciousness of our Intelligentsia has not wanted to know of history, as a concrete metaphysical reality and value. It always operated making use of abstract categories from sociology, of ethics or its dogmatics, it subordinates the historical concreteness to the abstract sociological, to the moral or dogmatic schemae. For such a consciousness, there did not exist nationality and ethnos, the historical fate and historical manifold and complexity, for it there existed merely the sociological classes or abstract ideas of the good and justice. The historical tasks, always concrete and complex, we loved to decide by the abstractly sociological, the abstractly moral or the abstractly religious, i.e. to simplify them, to arrange them into categories, taken from other areas. The Russian consciousness has an exceptional tendency to moralise over history, i.e. to apply to history moral categories, taken from personal life.

The moral meaning of the historical process can and ought to be discerned, but the moral categories of history are substantially different from the moral categories of personal life. Historical life is an independent reality, and in it are independent values. To such realities and values belongs nationality, which is a category concretely historical, and not abstractly sociological. In the Russian is the wont to demand, that everything in the world be thought of morally and that religiously it has its own truth. The Russian soul does not reconcile itself with the worship of thoughtless, immoral and godless power, it does not accept history, as some sort of natural necessity. But out of this limited, simplistic and schematising mindset there ought to be fashioned an healthy and valuable grain of good sense. We ought to open up our soul and our consciousness for concrete and manifold historical activity, an activity endowed with its own specific values. We ought to acknowledge the reality of nation and the value of national historical tasks. The question concerning the world role of Russia and about its destiny takes on tremendous significance, it cannot be diluted away into the question of the people's welfare, about social justice and suchlike questions. The horizon has become world-wide, world historical. And it is impossible to squeeze world history into the dictates of any abstract sociological or abstract moral categories, it knows instead its own goals. Russia has its own independent purpose in the world, not dilutable into other purposes, and Russia needs this purpose to reach Divine life.

The traditional transferal of abstract sociological categories over into historical life and historical tasks by the Russian Intelligentsia has always been but a peculiar and veiled form of a moralisation over history. When the war broke out, many of the Russian Intelligentsia then made attempts to evaluate it from the point of view of the interests of the Proletariat, to apply to it categories of the sociological doctrine of Economic Materialism or the sociological and ethical theories of Populism. The Intelligentsia of yet another camp likewise began to apply the doctrines of Slavophilism and to investigate it exclusively from a dogmatic Rightist perspective. And the Tolstoyans boycotted the war from the position of their abstract moralism. The Russian Social Democrats, or too the Populists, likewise simplistically moralised over history with the help of their sociological schemae, just like the Slavophils, just like the Tolstoyans, with the help of their own religio-ontological and religio-moral schemae. All these traditional and doctrinal perspectives fail to admit the independent historical reality and the independent historical goals. They fail to open their soul before the manifold of historical reality, and the energy of their thought works not towards new creative tasks, such as are availed by life and by history. Their thought does not work towards new appearances and themes, it does not penetrate into the concreteness of world life, it simplistically but rather applies their own old schemae, their own treasured categories, be they sociological, moral or religious. But world events demand an immersion within the concrete, a rise in the energy of thought, the accomplishing of new work over every new phenomenon in life. The Slavophil, the Populist or the Social-Democrat doctrinal schemae are quite unsuitable for the new happenings of world history, since they have been worked out for a more simple and elementary an actuality. Russian thinking has always been too monistic, too wrapped up in one aspect and hostile to the multiplicity, hidden away beneathe the concrete manifold. The world war is now producing a crisis for this exclusionary monism of Russian thought, always inclined as it is to violate the infinite complexity of being. It is necessary to begin thinking not by prepared schemes, not merely to apply the traditional categories, but to think creatively over the manifest tragedies of world history. And it is because the enormous moral and spiritual meaning will elude everyone, who attempts to force history into their doctrinal perspective. An absolute incapacity for the relative, the historical corporeal, is contained therein. All the relativity of the natural and historical process is reducable towards unity with the absolute only in the depths of spirit, and not in the external actuality.

III.

Another result of the war for our Intelligentsia ought to be a passover from a mindset primarily negative into a positive consciousness. In the traditional Intelligentsia consciousness there prevailed a redistributive, a non-productive attitude towards life, boycotting but not constructing. Our social consciousness has not been creative. The war with its bitter experience has an object lesson in this, that the people ought to gain itself a positive power and might, in order to realise its own mission in the world. In the Russian people and Russian society there ought to awaken a productive and constructive energy. In the life of the people, positive moments ought to win out over negative moments. And this presupposes a different condition of awareness -- more manly, responsible, free and independent. Historical creativity stands higher than the negative struggle of parties, currents, camps and groups. Only with the constructive, can there be a just reapportionment. The Russian Intelligentsia has not yet been called to power in history and therefore it is accustomed to an irresponsible boycott of everything historical. In it ought to be born a taste for being a constructive force within history. The future of a great people is dependent upon it itself, on its own will and energy, on its creative power and on the enlightenment of its historical consciousness. Upon "us", and not upon "them", depends our destiny. The settling of old accounts ought not so exclusively to govern our consciousness and will. And negative reaction ought not to hold back our creative energy. In the consciousness of the people, the debilitating idea of welfare and felicity ought to be conquered by the strengthening idea of values. The purpose to the life of the people -- is not welfare and felicity, but rather the creativity of values, the heroic and tragic living out of their own historical destiny. And this presupposes a religious attitude towards life.

Liberal imperialism appears among us as a positive and constructive consciousness, and in it there is a turning towards the historically concrete. But the liberal imperialism is too much constructed upon Western European models, it is too little of the Russian and national in its spirit. The soul of the Russian Intelligentsia is repulsed by it and does not want to see even the dram of truth, lodged within it. The mindset of our Intelligentsia needs to be reformed, regenerated and enriched by new values. I believe, that this will happen under the influence of the war. But in the soul of the Russian Intelligentsia there is its own non-transitory value, and this value -- is profoundly Russian. It ought to remain and be present in the inevitable process of the Europeanisation of Russia and its gravitation into the cycles of world history. This purpose ought to be freed of negative connections and limitations. The Russian Intelligentsia, freed from its provincialism, will emerge, finally, onto the historical stage and there carry on with its thirst for truth upon the earth, with its own partially subconscious dream about world salvation and its own will to a new, a better life for mankind.

Murky Wine[1]

I.

In Russian political life, in Russian statecraft lies concealed a murky irrational principle, it lays waste all the theories of political rationalism, it is not subject to any sort of rational explanations. The acting out of this irrational principle creates the unforeseen and the unexpected in our politics, it transforms our history into a fantasy, into an incoherent novel. That which lies at the basis of our state politics is not with a state sort of sense of reason and meaning, but rather something irrational and fantastic, -- there is a particularly sharp sense of this at the times most recent. The irrational priniciple jumbles up everything and creates the most fantastic correlations. The rightist, the conservative, even the reactionary Moscow court nobility have come into a position of opposition and it compulsively flees to democratic actions. The sole social stratum, which could be a support of the old power, slips away from under its feet. Even the Moscow Spiritual Academy, so accustomed to a fawning servility, demonstratively expresses its fear for the fate of Holy Church, stifled by murky influences. The genuine conservatism, the genuine churchliness shudders at the power of the dark element over the Russian state and the Russian Church.

Of interest has been the appointment of A. D. Samarin as the Uber-Prokurator of the MostHoly Synod. With this appointment, the genuine Orthodox set their hopes precisely on this, that it would precipitate the independence of the Church and that there would be made steps towards the renewal of the Church. These were conservative hopes, sincere hopes, the ideals of churchly conservatives, which had been reduced to despair by the ruination of churchly life, the domination over it by the dark powers. It was grievous for the Orthodox believers to look upon the servile dependency of churchly politics to outside influences, foreign to the inner

---

[1] TEMNOE VINO. First published in the newspaper "Birzhevye vedomosti", 20 October 1915, № 15159. (Klepinina № 212).

sanctities of the Church. Not long was Mr. Samarin in power, and his dismissal proved even more interesting, than his appointment.[1] A. D. Samarin -- is a rightist, a conservative churchman. His dismissal thus could not have been the result of a clash with the rightist nor even reactionary politics. He, in all probability, was himself not foreign to the restorational tendencies, and his inspired ideals were oriented backwards, not forward. But A. D. Samarin clashed with the dark, the irrational principle in churchly life, on the point of consolidation of church and state, he clashed with influences, which it would be wrong to even term reactionary, since for such influences there is no reasonable name. As an astute churchman and as a man of honour, Mr. Samarin could not put up with the servility. He thus had to take a stand in opposition, in his capacity as a rightist and conservative, as a firm Orthodox and churchman. The state is in danger -- this evokes in us a patriotic alarm. But the Church also is in danger. This evokes a religious alarm. The position of Russia was become unprecedentally tragic.

It had to vanquish not only an external enemy, but also a more internal dark principle. It is difficult even to say, that at present any planned-out reaction is occurring. This -- is not reaction, but rather a drunkennness of destruction. Even reactionaries, those even somewhat given to thought, are against what is happening. The rightists nonetheless can admit of a state sense of reason, its domination by dark elements. A. D. Samarin, evidently, is also a reasonable and thoughtful rightist, sufficiently alarmed, quite alarmed even. He, actually, is afraid of every too irrational a principle. And his reasonable and alarmed correctness, his rationalistic Slavophilism clashed face to face with the hidden power, drunken and insane, with the murky wine of the Russian land. The reasoned and cultured conservatism is powerless in Russia, the Russian power of authority is not inspired by it. And only the limitless adaptability of the Russian bureaucracy, its slavelike readiness to serve something, can

---

[1] *Translator note*: Aleksandr Dimitrievich Samarin served but a mere 3 months in 1915 as Uber-Prokurator, and was "sacked" for his hinted vocal opposition to the malign reputation and influence of Rasputin, who had become a figure of notoriety in public opinion. Berdyaev's present article appeared a mere month after the "dismissal" of Samarin. The murky and unnamed "irrational dark principle" infecting Russian life here likely refers to Rasputin as instigator.

properly harmonise with the dark influences. The Russian bureaucracy is a corrective to the Russian dark irrationality, its judgementally-active supplemental arm, without which this Russian element ultimately would perish. The bureaucracy molifies the irrational principle, and having adapted itself to the dark element, arranges for it the matters of this world. And with us the fantastic combines the coldly calculating Petrograd bureaucracy with the dark, the irrational and drunken power, lurking behind the fence.

II.

A far right and conservative current can defend a certain type of culture. In a very conservative type of culture the dark element runs its course through work and a surmounting by the human spirit and consciousness. But in Russia there is almost no suchlike cultural conservatism. Russian reactionism essentially is always hostile to every culture, to every consciousness, to every spirituality, and behind it stands always something darkly-elemental, chaotic, wild, drunken. Reaction with us is always an orgy, merely outwardly veiled over by the bureaucracy, dressed in their European frocks and coats. In Russia there is a tragic clashing of culture with the dark element. In the Russian land, in the Russian people there is a dark, in a bad sense irrational element, unenlightened and not subject to enlightening. Howsoever far ahead gets the enlightenment and subjecting to culture of the Russian earth, there always remains a sediment, with which it is impossible to do anything. In the life of the people this element has found itself a vivid, bordering even on genius I would say, expression in the Khlysty. There is in this element the murky wine, there is something drunken and orgiastic, and one who has tasted of this wine, has then difficult a time escaping the atmosphere, created by it. Khlystyism is a very profound phenomenon, and it is widespread in sects, bearing this name. Khlystyism, as a principle of the orgiastic elemental, exists also in our churchly life. All the drunkenness of the primitive element of the Russian land reflects a Khlysty wont.

In the Khlysty sect itself there is less of this unenlightened darkness, than in the non-similarly formed and concentrated elemental experiences of the people. In the mystical thirst of the Khlysty there is its own truth, indicative of its lack of satisfaction with the official churchly religion. In Russian literature, this element was artistically and with genius rendered in the novel by A. Bely, "The Silver Dove". A. Bely had artistic insight into the Russian people of a passionate mystical element, unnoted by the old Russian writers in creating their traditional popular representations of the people. This element was not to be felt either with the Slavophils, nor by L. Tolstoy. Only Dostoevsky knew it, but he revealed it not as among the life of the people, but rather in the life of the intelligentsia.

This dark Russian element is reactionary in the most profound sense of the word. Within it are eternal mystic reactions against all culture, against the personal principle, against the rights and dignity of the person, against every sort of value. This immersion in the element of the Russian earth, this intoxication with the element, its orgiastic experiences are not compatible with any sort of cultural values, nor with any sort of self-awareness of the person. Here the antagonism is irreconcilable. Every idealisation of the naturo-elemental mystique of the people is hostile to culture and developement. This reactionary idealisation for us frequently assumes the form of a rapture with the Russian lifestyle, by the warmth of the Russian muck itself, and it is accompanied by an hostility towards any sort of ascent. The Russian Khlysty element is twofold. Within it there lies concealed a genuine and truthful religious thirst to get out from this loathesome earth. In the Khlysty sectarian movement there is a valuable religious energy, though also lacking of enlightenment by an higher consciousness. But in the Khlysty element, overflowing into various forms throughout the Russian land, there is also a dark and dirty principle, which it is impossible to enlighten. In it is the source of the murky wine, imbibed by the Russian people in a bad and demonically-dark drunkenness. This chaotically-elemental, Khlysty-like intoxication of the Russian land has reached to the very summit of Russian life. We are experiencing a quite peculiar and exceptional phenomenon -- the Khlystyism of the ruling power itself. This is a path to the ultimate disintegration and rotting of the old ruling powers. Thus historically survives a remnant of the unenlightened darkness within an element of the Russian people. The dark irrationality in the pits of the people's life allures and pulls down the heights. Old Russia tumbles down into the abyss. But the new Russia, that which is to come has connection with other dark principles of the people's life, with the soul of Russia, and therefore Russia cannot perish.

III.

For Russia, there is present the great danger in the attraction of the organic ideals of the people, with the idealisation of the old Russian elemental aspect, the old Russian arrangement of the people's life, enraptured by natural traits of the Russian character. Such an idealisation holds a fatal tendency as regards the reactionary demonic darkness. The mysticism of the people's element ought to be opposed with a mysticism of spirit, transpiring through culture. The drunken and dark wildness in Russia ought to be opposed by a will towards culture, towards self-discipline, towards the formation of elements of a masculine awareness. The mysticism ought to enter into the depths of spirit, as it was for all the great mystics. In the Russian element there is an hostility towards culture. And this hostility has taken with us various forms of ideological justification. These ideological justifications have frequently been false. But one has been true. In the Russian spirit there is a genuine striving towards the extreme and the limit. But the path of culture -- is a middle path. And for the fate of Russia the most vital question -- is whether it has the discipline for culture whilst preserving all its uniqueness, all the independence of its spirit.

Will Russia end up in a naturo-Dionysian state of drunkenness amongst the people, in a quite latter-day and therefore ruinous for it paganism? That, which now is occurring in the Russian reaction, is an intoxicated paganism, a drunken orgy, reaching to the very top. The war has had the significance of a great deed -- doing away with the drunkenness. But with the Russian there is a murky wine, of which it is impossible to deprive him by any sort of external measures and reforms. In order for the Russian people to cease being intoxicated with this wine there is needed a spiritual regeneration of the people in the very roots of its life, there is needed a spiritual sobriety, through which only will it be served the new wine. With us they continue to intoxicate themself on the old wine, fermented and sour. The old Russia also has had to get itself drunk in the hour of its demise and historical end. The old life does not easily give way to the new life. Herein is that darkness of soul, that terror, which derives its power from the departing and dying, but which is incapable of sacrifice and self-denial, it drinks itself drunk, while giving the illusion of an higher life. And thus the end of the old historical power steals upon it unawares during the moment of orgy. And history surrounds this end with fantasy. It decays and approaches its end with a sort of dark principle in the Russian element, which eternally threatened a pogrom on values and a quenching of spirit. And there was a sort of small common thread, connecting the darkness at the top of Russian life with the darkness at its bottom. The top has crumbled, the soil beneathe it is gone, no sort of substantial power is there to support it. But beneathe everything is still the dark element, intoxicated on the murky wine, upon which it was attempted to prop up the top. This element long since already is still not dominant in national life, but it is all still capable of summoning forth its self-appointed ones, which bestow upon our churchly and state life a darkly-irrational character, not to be illumined by any sort of light. This has to be looked at more deeply and seriously, than generally it has, since this is something significant and not by chance for Russia. And for the struggle against the inner darkness there is needful a mobilisation of every spirit, having chosen the path of light.

The Asiatic Soul and the European Soul

I.

In the first issue of the journal, "Letopis" ("The Chronicle"), has been printed very characteristic an article by M. Gorky, "Dve dushi" ("Two Souls"), which evidently defines the direction of the new journal. The article centres round the eternal themes of Russian ponderings, around the problems of East and West. With this theme is connected the age-old dispute of the Slavophils and the Westernisers. The theme -- is basic for our national self-awareness and very appropriate; the theme -- is basic for a philosophy of history and demanding of a serious philosophic undertaking. Yet how does our acclaimed writer deal with it? M. Gorky writes in a tone, that should make it clear. He, evidently, feels himself the first radical Westerniser in Russia. "We suggest, that there has ensued a time, when history imperatively demands from honourable and intelligent Russian people, that they should subject this uniqueness to study on all sides, to a fearless criticism. It is necessary for us to fight against the Asiatic accretions upon our psyche". One might thus think, that the study and criticism of our uniqueness is only now to be initiated. But indeed with the long decades of Westernism, it have been the dominant current within Russian thought. No other people has attained to such self-negation, as have we Russians. Russians have almost become ashamed, that they are Russians. It is a phenomenon -- completely impossible in the West, where nationalism has blossomed extensively. And where indeed can we find such an apotheosis of Western Europe and Western European culture as a god, if not in Russia and by Russians? The denying of Russia and the idolatry regarding Europe -- is a phenomenon very Russian, an Eastern and Asiatic phenomenon. The quite extreme Russian Westernism is namely also a phenomenon of Asiatic a soul. There might even be expressed suchlike a paradox: the Slavophils, the views of which, suffice it to say, and without need for me to spell it out further, -- were the first Russian Europeans, since they attempted to think independently on their own like Europeans, and not merely mimic Western thought, as children are wont to mimic. The Slavophils attempted to do in Russia, the same thing, that

57

Fichte had done in Germany, to lead the German consciousness onto an original path. And here too is the reverse side of the paradox: the Westernisers have actually remained Asiatics, their consciousness has been child-like, they related to the European culture such as a people might relate to it, who are completely foreign to it, and for whom the European culture is a dreamy vision about the faraway, and not part of their inner being. For the Russian Westerniser-Asiatic -- the West is the promised land, a beckoning image of perfect life. The West remains completely on the outside, inwardly unfamiliar, remote. With the Westerniser there is almost a religious reverence, evoked by distance. It is thus that children relate to the life of adults, which presents itself to them so amazing and tempting, namely because, it is completely strange for them. Truly within the Russian soul there are "Asiatic accretions", and they are very much to be sensed in the radical Westernism of the Gorky type. In the radical Westernism of the Russian intelligentsia there was always very much not only of the completely Russian, foreign to the West, but also the completely Asiatic. European thought has been distorted within the Russian intelligentsia consciousness to the point of being unrecognisable. The Western science, the Western reason have taken on a character like some sort of gods, unknown to the critical West. Even G. Buchner, a third-rate populiser of superficial ideas, is transformed into a catechism, evoking a religious atitude to it. The value in itself of thought and of knowledge has however always been denied with us. It is time for Russian man, for cultured Russian man, that he should be freed of this Asiaticism. Western man does not bow down in idolatry before his cultural values, -- he creates them. And it befits us to create the cultural values from the depths. Creative originality is a trait of European man. And in this also Russian man ought to be like European man.

It would not be proper to confuse Russian originality with the Russian backwardness. Yet this distressful confusion is quite characteristic to the most varied currents. Russia -- is a land culturally backward. This fact is indisputable. In Russia there is much of the barbaric darkness, in it rages the dark and chaotic element of the East. The backwardness of Russia ought to be overcome by creative activity, by cultural developement. But the national originality has nothing in common with the backwardness, -- it ought to be manifest upon the higher, and not upon the lower steps of developement. That most original will be the coming, the new Russia, and not the old, the backward Russia. The authentic national consciousness can only be something creative, oriented forwards, and not backwards. And so it has been with all the peoples of Europe. Moreover, one ought not to confuse the dark, the wild and chaotic Asiatic East with the ancient cultural Asiatic East, representing an unique spiritual type, attracting the attention of the most cultured Europeans. In the East -- is the cradle of all the great religions and cultures. And at the summits of European culture the genuinely cultural European man cannot feel contempt for his ancient roots. This contempt is characteristic only to the barbarian, a man uncultured. The from of-old cultural European soul cannot bow down as to an idol afront the European culture nor can it scorn the culture of the East. Only an as yet dark Asiatic soul, not sensing in its blood and in its spirit the engraftings of the old European culture, could make a god of the spirit of European culture, as the perfect, the one and only. And it has no sense of the ancient cultures of the East. M. Gorky simplifies and makes a mishmash of everything. The old and basically true thought concerning the contemplativeness of the East and the activeness of the West is vulgarised by him and expounded in too elementary a manner. This is a theme demanding of great philosophic absorption. With Gorky, however, there is all the time sensed the insufficient informedness of the man, living amidst the concepts of the intelligentsia circles, and of his provincialism, not knowing the scope of world thought.

II.

Only one slightly and superficially in touch with European knowledge, can so simplistically bow down in worship to reason and science and see in them the panacea for all ills. One who however finds himself within it, in the very depths of the European process of knowledge, and not merely reverently gazing at it afar off on the side, such an one comprehends the inner tragedy of European reason and European science, their deep crisis, the tortuous dissatisfaction, the search for new paths. Gorky, evidently, seems to have bypassed the tremendous philosophic work, which has transpired in the West over the last decades and which has not left a stone set upon a stone for the naivo-naturalistic and naivo-materialistic worldview. Gorky reverently affirms reason in some very naive, non-critical, and altogether non-philosophic sense of the word. A large part of what there is in the scientifico-positivist currents does not admit of reason. In reason is what the metaphysicians believe in. And in

Gorky there is a sort of very naive metaphysical faith, having nothing in common with the investigations of positive science. For science and its aims, altogether unnecessary is this religious faith in reason. Gorky, typical of the Russian intelligentsia, has adopted European science in too Russian a manner, worshipping it like an Easterner, and not as a Westerner, just as never would worship it one, as actually creating the science. For Gorky, just as formerly for Pisarev, science -- is the catechism. But this is all still a childish condition of consciousness, the exhilaration of first encounters.

Europe is infinitely more complex, than it appears to Gorky, infinitely richer. There, in the West, is not only positive science and social action. There is also religion, and mysticism, and metaphysics, and romantic art, and there likewise is contemplation and visionary dreaming. The religious searchings in our era are characteristic not only of Rusia, but also of Europe. There also they seek God and the higher meaning of life, and the anguish is there also for the meaninglessness of life. The romanticism, which is not so pleasing to Gorky, is a phenomenon that is Western, and not Eastern. Western man namely -- is the romantic and passionate dreamer. Eastern man is not at all the romantic nor the dreamer, his religosity is of altogether different a type. Romanticism accompanies the Catholic type of religiosity, but it is not at all in the Orthodox type of religiosity. In the Orthodox East was impossible the search for the chalice of the Holy Grail. There is no romanticism in India either, in the non-Christian East. Is it possible to term yoga romantic? Romanticism for M. Gorky is always a bourgeois reaction, and upon this assertion can be seen, the extent of the blindness to which the schema of economic materialism tends to reach, in being out of touch with life. The romantic movement in the West arose then, when the bourgeoise was still at the very beginning of its life's path, when there stood before it an entire century of brilliant successes and of might within the earthly life. Concerning the disintegration of the European bourgoise in that period of time it would be absurd to speak, just as it is absurd to speak about the disintegration of the bourgeoise in Russia in our time, when it is still only at the beginning of its developement. I shall not speak further about the offensive lack of taste of suchlike explanations of spiritual life.

M. Gorky accuses the Russian "God-seeking" of wanting to situate the centre of things outside oneself and thereby remove from oneself the responsibility for meaningless life. He even reckons it possble to assert, that it is religious people namely that deny the meaning of life. What an astonishing example of blindness! It is namely those, whom Gorky mocks with the misplaced term "God-seekers", that for many a year already are striving to transfer the centre of gravity within man, into his depths, and to impose upon the human person the enormous responsibility for life. These are the very ones that fight against the irresponsibility, such as is involved in placing the responsibility upon powers, situated outside of man. To Gorky it even begins to seem, that religious people deny the meaning of earthly life, at but the same time that they acknowledge it. Positivism and materialism deny responsibility, freedom, the creative will, they deny man and construct an involunarist theory of the social mean and the force of necessity, the might of external circumstances. The religious consciousness, however, has to contend against these disintegrative and enervating theories of the social mean in the name of the creative activity of man, in the name of his higher freedom, in the name of an higher meaning of life. In Russia these materialistic theories are tangled up with the social mean, and these accepted theories about the necessity of everything happening only but encourage the Eastern lethargy, the weakness of will, the irresponsibility. The faith in man, in his creative freedom and creative might is possible only for the religious consciousness, and never for the positivistic consciousness, which looks upon man, as upon a reflex of material means, both natural and social. Truly needed and urgent in Russia is the call for the promoting of human activity, of human creativity, human responsibility. This however is possible upon a grounding rather quite other, than those, upon which M. Gorky stands. The radical Russian Westernism, the distortive and slave-like accepting of the complex and rich life of the West, is a form of Eastern passivity. In the East there has to be roused original creative activity, creating a new culture, and this is possible only upon religious a foundation. We are already at that age in our being, when it is time for us to leave off with the childish Westernism and the childish Slavophilism, when we ought to advance to a more mature form of national self-consciousness. Great worldwide events are leading us out into the expanse of the world, towards worldwide perspectives. The upheavals of the current world war is leading Europe also out beyond its set borders, they reveal the deep-rooted contradictions within Europe itself and they topple over the idols of Westernism. The dragging of Russia into world events signifies the end of its settled provincial existence, with its Slavophil self-conceit and Westerniser servility. But M. Gorky remains within the old mentality, he

61

wants to learn nothing from what is happening in the world and so he continues to dwell in the old opposition of East and West.

Concerning the Power of the Expanse upon the Russian Soul

I.

Much is enigmatic within Russian history, in the fate of the Russian people and the Russian state. The relationships obtaining amidst the Russian people, whereby the Slavophils acclaimed the people as stateless, and the enormous aspect of the Russia state -- remains up to the present a riddle within the philosophy of Russian history. More than once already has it been pointed out, that in the fate of Russia there was the tremendous significance possessed by geographic factours, its position upon the earth, its immense expanse. The geographic position of Russia was such, that the Russian people was compelled to form an enormous state. Upon the Russian expanse of the steppes there had to be formed an immense East-West, an unified and organised state entirely. The enormous expanses came easily for the Rusian people, but what came not easily for it was the organisation of these expanses into the most immense state in the world, the sustaining and guarding of the order within it. Into this effort went a large portions of the powers of the Russian people. The proportions of the Russian state presented the Russian people with tasks almost impossible, held the Russian people in the grip of an excessive strain. And in the enormous deed of creating and guarding their state, the Russian people exhausted its powers. The demands of the state left too little for the free profusion of powers. All the outward activity of Russian man went to the service of the state. And this set an hapless seal upon the life of Russian man. Russians have almost not the wherewithal to be happy. There is not in Russian people any creative play of powers. The Russian soul is choked up with the vast Russian fields and the vast Russian snows, it drowns and dissolves away into this vastness. The formation of his soul and the formation of his creativity was difficult for Russian man. The genius of form -- is not a Russian genius, with difficulty only it is combined with the power of the expanse over the soul. And Russians almost not at all know of any happiness of form.

The state domination of the vast Russian expanses was accompanied by a terrible centralisation, subjecting the whole of life to state interests and stiffling the free personal and societal powers. Always weak among Russians has been the consciousness of personal rights and undeveloped was the self-initiative of classes and groups. It was not easy to uphold the largest state in the world, especially indeed for a people, not endowed with any genius for formal organisation. For a long time it had to defend Russia from enemies attacking from all sides. Attacking waves from the East and from the West threatened to engulf Russia. Russia suffered the Tatar-Mongol Yoke, it suffered the Times of Troubles and ultimately it grew strong, it grew into a colossal state. But the vast expanse of Russia imposed an heavy burden upon the soul of the Russian people. Into its psychology entered in both the boundlessness of the Russian state and the boundlessness of the Russian fields. The Russian soul was thrust upon by the vastness, it did not see any borders, and this boundlessness does not liberate, but the rather enslaves it. And here the spiritual energy of Russian man went inwards, into contemplation, into the soul, it could not orient itself towards history, as is always connected with form, with a path, in which the boundaries are denoted. The forms of the Russian state rendered Russian man formless. The humility of Russian man became his self-protection. The refusal of historical and cultural creativity was demanded by the Russian state, by its protagonists and preservers. The vast expanses, which from all sides encircle and press upon Russian man -- are not outward and material, but instead inward, a spiritual factour of his life. These vast Russian expanses are situated also within the Russian soul and possess over it an enormous power. Russian man, the man of the land, senses himself powerless to control these expanses and organise them. He is too accustomed to pass off this organisation onto the central powers, as though it were something transcendent for him. And in his own soul he senses the vastness, with which it is difficult for him to deal. Russian man is expansive, as expansive as the Russian earth, as the Russian fields. The Slavic chaos storms about in it. The enormity of the Russian expanses has not permitted the working out of self-discipline and self-initiative in Russian man, he has instead flowed off into the expanse. And this has not been an external, but rather the internal fate of the Rsusian people, since everything external is but a symbol of the internal. From the external, the positivistic-scientific point of view the enormous Russian expanses reflect a geographic factour of Russian history. But from a deeper, an inner point of view these expanses can be viewed as an inner, a spiritual fact in the Russian fate. This -- is a geography of the Russian soul.

II.

In Russian man there is not the narrowness of European man, who concentrates his energy upon a not-large expanse of soul, there is not that thriftiness, the economising of space and time, the intensiveness of culture. The power of the breadth over the Russian soul engenders a whole series of Russian qualities and Russian insufficiencies. The Russian lethargy, the carelessness, lack of initiative, the weakly developed sense of responsibility is connected with this. The breadth of the Russian land and the breadth of the Russian soul have provided the Russian energy, opening the possibility of movement on the side of extensiveness. The breadth has not demanded intensive energy and intensive culture. From the Russian soul, the vast Russian expanses have demanded humility and sacrifice, but they have safeguarded Russian man and provided him a sense of security. Russian man has sensed himself surrounded on all sides by enormous expanses, and there has not been terror for him in the bosom of Russia. The enormous Russian land, broad and deep, always comes through for Russian man, and saves him. Always he is quite reliant upon the Russian earth, upon Mother Russia. He almost confuses and identifies his mother-earth with the Mother of God and trusts on Her intercession. The Russian land rules over Russian man, and it is not he that rules over it. Western European man senses himself squeezed in by the small extents of expanse and just the same by small expanses of soul. He is accustomed to rely upon his own intensive energy and activeness. And in his soul it is cramped in, not expansive, everything has to be considered and rightly distributed its place. The organised arrangement of everything to its place creates the philistinism of Western European man, always so striking and repelling for Russian man. These philistine fruits of western culture evoked the indignation of Hertsen, evoked the loathing of K. Leont'ev, and for every characteristically Russian soul these fruits lack sweetness. Let us consider the German. He feels himself hemmed in on all sides, like in a mousetrap. Wide spaces are not around him, nor within him. He seeks salvation in his own organisational energy, in his directed activity. Everything for the German has to be in its place, everything distributed and set. Without self-disciple and responsibility the German cannot exist. Everywhere he sees boundaries and everywhere he sets boundaries. The German cannot exist in the unboundedness, foreign and contrary to him is the Slavic expansiveness. Only with a great exertion of energy would he want to widen his boundaries. The German is wont to despise the Russian man over this, that he has not a stable life, that he tends not to arrange and organise life, knows neither measure nor place, nor tends to attain the possible. And to the Russian is contrary the German pathos of a philistine ordering of life. The German senses, that Germany will not save him, that he himself has to save Germany. The Russian however thinks, that he cannot save Russia, but rather that Russia will save him. The Russian never senses himself an organiser. He is accustomed to be organised. And even in this terrible war, when the Russian state is in peril, it is not easy to bring Russian man to the awareness of this danger, to inspire in him the sense of responsibility for the fate of his native land, to evoke an exertion of energy. Russian man comforts himself in this, that beyond still stands the vast expanses to save him, so that it is not very frightful for him, and he is not very inclined to overly exert his efforts. And so it is with difficulty that Russian man reaches the awareness of the necessity to mobilise all his energy. The question about an intensive culture presupposes an exerted activity, still has not rendered itself for him into a question of life and fate. He is immersed in its bosom and in its expanses. And it mustneeds be said, that every self-initiative and activity of Russian man is beset with insurmountable hindrances. The enormity, transformed into the self-sufficing power of the Russian state was afraid of the self-initiative and activity of Russian man, it lifted from Russian man the burden of responsibility for the fate of Russia and imposed upon him service, it demanded of him humility. Through the historical formation of the Russian state the Russian expanses themself have limited every responsible self-initiative and creative activity of Russian man. And this enslavement of the powers of Russian man and all the Russian people was considered justified for the guarding and maintaining of the Russian expanses.

III.

The demands, placed on Russia by the world war, ought to lead to a radical change of awareness for Russian man and for the directing of his will. He ought, certainly, to free himself from the power of the expanse and himself instead be master with the expanses, changing no little with the Russian uniqueness, connected with the Russian breadth. This signifies a radically different attitude towards the state and culture, than that, which has obtained with the Russian people. The state should become an inward power with the Russian people, its own proper positive might, its instrument, and not an external priniciple over it, not its lord. Culture also ought to become more intensive, actively taking hold in the bosoms and the expanses and cultivating them with Russian energy. Without such an inner impetus the Russian people cannot have a future, cannot pass over into a new phase of its historical being, that truly of an historical being, whilst the Russian state itself is subject to a danger of disintegration. If the Russian state up til now has been wont to exist with the passivity of the Russian people, then from hence it would exist only by the activity of the people. The expanses ought not to frighten the Russian people, who themself ought to have an energy, not that of the German, but rather a Russian energy. Crazy are those, who connect the Russian originality and uniqueness with a technical and economic backwardness, with the elemental level of social and political forms, and who want to preserve Russian appearances through a preservation of the passivity of the Russian spirit. Originality cannot be bound up with weakness, with a lack of developement, with deficiencies. The unique type of the Russian soul has already been wrought and forever affirmed. Russian culture and Russian sociality can be created only from the depths of the Russian soul, from its unique creative energy. But the Russian originality ought, certainly, to manifest not negatively, but positively rather, in might, in creativity, in freedom. The national originality ought not to be timid, guarding itself suspiciously, and in chains. In a mature period of the historical existence of the people the originality ought to be freely expressed, bold, creative, oriented forward and not backwards. Certain among the Slavophil mindset even in our woeful days tend to think, that if we, as Russians, become instead active in regard to the state and to culture, with mastery and well-ordered, if we begin from the depths of our spirit to create a new, a free societal order and the material tools needful for us, if we enter upon the path of technical developement, then we shall merely be like the Germans in everything and therein lose our originality. But this is a lack of faith in the spiritual might of the Russian people. An originality, which can be preserved only by attaching it to backward and elementary material forms, is not something that will stand on its own, and it is impossible to base anything upon it.

Guardians always little believe in that what they guard. A true faith however is only of the creative, of the free. The unique Russian spiritual energy can create only but unique life. And it is time to stop frightening Russian man with the enormity of the state, with the vast expanses, and holding him down in slavery. It is namely then, when Russian man has been held down in slavery, that he has been under the grip of the Germanism, which has set its seal upon all the detritus of the Russian state. Setting free the energy of the Russian people and directing it towards an active mastery and formation of the Russian expanse would also liberate the Russian people from German slavery, would be an affirmation of its creative orginality. It is impossible to suppose that the Russian originality should consist in this, that the Russians would be slaves to a foreign activity, whether it be German, or merely in reaction to the Germans, who themself are active! God preserve us from such an originality -- from it we would perish! The historical period of the power of the expanse over the soul of the Russian people is at an end. The Russian people is entering upon a new historical period, when it has to become master of its own earth and creator of its own fate.

Centralism and the Life of the People

I.

A large portion of our political and cultural ideologies suffer from centralism. Always there is a sense of something incommensurable between these ideologies and the vastness of Russian life. The inner life of the people within the enormity of Russia all still remains enigmatic, mysterious. The people itself is all still as it were mute, and the people at the centres riddle out its will only with difficulty. Such currents of ours, as Slavophilism and Populism, relate with an especial esteem and attention to the people's life and seek variously to ground themself upon the verymost essentials of the Russian earth. But both in Slavophilism and in Populism there has always been a remarkable amount of the utopianism of centralising ideologies, and these intellectual currents oriented towards the people's life have failed to cover all the vastness and enormity of the life of the Russian people. Populism, so characteristic a thought and manifest in various forms, presupposes already a rebelliousness and being sundered off from the life of the people. It was a search for the true people and the true life of the people on the part of the intelligentsia, itself having lost its connection with the people and itself incapable of truly knowing the people. This -- was an aspiration for a merging together with the people and an idealisation of the people from off on the side and at a distance. Populism -- is purely intellectual a current. In the very depths of the life of the people, with the finest people from amongst the people itself, there was no sort of populism, there is instead a thirst for developement and ascent, a striving towards the light, and not towards any populism. Quite the same thing, where in the West there are no Westernisers. One of the deep-rooted mistakes of the populism was its identification of the people with only the common people, with the peasantry, with the working classes. Our cultural and intellectual segment lacks ability to recognise itself as among the people and so with envy and with longing it looks upon the populace of the common people. But this -- is an impaired self-awareness. People of the cultural and intellectual centres too often think, that the centre of gravity of the spiritual and social life of the people -- is in the common people, somewhere far off in the depths of Russia. But the centre of the people's life is everywhere, it is in the depths of each Russian man and in every span of the Russian earth, it is not in some sort of special place. The life of the people is something national, an in-common Russian life, the life of all the Russian land and all the Russian people, taken not at a superficial, but rather deep level. And each Russian man ought to have a sense of himself and be conscious of himself as of the people and in his depths have a feel for the people's element and the people's life. The highly cultured man, living at the centres, both ought and can sense himself no less a man of the people, than a muzhik-peasant somewhere off in the depths of Russia. And of the people most of all -- is the genius. The highly cultured stratum can be of the people just the same, as is the deeply agrarian segment of the people's life. The people -- is first of all I myself, in my own depths, connecting me with the depths of the great and vast Russia. And only insofar as I am fallen off into the periphery, can I sense myself as sundered off from the bosom of the people's life. The true life of the people mustneeds be sought not in the expanses and external distances, but in the stirrings in the depths. And in the depths, I -- a cultured man -- am the people the same, just like the Russian muzhik-peasant, and it is easy for me to make common with this muzhik spiritually. The people is not a social category, and social oppositions do but cloud over the perception of the people. The anguished dream about the true life of the people somewhere outside myself and remote from me -- is something sick and impotent. The true centre always indeed can be found only within man, and not outside him. And all the people's Russian earth is but a deep layer within each Russian man, it is not some promised land outside him set afar off. The true centre is not in the capital and it is not in the province, it is not at the top and not in the bottom layer, but in the depths of each person. The life of the people cannot be the monopoly of some particular segment or class. The spiritual and cultural decentralisation of Russia, which is quite inevitable for our national health, is impossible to understand as purely an external ripple-effect movement from the capital centres to the deep provinces. This is first of all an inward movement, the raising of consciousness and the growth of collective national energy in each Russian man throughout all the Russian earth.

II.

Russia combines within itself certain historical and cultural periods of growth, from the early Middle Ages up through the XX Century, from the most primitive stages, preliminary to a cultural condition, up to the very summits of world culture. Russia -- is a land of great contrasts predominantly -- nowhere are there such contrasts of heights and depths, of dazzling light and primordial darkness. Herein is why it is so difficult to organise Russia, to bring order to the chaotic elements in it. All lands combine many periods of growth. But the vast immensity of Russia and the peculiarity of its history have begotten unseen contrasts and oppositions. With us, there is almost no strong middle societal segment, which might everywhere organise the people's life. The immaturity of the deep province and the oppression from the state centre -- herein lies the polarity of Russian life. And Russian societal life is too tightly set within this polarity. The life of the vanguard circles of Petrograd and Moscow and the life of the deep corners of the remote Russian province belongs as it were to different historical epochs. The historical structure of the Russian state has centralised state-societal life, poisoning with its bureaucracy and smothering provincial societal and cultural life. In Russia has occurred a centralisation of culture, dangerous for the future of so enormous a land. All our cultural life is tied to Petrograd, to Moscow, and only partly to Kiev. Russian cultural energy has no wish it would seem to spread through the vast expanses of Russia, it is afraid of drowning in the darkness of the deeps of the provinces, and so it seeks to guard itself in the centres.There is a sort of fear afront the gloomy darkness and of being engulfed in the bosom of Russia. This phenomenon -- is a sickness and a menace. Russia -- is not France. And in France the exceptional concentration of culture in Paris begets an immeasurable differentiation of developement in Paris and in the French province and makes for fickle and superficial political turnabouts. In Russia however the same concentration is altogether already debilitating and holds Russia down at the lower stages of developement. Essentially needful in Russia is a spiritual-cultural decentralisation and a spiritual-cultural ascent of the innermost aspects of the life of the Russian people. And this is not at all a matter of populism. Simultaneously there ought to be surmounted both the false centralism of the capital, of its spiritual bureaucratism, and the false populism, with its spiritual provincialism. Simultaneously incredible are both the orientations of the life of the capital, and the provincial orientations. These are two sides of one and the same rift within the life of the people. There ought to be started the whole-nation orientation of life, transpiring within every Russian man, every person, having become aware of his own connection with the nation. The bosom of Russian life is not some wherever, but rather everywhere, everywhere there can be revealed the depths of the people's spirit. There will always exist spiritual centres upon the surface of national life, but this ought not to convey the character of a spiritual bureaucraticising of life.

The varied stages of developement in Russia present first of all tasks of a spiritual, moral and societal nurturing and self-nurturing of the nation. These tasks presuppose a great flexibility and do not permit of coercion over the life of the people. If the bureaucratic-absolutist centralisation and a revolutionary-jacobin centralisation be both dangers in common for the healthy developement of the people, then still all the more are they dangers in so collosal and mysterious a land, as Russia. Reactionary centralism and revolutionary centralism can alike fail to correspond with what is transpiring in the depths of Russia, in the bosom of the life of the people. And grant that it may not happen, that the old bureaucratic violence over the life of the people should find its substitute in a new jacobin violence! Let the life of the people develope from within, corresponding with our real being! The Petrograd bureaucratism has infected also our liberal and revolutionary movement. The bureaucratism reflects a peculiar metaphysics of life, and it is deeply pervasive in life. But the provincialism reflects a different metaphysics of life. Extreme centralising bureaucratism and extreme provincialism -- are correlative and mutually condition each the other. Russia is perishing from the centralistic bureaucratism on the one side and from the dark provincialism on the other side. The decentralisation of Russian culture would signify not a triumph of provincialism, but rather the surmounting of both the provincialism and the bureaucratic centralism, the spiritual ascent of all the nation and of each person. Within Russia overall there should begin a cultivation of its interiour, spiritually as well as materially. And this presupposes a lessening of the differences between the centralists and the provincialists, between the upper and the lower segments of Russian life, it presupposes a respect for those vital processes, which transpire in the unknown deeps and faraway in the life of the people. It is impossible to dictate freedom from the centre -- it ought instead to be the will to freedom within the life of the people, tending to their own roots in the bosom of the earth. This will to freedom and to the light resides there also in the agrarian element itself and in the as yet moreso ignorant levels of the people. It is needful but to approach this as yet ignorant soul of the people with attentive love and without coercion. There ought now to awaken not the intelligentsia, not the upper cultural segment, not some sort of demagogic developed class, but rather the enormous, the unknown, popular, provincial, "ordinary" Russia, not as yet having said its say. The upheavals of the war facilitate this awakening. And the light of awareness, which ought to go forth to meet this awakened Russia, ought not to be an external, centralistic and coercive light, but rather a light inward for every Russian man and for all the Russian nation.

Concerning Sanctity and Honour

I.

K. Leont'ev says, that Russian man can be a saint, but he cannot be honourable. Honour -- is a Western European ideal. The Russian ideal -- is sanctity. In the formula of K. Leont'ev there is a certain aesthetic exaggeration, but there is also an indisputable truth, in it there is posited a very interesting problem in the psychology of the Russian people. With Russian man there is an insufficiently strong awareness, that honour is obligatory for each man, that it is connected with the integrity of a man, that it forms the person. The moral self-discipline of the person among us has never been considered as an independent and higher task. In our history was absent the knight-chivalry principle, and this absence was unfavourable for the developement and forming of the person. Russian man has not set himself the tasks to work out and discipline the person, he instead is too inclined to rely on this, that the organic collective, to which he belongs, renders it all for him morally healthy. Russian Orthodoxy, to which the Russian people are connected by their moral upbringing, has not set too high the moral tasks of person for the average Russian man, and in this has been an enormous moral condescension. Prescribed first of all for Russian man was the demand for humility. In reward for the virtue of humility everything was permitted and everything was decided. Humility also was the sole form for the discipline of person. Better to humbly sin, than proudly to seek becoming perfected. Russian man has been accustomed to think, that dishonour -- is no great evil, if amidst this he were humble of soul, not proud, did not exalt himself. Even in a large transgression it was possible to humbly repent, while the little sins are readily lifted by a candle, set before a saint. The higher supra-human tasks were for the saints to do. The ordinary Russian man thus ought not to set himself too high a goal even remotely approaching this ideal of sanctity. For this -- would be pride. The Orthodox Russian starets-elder never would direct one onto such a path. Sanctity is the portion of but few, it cannot be the path for the mere man. Every too heroic a path of person is acknowledged by the Russian Orthodox consciousness as pride, and the ideology of Russian Orthodoxy is prepared to see in this path an inclination towards man-godhood and demonism. Man ought to live in the organic collective, needful of its its order and harmony, to be schooled in its condition, its traditional professions, in all its tranditional arrangement among the people.

In what sense is it then, that the popular Russian Orthodox consciousness believes in Holy Rus' and always asserts, that Rus' lives by sanctity, in contrast to the peoples of the West, which live only by honour, i.e. by a principle less lofty? In this regard, within the Russian religious consciousness there is a deep-rooted dualism. The Russian people and the truly Russian man lives by sanctity not in a sense, that they would see sanctity as their own path or consider sanctity for themself in whatever the measure as proper and obligatory. Rus' is not at all holy and does not regard it obligatory to be made holy and realise the ideal of sanctity, it -- is holy merely in the sense, that endlessly it venerates the saints and sanctity, only in sanctity does it see an higher condition of life, whereas in the West they see the higher condition in likewise the attainments of knowledge or of societal justice, in the triumph of culture, in creative genius. For the Russian religious soul there is made holy not so much the man, as rather the Russian earth itself, unto which "in the form of a servant the Heavenly King hath come, bestowing blessing". And in the religious mindset of the Russian people the Russian earth comes to represent the Mother of God Herself. Russian man generally does not traverse the paths of sanctity, indeed never would he set himself such lofty goals, but he bows down before the holy and the sacred, for with such is bound up his ultimate love, he relies upon the saints, upon their intercession and help, and to be saved by this, in that the Russian land has so much that is holy. The soul of the Russian people has never worshipped the golden calf and, I believe, never could worship it in its ultimate depths. But the Russian soul is inclined to sink into the lower conditions, there to indulge in prodigality, to allow dishonesty and dirt. Russian man may tend to plunder and get rich by impure paths, but amidst this never would he esteem material riches an an higher end, he would continue to believe, that the life of St. Seraphim of Sarov is higher than all earthly blessings and that St. Seraphim will save him and all the sinful Russian people, interceding before the MostHigh on behalf of the Russian land. Russian man can be a desparate crook and transgressor, but in the depths of his soul he reverences the holy and seeks salvation of the saints, from their intercession. Some robber and killer --

can very sincerely, and indeed reverently bow down before the sacred, set candles before the images of the saints, drive off into the wilderness to starsi-elders, having forsaken being a robber and murderer. It is impossible even to term this hypocrisy. This -- is the age-old dualism in upbringing, having entered into the flesh and blood, a particular ordering of the soul, a peculiar path. This -- is a soul-flesh engrafting, and insufficently spiritual a religiosity. But in the Russian soul type there is an enormous superiourity over the European type. The European bourgeois makes his wealth and gets rich with the consciousness of his own great accomplishment and excellence, with faith in his own bourgeois virtues. The Russian bourgeois, in making his wealth and getting rich, always senses himself somewhat a sinner and somewhat scorns the bourgeois values.

II.

Sanctity remains for the Russian man a transcendent principle, it does not become his inner energy. The veneration of sanctity accords with the type, which is there also in the veneration of icons. To the saint is imputed an attitude, as towards the icon, his face becomes an iconographic face, and has ceased to be human. But this is a transcendent principle of sanctity, having become intermediary betwixt God and man, and it ought to do something for Russian man, to help him and save him, and beyond him to accomplish a moral and spiritual working. But Russian man is not at all mindful of this, that the sanctity should become an inward principle, transforming his life, it always acts on him from the outside. The sanctity is too lofty and impermissible, it -- is already a non-human condition, before which it is possible only to bow down and seek help and intercession for the hopeless sinner. The veneration of the saints has come to screen out any direct communion with God. The saint -- is greater, than a mere man, yet the saint as venerated, seeking in him only the intercession, -- is less, than the mere man. Where indeed the man? Every human ideal of perfection, of nobility, honour, integrity, purity, of light, presents itself to Russian man as of little value, too worldly, moderately-cultural. And Russian man thus sways back and forth between the beastly and the angelic principles, bypassing the human principle. For Russian man it is so characteristic, this oscillation between sanctity and swinishness. To Russian man it often seems, that if it is impossible to become a saint and ascend to the supra-human heights, then better it is to remain in a swinish condition, and then it is not all that important, whether one be a swindler or honourable. And since the supra-human condition of sanctity is attained but by very few, then it transpires that the very many do not attain even the human condition, they remain in the swinish condition. Active human perfecting and creativity become paralysed. In Russia the human principle has still all been insufficiently revealed, it is all still in its potentials, great potentials, but only potentials.

Russian morality is pervaded by dualism, inherited from our characteristic religiosity of the people. The idea of Holy Rus' has had deep roots, but it has included within it also a moral danger for Russian man, it frequently has sapped him of moral energy, paralysed his human will and impeded his ascent. This -- is a feminine religiosity and feminine morals. The Russian weakness, the lack of character is to be sensed in that eternal wish to take cover within the folds of the garb of the Mother of God, to recourse to the intercession of the saints. The Divine principle has not revealed itself from within, in the Russian will itself, the Russian vital impulse. The experiences of one's weaknesses and one's desperation are also representative of the religious experiences predominantly. And so all the more we have need of developing within ourself of the masculine religious principle in all regards. We ought to develope in ourself an awareness of responsibility and get accustomed to rely as is possible moreso upon ourself and our own activity. On this depends the future of Russia, the fulfilling of its vocation in the world. It is impossible to see the uniqueness of Russia in weakness and backwardness. In power and in developement ought to be revealed the true uniqueness of Russia. Russian man ought to stop relying on this, that someone will do and accomplish everything for him. The historical hour of the life of Russia demands, that Russian man reveal his own human spiritual activeness.

It is very characteristic, that not only in the Russian people's religiosity and its representatives of the old Russian piety, but also with the atheistic intelligentsia, and with many of the Russian writers, there is to be sensed all this same transcendent dualism, all the same admitting of the value only of supra-human perfection and the insufficient appreciation of the human perfecting. And so the average radical member of the intelligentsia tends to think, that he either is called to overturn the world, or he is compelled to remain in a rather lowly condition, to dwell sinking down into a moral slovenliness. Consideration of activity he entirely writes off as "bourgeois", which, in his opinion, cannot reflect any moral qualities. The Russian man gets too easily "entangled with the means". He is accustomed to rely not upon himself, upon his own activity, not upon any inward discipline of person, but upon the organic collective, upon something external, to lift him up and save him. The materialistic theory of the social mean in Russia is a peculiar and distorted remnant of religious transcendence, of placing the centre of gravity outside the depths of man. The principle of "all or nothing" in Russia usually remains a victory for "nothing".

III.

It mustneeds be acknowledged, that personal worth, personal honour, personal integrity and purity entice very few of us. Every appeal for personal discipline merely irritates Russians. The spiritual effort over the formation of one's person seems for Russian man neither necessary nor enticing. When Russian man is religious, then he believes, that the saints or God Himself will do everything for him, and when however he is an atheist, then he thinks, that everything is to happen for him through social means. The dualistic religious and moral upbringing, always calling exclusively for humility and never appealing to honour, pays no regard to the purely human principle, the purely human activity and worth, it always disintegrates man into the angelic-heavenly and the beastly-earthly, as shewn indirectly now, during the time of war. Russian man all still bows down to sanctity in the finer moments of his life, but he is still lacking in integrity, human integrity. But even the veneration of sanctity, that chief source of moral nourishing of the Russian people, is on the decline, the old faith is weakening. The beastlike-earthly principle in a man, unaccustomed with spiritual attention to himself, to the transforming of the lower nature into an higher, leaves him at the mercy of fate. And having fallen away from faith, in the modern bourgeois manner, Russian man remains under the grip of the old religious dualism. But the grace is withdrawn from him, and he remains at the mercy of his own unenlightneed instincts. The orgy of chemical instincts, the ugly profiteering and speculation during the days of the terrible world war and the great tribulations for Russia is our greatest disgrace, a dark blot upon national life, an ulcer upon the body of Russia. The thirst for profiteering has taken hold with too broad a segment of the Russian people. It lays bare the age-old lack of honour and integrity in Russian man, a deficiency in the moral upbringing of the person as regards free self-restraint. And in this is something akin to the slave, not the citizen, a pre-citizen condition. For the average Russian man, be he a land-owner or merchant, there is a lack of citizen's integrity and honour. Free citizens would not speculate, and pilfer products most urgently needed etc, during the time of great tribulation for the spiritual and material powers of Russia. This is an indelible disgrace, which future generations will remember with shudders of indignation alongside their remembrance about the heroic efforts of the Russian army, about the unselfish activity of our social organisations. I believe, that the core of the Russian people is morally healthy. But in our bourgeois-ordinary segment there is not evidenced a sufficiently strong moral awareness of citizenship, of the moral and citizen undertakings of the person. Facing this segment stands not only great tribulations, but also great temptations. Russian man can endlessly endure and bear up, he has passed through the school of humility. But he easily succumbs to temptations and does not withstand the temptation of easy profit, he has not passed through the genuine school of integrity, he has not had the proper tempering of the citizen. This does not mean, that in being so easily tempted and swayed off the path of integrity proper to person and citizen, that Russian man does not at all love Russia. In his own way he loves Russia, but he is not accustomed to feel himself responsible for Russia, since he was not raised in the spirit of the free citizen in regard to it.

It is indeed sad to say, that Holy Rus' has its correlative in the Rus' of the swindler. This is no different, than where the monogamous family would have its correlative in prostitution. This dualism herein ought to be surmounted and ended. It is necessary to get down to the depths of the spiritual sources of our contemporary moral ulcers. In the depths of Russia, in the soul of the Russian people there ought to be manifest an immanent religiosity and immanent morality, for which the higher Divine principle is rendered inwardly a transfigurative and creative principle. This means, that in all his stature he ought to become a man and citizen, fully free. A free religious and social psychology ought to win out inwardly for each man over the slave-like religious and social psychology. This likewise means, that Russian man ought to get out beyond that condition, wherein he can be a saint, but he cannot be honourable. Sanctity will forever remain among the Russian people, as its inheritance, but it has to enrich itself with new values. Russian man and all the Russian people ought to be conscious of the Divine aspect within human honour and integrity. And then creative instincts will win out over the plundering instincts.

Concerning the Relationship of Russians towards Ideas[1]

I.

Much in the mentality of our social and populist psychology leads to sad considerations. And one of the saddest facts needful is to recognise the indifference towards ideas and towards ideational creativity, to recognise the ideational backwardness of broad segments of the Russian Intelligentsia. In this is evidenced a desiccation and inertia of thought, a dislike for thought, a disbelief in thought. The moralistic frame of mind of the Russian soul begets a suspicious attitude towards thought. Life amidst ideas is accounted by us as a luxury, and in this luxury they do not see any essential relationship to life. In Russia from quite contrary points of view is preached an ascetic abstinence from ideational creativity, from the life of thought, from going over beyond the limits of the necessary useful for goals whether social, moral or religious. This asceticism in relationship to thought and to ideational creativity is affirmed for us simultaneously both from the religious perspective, and from the materialistic perspective. This is quite characteristic to Russian populism, taken both in its extreme left, and its extreme right forms. This frame of mind for the Russian soul has been clearly expressed by the Tolstoyans. Some reckon it alone sufficient for us that minimum of thought, which is enclosed in the Social-Democrat brochures, while with others, -- that which can be found in the writings of the holy fathers. The brochures of the Tolstoyans, the brochures of the "Religio-Philosophic Bibliotek" of M. A. Novoselov and the brochures of the Social Revolutionaries all show a completely identical dislike and contempt for thought. The value in itself of thought is denied, the freedom of ideational creativity was cast under suspicion at one point from the perspective of the Social Revolutionaries, and at another point from the perspective of the religious guardians. They love for us to have only catechisms, which superficially and simply are applied to every instance of

---

[1] OB OTNOSHENII RUSSKIKH K IDEYAM. First published in the journal "Russkaya mysl'", Jan. 1917, p. 66-73. (Klepinina № 256).

life. But the love for catechisms is also a dislike for independent thought. In Russia there was never a creative abundance, there was never anything of a renaissance, there was nothing of the spirit of the Renaissance. How sad and melancholy has Russian history been constituted and rendered for the soul of Russian man! All the spiritual energy of Russian man was directed to the sole thought about salvation, about the salvation of his soul, about the salvation of the people, about the salvation of the world. In truth, this thought about universal salvation -- is a characteristically Russian thought. The historical destiny of the Russian people has been sacrificial -- it saved Europe from the invasions of the East, from the Tatar-Mongol Yoke, and in it there did not take hold the strength for free developement.

Western man creates values, he forms rich cultures, and he has an independent love for values; Russian man searches for salvation, and the creativity of values for him is always a little suspicious. Not only do believers of Russian soul seek salvation, the Orthodox and the sectarians, but it is also the Russian atheists, the socialists and anarchists, they all seek after salvation. For the matter of salvation catechisms are necessary, but free and creative thought is dangerous. It is a mistake to think, that the best, the most sincere element of the Russian leftist revolutionary intelligentsia is socially in accord with the directives of its own will as concerned with politics. It is impossible within it to find the least signs of social thought, of a political consciousness. It -- is apolitical and non-societal, by distorted paths it seeks salvation of soul, purity, to be able to seek out ascetic deeds and service to the world, but bereft of the instincts of civil and social organisation. The "social" world-concept of the Russian Intelligentsia, subordinating everything of value to politics, is merely the result of a great confusion, a weakness of thought and awareness, an hodgepodge of the absolute and the relative. The maximalism, the revolutionism, the radicalism of the Russian Intelligentsia is a peculiar form of moralistic asceticism in relation to the civil, the social and historical life generally. It is very characteristic, that Russian tactics usually take the form of boycotts, strikes and work-stoppages. The Russian intelligent is never certain, whether he ought to accept history with all its tormenting, violent and tragic contradictions, none the more correct, or whether to repudiate it entirely. He refuses to ponder over history and its tasks, and he prefers to moralise over history, to impose upon it his own sociological schemae, very reminiscent of theological schemae. And in the Russian intelligent, torn away from his native soil, he remains characteristically a Russian man, having never the taste for history, for historical thought and for the drama of history. Our social thought has been intensely primitive and elementary, it has always striven after simplicity and feared complexity. The Russian Intelligentsia has always been confessing some sort of doctrine, containable in a pocket catechism, and an utopia, promising an easy and simplistic method of universal salvation, but it was not fond of and it feared creative thought as being of value in itself, before which might open infinitely complex perspectives. Among the broad masses of the so-called radical Intelligentsia, thought was not only made simplistic, but also neglectful and flippant. The reduction of old ideas among the half-indifferent masses -- was poisonous. The catechisms are tolerable only for an heated atmosphere, and it is in the hot-house atmosphere that they are produced and born. Creative thought, which posits and considers all ever new and newer tasks -- is dynamic. Russian thought however has always been too static, despite the shifting of various beliefs and currents. This is valid identically both in regard to the theocratic-guardian doctrines, and in regard to the positivist-radical and socialist doctrines.

II.

The Russian dislike for ideas and indifference towards ideas is often transformed into an indifference towards truth. The Russian man does not very much seek truth (istina), he seeks just-truth (pravda), which he thinks of now religiously, now morally, and then socially, he seeks salvation. In this there is something characteristically Russian, and there is its own genuine Russian just-truth (pravda). But there is also a danger, there is a turning-away from the paths of knowledge, there is a tendency towards a populism-based churlishness. Bowing before an organic wisdom of the people has always paralysed thought in Russia and cut short ideational creativity, wherein the person tends to be on his own responsibility. Our conservative thought has been still a native thought, and in it there has been no self-consciousness of personal spirit. But this self-consciousness of personal spirit also has little been sensed in our progressive thought. Thought, the life of ideas was always subordinated to the Russian soul-emphasis, a mixing up of rightful-truth (pravda-istina) with rightful-justice (pravda-spravedlivost'). But the Russian soul-emphasis was not subordinated to spirituality, it did not pass through spirit. Upon the basis of this soul-emphasis unfold all sorts of psychologism.

Nicholas Berdyaev

Native thought, thought, connected with the element of the soil, is always of soul, and not spiritual thought. But the thinking of the Russian revolutionaries has always transpired in an atmosphere of soul-emphasis, and not spirituality. The idea, the meaning reveals itself in the person, and not in the collective. And the people's wisdom reveals itself at the summits in the spiritual life of persons, expressing the people's spirit. Without great responsibility and the daring of personal spirit there cannot be realised developement of the people's spirit. The life of ideas is the uncovering of the life of spirit. In creative thought spirit transcends the soul-body elements. The exclusive dominance of soul-emphasis with its brutal heatedness opposes itself to the liberating life of spirit. The greatest Russian geniuses were afraid of this responsibility of personal spirit, and from the heights of the spiritual they fell downwards, they fell all the way to the ground, and they sought salvation in the elementary wisdom of the people. Thus it was with Dostoevsky and Tolstoy, and thus it was with the Slavophils. In Russian religious thought only Chaadaev and Vl. Solov'ev stood out as exceptions.

The Russian people's elemental soul-emphasis has assumed very manifold, very contradictory forms -- the protective and the seditious, the nationally-religious and the internationally-socialist. This -- is at the root of Russian populism's hostility to thought and ideas. In the mentality and the tendency of the Russian people's soul-emphasis there is something anti-gnostic, holding the process of cognition under suspicion. The heart has been victorious over the mind and the will. The Russian populist soul-emphasis type is moralistic, it applies to everything in the world a moralistic evaluation. But this moralism is incapable of results of a personal character, it does not create the tempering by spirit. In this moralism there predominates a vague soulfulness, a tender cordiality, often very charming, but there is no sense of courage of will, responsibility, self-discipline, firmness of character. The Russian people, perhaps, is the most spiritual people on earth. But its spirituality floats on some sort of elemental soulfulness, even moreso on corporeality. In this spirituality, the masculine principle adrift does not embrace the feminine principle, it does not give it form. But this means also, that spirit does not embrace the soulful. This is valid not only in regard to the "people", but also in regard to the "intelligentsia", which is broken away and external to the people, but preserving very characteristic features of the people's psychology. Upon this ground also is born the mistrust, the indifferent and hostile attitude

84

towards thought, towards ideas. Upon this very ground also is born moreover the reknown weakness of the Russian will, of the Russian character. The far right Russian Slavophils and the far left Russian populists (to them with few exclusions mustneeds on the basis of soul mentality be included also the Russian Social Democrats, dissimilar to their Western comrades) both alike rise up against "abstract thought" and demand thought that is moral and salvific, having essentially a practical application to life. In the rising up against abstract thought and in the demand for integral thought there has been very great truth and the presentiment of an higher type of thought. But this truth has foundered on the adrift soul-emphasis and the incapacity for analysis and differentiation. Human thought upon the pathways of the human spirit ought to proceed through dichotomy and analysis. The primordial organic integrality cannot be preserved and carried over into an higher type of spirituality without a tortuous differentiation process, without a falling-away and secularisation. Without the consciousness of this truth organic integral thought passes over into an hostility towards thought, into thoughtless nonsense, into an obscure moralism. The unique originality of the Russian soul cannot be killed by thought. Such a fear displays a lack of belief in Russia and in Russian man. The non-differentiation of our conservative thought has carried over into our progressive thought.

III.

In Russia a genuine emancipation of thought has still not been accomplished. Russian nihilism has been an enslaving, not liberating, thought. Our thought has remained servile. Russians fear the sin of thought, even when they do not believe in any sort of sin. Russians have still not altogether risen up to the awareness, that in living creative thought there is light, a transfigurative element, transfixing the darkness. Knowledge itself is life, and therefore it is impossible to say moreover, that knowledge ought to be subordinated to life in an utilitarian manner. There mustneeds be for us a liberation from Russian utilitarianism, so enslaving for our thought, be it religious or materialistic. The slavery of thought has led in wide circles of the Russian Intelligentsia to an ideational poverty and an ideational backwardness. The ideas, to which many still continue to point to as "foremost", in essence are very backward ideas, which do not measure up to the heights of contemporary European thought. The adherents of a "scientific" world-concept have lagged half a century behind the actual developements in science. Both the intelligent and the half-intelligent masses also attempt to live by antiquated ideas of stuff, long already relegated to the archives. Our "vanguard" intelligentsia remain hopelessly behind from the developements in European thought, hopelessly behind from the all more and more complicated and intricate philosophic and scientific creativity. It believes in ideas, which were current in the West more than fifty years back, and it is quite seriously capable of confessing the positivist world-view, the old theory of the social mean, etc. But this is the ultimate terminus and ossification of thought. Traditional positivism long ago already tumbled down not only in philosophy, but also in science itself. If it be never possible to speak seriously about materialism, as a directive for the half-literate, then it is impossible too to speak seriously about positivism, and soon it will be impossible to speak about criticism of the Kantian type. And it will be likewise impossible to support that radical "sociologism" of world-sense and world-concept, which all the masses of the intelligentsia in Russia still adhere to. New "cosmic" perspectives of world-sense and world-concept are unfolding. The social cannot be sundered and isolated from cosmic life, from the energies, which spill forth into it from all the planes of the cosmos. Thus impossible is even the social utopianism, always grounded in a simplification of thought concerning social life, in the rationalisation of it, whilst disregarding irrational cosmic forces. Not only in creative Russian thought, which in a small circle survives the period of transition, but also in Western European thought there has occurred a radical shift, and the "vanguard" in thought and consciousness appears altogether otherwise, than what too many among us continue to believe -- idle and inert thoughts.

The uppermost of mankind has already entered into the night of a new Middle Ages, when the sun ought to shine itself within us and bring us towards a new day. The external light fades out. The crash of rationalism, the rebirth of mysticism is also of this nocturnal moment. However, when the crash of the old rational thought occurs, it is quite necessary to appeal to creative thought, to a revealing of the idea of spirit. The struggle moves to the spiritual summits of mankind, it is there that the fate of human consciousness is determined, it is a genuine life of thought, a life of ideas. In the middle yet prevails the old inertness of thought, there is no initiative in the creativity of idea, and shreds of the old world of thought drag on in their miserable existence. Middling thought, imagining itself as the intelligent, arrives at a condition of complete absurdity. We are endlessly bumping up against static thought, while dynamic thought is nowise apparent. But thought by its nature is dynamic, it is an eternal developing of spirit, before it stand eternally new tasks, eternally new worlds are disclosed, and it mustneeds bestow eternally creative solutions. When thought is made static -- it shrivels up and dies. For many of our foremost Westernisers thought came to a stop 60 years ago, and they -- are the guardians of this old thought, they halted at a very elementary stage of enlightenment, which arose back in the West during the XVIII Century. These people in the area of thought are neither progressive nor revolutionary, they are rather conservators and guardians; they aspire backwards, towards the rational enlightenment, they re-warm long since chilled-down thoughts and are hostile to any heated blazing of thought.

IV.

The creative developement of ideas does not occasion for itself any sort of strong interest in the broad circles of the Russian Intelligentsia community. For us it has even included the conviction, that for social actions, ideas are altogether unnecessary or needed only in minimum supply, which always it was possible to find in the supplies of the traditional, the long ago cooled-off and static-ossified thought. All our developements in 1905 were not inspired by vitally creative ideas, it fed itself off ideas that were tepidly warm-cold, but was torn asunder by heated passions and interests. And this ideational poverty has been fateful. In the last fifty years for us there has been expressed many a creative idea, and ideas not only abstract, but of life and concrete. But surrounding all these ideas there has still formed no sort of cultural atmosphere, nor has there arisen any sort of social stirring. These ideas hold on in a few circles. The world of ideas and the world of sociality remain disconnected. On the part of the social element there has been no demand for ideas, there were no commands for ideational creativity, it had enough with the pitiful remnants of the old ideas. All the abnormality and sickness of the spiritual condition of our society was particularly sensed, when the world war started, requiring the exertion of all powers, not only material, but also spiritual. It was impossible to engage the world tragedy with the stock of old enlightenment ideas, of the old rationalist-sociological schemata. Man, armed with but these antiquated ideational armaments, was left to sense himself crushed and cast off onto the beehive of history. The humanitarian-pacifist current, always very elemental and simplistic, was powerless before the gruesome face of the historical destiny, the historical tragedy. If for us there had been an insufficient material preparation for the war, then also there was not a sufficient ideational preparation. The traditional ideas, for decades prevailing for us, were completely useless for the measures being played out in the world of events. Everything was shifted from its usual place, everything requires a completely new creative work of thought, a new ideational inspiration. Our social element during the time of unprecedented world catastrophe was poor in ideas, insufficiently inspired. We are paid back for the long period of indifference towards ideas. The ideas, upon which the old authority rested, have ultimately crumbled. It was impossible to revive them by any means. No sort of poisoned mystical justifications can help, drawn forth from the old supply. But the ideas of the Russian social element, appealing for the rebuilding of Russian life and the renovation of authority, had become chilled off and weather beaten earlier than the hour which transpired for their realisation in life. It remains to turn things around towards a creative life of idea, which imperceptibly impends in the world. Shaken loose are the ideological bases of Russian conservatism and Russian radicalism. There is need to pass over into another ideational format.

In the world struggle of peoples the Russian people ought to have its own idea, ought to bear into it its own tempering of spirit. Russians cannot be content by negative ideas of repelling German militarism and gloomy defeat by an internal reaction. Russians in this struggle ought to rebuild not only civilly and socially, but also to rebuild ideationally and spiritually. The shameful indifference towards ideas, reinforcing the backwardness and stony petrification of thought, ought to be replaced by a new ideational inspiration and ideational ascent. The soil is harrowed loose, and the time is propitious for ideational propagation, upon which all our future depends. In this very difficult and demanding hour of our history we find ourselves in a condition of ideational anarchy and muck, in our spirit takes place a rotting process, bound up with the putrefaction of thought both conservative and revolutionary, of ideas both of the right and of the left. But in the depths of the Russian people there is a living spirit, concealing great possibilities. In the loosened soil there ought to sprout the seeds of new thought and new life. The maturing of Russia towards a world role presupposes its spiritual rebirth.

II. THE PROBLEM OF NATIONALNESS.
EAST AND WEST

Nationalness and Humanity

I.

Our nationalists and our cosmopolists are situated within the grip of quite lowly concepts of nationalness, and they both alike disunite national existence from the existence of all the one mankind. The passions, which the national problems usually evoke, hinder clarity of consciousness. The ruminations of thought over the problem of nationality ought, first of all, to establish, that it is both impossible and thoughtless to set an opposition of nationality and humanity, or a national multiplicity and an all-human unity. Moreover, this false opposition is made from two sides, from the side of nationalism and from the side of cosmopolitism. It would be impermissible, on principle, to oppose the part to the whole or an organ to its organism and to think it itself -- a perfectly whole organism, amidst the disappearance and apparent surmounting of the multiplicity of parts and organs. Nationalness and the struggle for its existence and developement do not signify a quarrel between mankind and man, and it cannot on principle be bound up with the incomplete and unrealised united condition of mankind, subject to disappear amidst the onset of complete unity. False nationalism feeds upon such concepts about nationalness. Nationalness is individual existence, outside of which is impossible the existing of mankind, it is lodged within the very depths of life, and nationality is a value, creative within history, dynamically oriented. The existence of mankind in forms of the national existence of its parts does not at all mean an indispensible zoological and lower condition of mutual hostility and infringement, which would disappear with the measure of growth of humanness and unity. Behind nationalness stands an eternal ontological basis and an eternal valuable value. Nationalness is existant individuality, one of the hierarchical degrees of being, an other degree, an other circle, than the individuality of man or the individuality of mankind, as a certain collective of persons. The establishing of perfect brotherhood between people would not mean the disappearance of human individualities, but instead would be their full affirmation. And the establishment of an all-human brotherhood of peoples would not mean their disappearance, but rather the affirmation of the national individualities. Mankind involves a certain positive all-unity, but it would be transformed into an empty abstraction, if by its own existence it extinguished and diminished the being of all the degrees of reality entering into it, of the national individualities and the individualities of persons. And in the Kingdom of God, it ought to be thought of as the perfect and beautiful existence of person-individualities and nation-individualities. Every being -- is individual. An abstraction is however not a being. There is no spirit of being in an abstract humanism, freed of all its concrete multiplicity, there is only emptiness. Mankind itself is a concrete individuality of an higher hierarchical degree, a collective person, and not an abstraction, not a mechanical sum. God too is not the extinguishing of all the individual degrees of the manifold of being, but rather their plenitude and perfection. It is impossible to replace the multiplicity of individual degrees, all the complex hierarchy of the world, by the unity of an higher degree, by the individuality of the unity. Perfect unity (the national in general, the human in general, the cosmic or Divine) is an higher and most full form of being of all the multiplicity of individual existences in the world. Every nationality is a richness of a singular and brotherly united mankind, and not an hindrance to its path. Nationality is a problem historical, and not social, a problem of concrete culture, and not abstractly societal.

Cosmopolitism both as regards philosophy and life is inconsistent, it is merely an abstraction or utopia, the application of abstract categories to an area, where everything is concrete. Cosmopolitism does not live up to its own name, in it there is nothing of the cosmic, since also the cosmos, the world, is a concrete individuality, one of the hierarchical degrees. In the cosmopolitan consciousness, the image of the cosmos is absent just the same, as is the image of the nation. To sense oneself a citizen of the universal does not at all mean the loss of a national feeling and a national citizenship. Man communes with cosmic and universal life through the life of all the individual hierarchical degrees, through the national life. Cosmopolitism is a monstrous and unrealisable expression about a dream concerning an united, brotherly and perfect mankind, replacing the concretely live mankind with an abstract utopia. Whoever does not love his own people and for whom its image is not dear, that one also cannot love mankind, cannot hold dear the concrete image of mankind. Abstraction begets abstraction. Abstract feelings take hold in such a man, and consequently everything alive, in flesh and blood, disappears from the field of vision for the man. Cosmopolitism is likewise a denial and extinction of the value of the individual, of every image and its detection, with the preaching of an abstract man and abstract humankind.

II.

A man enters into mankind through his national individuality, as a national man, and not as an abstract man; he enters it as a Russian, a Frenchman, a German or Englishman. A man cannot skip and overleap through an entire step of being, in doing so he would have impoverished and desolated himself. The national man -- is more, and not less, than simply man, in him there are the innate features of man in general and moreover still features individually-national. One might desire the brotherhood and unity of Russians, French, English and Germans and all the peoples of the earth, but it is impossible to desire, that from the face of the earth there should vanish the expressions of national images, of national spiritual types and cultures. Such a vision concerning man and humankind, abstracted from everything national, is a thirst for the extinction of an entire world of values and richness. Culture never was and never will be abstractly-human, it is always concretely-human, i.e. national, individually of a people and only in such capacity ascending into mankind in general. That which is totally non-national, the abstractly human, the easily transported from people to people, is the least creative, the external technical side of culture. Everything creative within culture bears upon it the seal of national genius. Even the great techical inventions are national, and non-national only are the technical applications of the great inventions, which readily are adopted by al the peoples. Even so is the scientific genius, the initiative, creating national-methods. Darwin could only have been an Englishman, and Helmholtz -- characteristically a German. The national and the generally-human in culture cannot be set in opposition. The high points of national creativity have especially a significance common to all mankind. In the national aspect, the genius reveals the all-human, through his own individual aspect he penetrates into the universal. Dostoevsky -- is a Russian genius, and there is a national image imprinted upon all his creativity. He reveals to the world the depths of the Russian spirit. He himself was a Russian's Russian -- yet he is also very all-human, a most universal of Russians. Through the Russian depths he reveals depths that are all-human, of all the world. The same thing can be said about every genius. Always he bears upwards the national to a significance common to all mankind. Goethe -- is an universal man not in the capacity of an abstract man, but in the capacity of a national man, a German.

The unification of mankind, its developement towards an all-unity is accomplished through a tormentive and painful education and struggle of national individualities and cultures. Another historical path there is not, though an other path -- is abstraction, emptiness or the purely individual withdrawal into the depths of spirit, into an other world. The fate of nations and national cultures ought to taken to completion. The acceptance of history is already the acceptance of the struggle for national individualities, for types of culture. The Greek culture, the Italian culture during the era of the Renaissance, the French culture and the German culture during their flourishing period is also the path of the world culture of all mankind, but they are all profoundly national, individually unique. All the great national cultures -- are of all-humankind in their significance. The levelling down of civilisation is an ugly thing. An artificial language Volapuk culture cannot have any siginificance, in it there is nothing universal. The entire world path of existence is a complex interaction of various degrees of the world hierarchy of individualities, the creative outgrowth of one hierarchy into another, of the person into the nation, the nation into mankind, mankind into the cosmos, the cosmos into God. The disappearance of classes and coercive states can and ought to be thought of in context of the perfecting of mankind, but it is impossible to think of the disappearance of nationalities. The nation is a dynamic substance, and not a transitory historical function, it grows with its roots within the mysterious depths of life. Nationality is a positive enrichment of being, and it deserves to be struggled for, as a value. National unity goes deeper than the unity of classes, parties and all the other transitory historical forms in the life of peoples. Each people struggles for its own culture and for an higher life in an atmosphere of national mutual responsibility. And it is a great self-delusion -- to want to create something parallel to nationality. Even the Tolstoyan non-resistance, the fleeing from everything connected with nationality, proves itself profoundly national and Russian a thing. The withdrawal from national life, the wont for wandering -- is a purely Russian phenomenon, bearing the imprint of the Russian national spirit. Even the formal denial of nationality can be national. National creativity does not signify a consciously-deliberate nationalising, it is freely and elementally national.

III.

All the attempts at a rational definition of nationalness lead to failure. The nature of nationalness is undefinable by any rationally expedient signs. Neither race, nor territory, nor language, nor religion are manifest by signs, determinative of nationality, though they all play some role or other in its determination. Nationalness -- is a complex historical learning process, it is formed as the result of a bloody mix of races and tribes, many a redistribution of lands, with which its destiny is bound up, and a spiritual cultural process, creating its unrepeatable spiritual visage. And as the result of all the historical and psychological investigations there remains still an indefinable and elusive residue, in which also consists all the mystery of national individuality. Nationality -- is mysterious and mysteried, irrational, just like every individual being. It is needful to be in the nationality, to participate in its creative vital process, in order ultimately to know its mystery. The mystery of nationality is preserved behind all the swells and surges of historical elements, behind all the vagarities of fate, behind all the dynamic movements, destroying the past and creating the hitherto non-existing. The soul of medieval France and the France of the XX Century -- is one and the same national soul, though within history everything has changed to the point of being unrecognisable.

The creativity of national cultures and the types of life does not allow of an external and compulsory regulation, it is not the fulfilling of obligatory law, it is free, within it is a creative capriciousness. The legal, the official, the outwardly obligatory nationalism only but hinders the national vocation and denies the mystery of national existence. A legalistic nationalism and a legalistic humanism alike hamper the creative impulse, they are alike hostile to an understanding of a national mode of existence, as a creative task. There does exist an Old Testament sort of nationalism. The Old Testament protective sort of nationalism is very much against that, what they term the "Europeanisation" of Russia. They cleave to those features of national existence, which are connected with the historical backwardness of Russia. They are afraid, that European technology, the machine, developements in manufacturing, new forms of society, derived from the Europeans, can kill the uniqueness of the Russian spirit, can depersonalise Russia. But this -- is a faint-hearted nationalism of little faith, this -- is a lack of faith in the power of the Russian spirit, in the invincibility of national strength, this -- is materialism, setting our spiritual existence into a servile dependency on the external material conditions of life. That which is considered as the "Europeanisation" of Russia does not at all signify the denationalisation of Russia. Germany was an economically and politically backward land in comparison with France and England, it was the East in comparison with the West. But there came the hour, when it accepted the more advanced Western civilisation. Did this make it less national, did it lose its unique spirit? Certainly not. The machine, itself per se formless and unsightly, international, was especially welcomed in Germany and became a tool of the national will. That which is evil and violent in the German machine, is very national, very German. In Russia the machine can play an altogether different role, it can become a tool of the Russian spirit. The same as in everything. That which is called European or international civilisation, is essentially a phantom. The growth and developement of every national mode of existence is not a matter of its transfer over from a national uniqueness into some international European civilisation, which does not at all exist. The levelling effect of Europeanism, the international civilisation -- is a purest abstraction, in which is contained not a single drop of concrete reality. All peoples, all lands pass through a certain stage of developement and growth, they arm themself with the weapons of technology both scientific and social, in which per se there is nothing individual nor national, since in the end the only thing individual and national is the spirit of life. But this process of growth and developement is not some sideways movement, towards some "international Europe", which nowhere is to be found in the West, this -- is a movement upwards, a movement all-human in its national particularity. There is only one historical path to the attainment of the utmost all-humanity, to the unity of mankind -- the path of national growth and developement, of national creativity. The all-humanity reveals itself only under the guise of nationalities. Denationalisation, as pervaded by the idea of an international Europe, of an international civilisation, of an international mankind is a purest void, non-being. Yet neither can a people have its developement via a detour, on the sidelines, to grow along a foreign path and a foreign growth. Betwixt my nationality and my humanity lies no sort of an "international Europe", of an "international civilisation". The creative national path also is a path towards all-humanity, it is a revealing of all-humanity in my nationalness, just as it is revealed in every nationality.

IV.

That which usually gets termed as the "Europeanisation" of Russia, is inevitable and beneficial. There is much that is grievous and hurtful in this process, involving a difficult transition from the old integrality through the splitting and disintegration of everything organic towards a new and yet non-existant life. But least of all does the process of "Europeanisation" signify, that we shall become the like of the Germans and the English or the French. Quite bereft of any meaning is an opposition of the orientation of the life of mankind in general against a national orientation. The appeal to forget about Russia and the national and instead to serve mankind, to be inspired only by mankind in general, has no signifcance, and is an empty appeal. The reality of all mankind is dependent upon the reality of Russia and other nationalities. Russia -- is a great reality, and it enters into an other reality, mankind namely, and enriches it, fills it with its own values and riches. The cosmopolitan denial of Russia in the name of mankind is a robbing of mankind. Russia -- is an existential fact, through which we all dwell within mankind. And Russia ought to be elevated to significance for mankind in general. Russia -- is a creative task, set before mankind, a value, enriching the life of the world. Mankind and the world expect a ray of light from Russia, its say, its unrepeatable deed. All-mankind has great need of Russia, and for all-mankind it would be an hideous thing to have Russian man transformed into an international and cosmopolitan man. For all-mankind there is needful the elevation of Russian man to all-human significance, and not the transforming of him into an abstracted and empty man. All-mankind has nothing in common with internationalism, all-humanity is to an utmost a fullness of all the national. And we ought to create a concrete Russian life, not upon something dissimilar, and not upon abstract social and moral categories. All our life ought to be oriented upon concrete ideas of nation and the person, and not upon abstract ideas of class and mankind. The fate of Russia is infinitely more dear than the fate of classes and parties, doctrines and teachings. The zoological national feeling and instinct, which so frightens the humanist cosmopolitans, is an elementary and dark still elemental condition, which ought to be transformed into a creative national feeling and instinct. Without an initial and elemental love for Russia it is impossible to have any creative historical path. Our love for Russia, just like any love -- is arbitrary, it is not only love for quality and worth, but this love ought to be a source of the creative realising of qualities and worthiness of Russia. The love for one's people ought to be a creative love, a creative instinct. And least of all does it mean hostility and hatred towards other peoples. The path towards all-humanity for each of us lies through Russia. And truly indeed every denationalisation separates us from the all-mankind. The visage of Russia should be imprinted upon the celestial mankind itself. Within the one mankind there can only be united individualities, and not empty abstractions. The truth about the positive connection of nationality and mankind can be expressed from another and opposite side. If impermissible be the opposition of the idea of mankind to the idea of nationalness, then impermissible also is the reverse opposition. It is impossible to be an enemy of the unity of mankind in the name of nationality in the capacity of a nationalist. Such a turning of nationality against mankind is an impoverishment of nationality and its ruination. Such a sort of false and renegade nationalism ought to share the fate of the empty internationalism. The creative assertion of nationality is also an assertion of mankind. Nationality and mankind -- are one.

Nationalism and Messianism[1]

I.

Nationalism and messianism are contiguous and tend to get confused. Nationalism in its positive assertion, at the moment of an exceptional spiritual ascent, gets transfused into messianism. Thus in Germany at the beginning XX Century, the spiritual national ascent with Fichte broke down its borders and was transformed into a German messianism. And the nationalism of the Slavophils imperceptibly passed over into messianism. But nationalism and messianism are profoundly contrary in their nature, their origin and their tasks. The contrary nature of nationalistic and messianic aspirations always was very felt in Russia. It would be difficult to discover the messianic idea in the nationalism of the "Novyi Vremya" ("New Times") or of our thoughtful nationalists. To the nationalists of such a sort, all messianism with its foolishness and sacrifice seems not only inimical, but also dangerous. The nationalists -- are sober, practical people, well set upon the earth. Nationalism can be consolidated upon very positivist grounds, and can have a basis biological. Messianism however is conceivable only upon a religious grounding, and its basis can only be mythical. There is possible the existence of many a nationalism. In its idea, nationalism makes no pretense to universality, it involves uniqueness and exclusion, though in practice it can easily reach the point of denial and destruction of other nationalitics. But by its nature nationalism is particular, it is always partial, by its own denials and destructions there is thus quite little pretense to universality, as rather the biological struggle of individualities within the animate world. Messianism does not tolerate co-existence, it -- is singular, yet always universal in its scope. But messianism never denies nor biologically destroys other nationalities, it seeks to save them, to subjoin them to its universal idea.

---

[1] NATSIONALIZM I MESSIANIZM. Originally published separately as a pamphlet, Moscow, G. A. Leman & S. N. Sakharov, 1917, (Klepinina № 12).

The religious roots of messianism -- are in the messianic consciousness of the Hebrew people, in its consciousness of itself as the chosen people of God, into which would be born the Messiah, the Deliverer from all evils, creating the holy kingdom of Israel. The ancient Jewish messianism -- was exclusive, tied in with one nationality and spurning all other nationalities. In the Hebrew messianism there was still not the idea of all-mankind. For Christianity, however, there is no distinction between Greek and Jew. The Hebrew type of messianism is impossible for the Christian world. With the appearance of the Messiah-Christ the religious mission of the Hebrew people was completed and thus ended the Hebrew messianism. In the Christian world impermissible further became the fierce religio-national hatred. It was possible only as a fact biological, and not as a fact religious. The kingdom of Israel within the Christian world has become an all-mankind kingdom. Christianity no little involves the denying of race and nationalities, as natural aspects, as spiritual-biological individualities. But Christianity is a religion of salvation and delieverance of all mankind and of all the world. Christ came for all and for everyone. But although impossible amongst Christian mankind is an exclusive national messianism, denying the very idea of humankind, an Old Testament type of messianism, there yet remains the New Testament transfigurative messianism, deriving from the appearance of the Messiah for all mankind and for all the world. Amongst Christian mankind the messianic consciousness can be oriented only forwards, only towards the Coming Christ, since in essence this consciousness -- is prophetic. And the purely religious, the purely Christian messianism always takes on an apocalyptic hue. A Christian people can conceive of itself as a people God-bearing, Christian, a people of the Messiah among peoples, it can sense its own unique religious vocation for resolving the fates of world history, and no wise by this denying the other Christian peoples. Russian messianism, if within it there be distinguished the element purely messianic, is preeminently apocalyptic, oriented towards the Christ to Come and His antipode -- the Anti-Christ. This has existed among our schismatics, in the mystical sectarianism and in our Russian national genius, as with Dostoevsky, and by this is tinted our religio-philosophic searchings. The messianic consciousness within the Christian world tends towards antinomy, just as everything within Christianity. In the spiritual composite of the Russian people there are features, which render it an apocalyptic people within the highest aspects of its spiritual life. The

Polish messianism also bears an apocalyptic imprint, and this is something inherent to the nature of the Slavic peoples. But the messianic idea can be torn away from its religio-Christian foundation and be experienced by peoples, as an exceptional spiritual-cultural vocation. And thus the German messianism has become predominantly racial, with a strongly biological hue. The German people at its spiritual heights has come to conceive of itself not as the bearer of the Spirit of Christ, but as the bearer of an higher and singular spiritual culture. The German race -- becomes the chosen higher race. The apocalyptic disposition is completely foreign to the Germanic spirit, nor was it there in the old German mysticism. In this -- is a basic difference of the Slavs from the Germans. But the German consciousness, deriving from Fichte, and from the old idealists and romantics, from R. Wagner and in our own time from Arthur Drews and H. S. Chamberlain, with such an exceptional intensity involves an experience of the chosenness of the German race and its summoned vocation to be the bearer foremost of an higher spiritual world culture, and in this it includes within itself features of messianism, though distortedly. Drews reckons it possible even to speak about the consciousness of a Germanic religion, a religion of Germanism, purely Aryan, but neither Christian nor anti-Christian.

II.

In the XIX and XX Centuries the messianic and the nationalistic experiences became intertwined, mixed together and passed over one into the other. It mustneeds be remembered, that nationalism -- is a comparatively recent phenomenon, it developed only during the XIX Century, it came as the replacement to the medieval and the old Roman universalism. Nationalism, in its pretensions reaching the extent of a denial of other national souls and bodies, to the impossibility of any positive intercourse with them, is an egoistic self-assertion, a self-limiting isolation. Its basis -- is elementally biological. And wherein such a nationalism makes pretense to unlimitedness, it becomes all the more limited. The unbounded pretensiveness of nationalism renders it something negative, narrow, separates it from universality, deprives it of creative spirit. Suchlike is the nationalism of Katkov and Danilevsky. The national organism, always manifesting itself as particularised being, and not the universal, does not comprise within itself the universal and all-human spirit, but it has the pretension to be everything and swallow up all. Every mixing up of nationalism with messianism, every projecting of nationalism as messianism begets a darkened consciousness and bears evil in the wotld. The substitutions always become evil-bearing. And strict distinctions here are needful, since the partial ought not to pass itself off as all-inclusive. Nationalism is a positive good and value, as a creative assertion, the revealing and developing of the existence of an individual people. But in this individual image of a people there ought to be revealed all-mankind. It is pernicious, when nationalness as an unbounded self-conceit and greedy self-assertion, opines itself universal to the extent that no one and nothing can compare alongside it. Suchlike is the trend of German nationalism. But it is a fruitful thing, when nationalness by its creative efforts reveals in itself the universal, its non-impersonal individually unrepeatable image, carrying it to the level of universal a significance. Nationality cannot pretend itself to be exclusive in its universality, it allows for other national individuums and enters into intercourse with them. Nationality belongs within an hierarchy of degrees of being, and it ought to take its own assigned place, for it hierarchically is co-subordinate to mankind and the cosmos. And it is necessary strictly to distinguish between nationalism and messianism.

Messianism belongs to a completely different spiritual order. Messianism relates to nationalism, just as the second birth for the mystics relates to the first birth within nature. National existence is a natural existence, for which it is needful to struggle, which it is necessary to reveal and develope. But the messianic calling lies already outside the lines of the natural process of developement, this -- is a brilliant flash of light from the heavens, a Divine fire, in which is consumed all the earthly order. A prudent-minded messianism, setting the earthly affairs in fine order, cannot be. In the messianic consciousness always there is an ecstatic turning towards the miraculous, towards a catastrophic rupture within the natural order, towards the absolute and finalative. Nationalism however involves a dwelling within the natural and relative, within historical developement. Nationalism and messianism tend no little to negate each the other, since they are situated upon different planes. Nationalism can but affirm and develope that which is of the natural historical existence of the people, in the depths of which can blaze forth the messianic idea, like lightning, come down from the spiritual heavens. But it is possible to have a substitution of messianism by nationalism, with the phenomena of this world for the phenomena of the other world. A purified and creative national work can but ready the recepticle for the messianic idea. But the messianic idea itself comes rather from the other world, and its element -- is the element of fire, and not of earth.

III.

Within the actual messianic consciousness there transpires a mixing together of the Christian messianism with the Hebrew messianism. And if pernicious be the replacement of messianism by nationalism, of universalism -- by particularism, then no less pernicious is the replacement of Christian messianism -- by the Hebrew sort. The Hebrew messianism has become forever impossible after Christ. Within Judaism itself its role has been rendered negative, since it would involve the awaiting of a new messiah, opposed to Christ, to assert the kingdom and felicitude of Israel upon the earth. But the Jewish messianism has penetrated into the Christian world, and there it replaces the sense of service -- by demands, it replaces the sense of sacrifice -- with a thirst for a privileged earthly happiness. But the Christian messianic consciousness of a people can be exclusively a sacrificial consciousness, a consciousness of the vocation of a people to serve the world and all the peoples of the world by their deed of deliverance from evil and suffering. The Messiah by His mystical nature -- is sacrificial, and the people of the Messiah can only but be a sacrificial people. The messianic awaiting is an awaiting of deliverance through sacrifice. The Jewish chiliasm, however, which expects felicitude upon earth without sacrifice, without Golgotha, is profoundly different from the Christian messianic idea. And the awaiting of the Coming Christ presupposes a passing through Golgotha, the acceptance of Christ Crucified and the heroic creative path upwards. With the Polish messianists, with Adam Mickiewicz, with Andrzej Towianski, August Cieszkowski, there was a very pure sacrificial consciousness, it blazed at the heart of the people amidst its great suffering. But all too quickly the sacrificial messianism in Poland was replaced by an extreme nationalism. The messianic consciousness of a people can only be through the fruition of great sufferings of the people. And the messianic idea, lodged within the heart of the Russian people, was in the fruition of the suffering-laden fate of the Russian people, its search for the City to Come. But in the Russian consciousness there has occurred a mixing together of the Christian

103

messianism with the Hebrew messianism and with a nationalism transgressive of its limits. With us there has not been healthy a national consciousness and national feeling, always there has been a sort of fracture, always either an excess of self-assertion or self-denial. Our nationalism too oten has made pretense to be of the nationalism of the ancient Hebrew type, raging, exclusive and demanding. Its reverse side however has been a complete denial of nationality, an abstract and utopian internationalism.

Distinctions and clarifications within our national self-consciousness need to be made. Nationalism affirms the spiritual-biological basis of the individually-historical existence of peoples, outside of which is impossible the fulfilling of any sort of mission. A people has to exist, has to preserve its own image, has to develope by its own energy, has to have the possibility to create its own values. But the most refined, the most positive nationalism still yet is not messianism. The messianic idea -- is an universal idea. It defines itself by the power of the sacrificial spirit of the people, by its exclusively being inspired by the kingdom not of this world, it cannot pretend upon external force over the world nor pretend upon what provides the people earthly felicitude. And I think, that in Russia, in the Russian people there is exclusionary nationalism, transgressive of its own borders, there is the raging exclusionary Hebrew type messianism, but there is also the truly Christian and sacrificial messianism. The image of Russia is twofold, within it are mixed the greatest of contradictions. The extreme assertion of nationalism with us is frequently combined with a denial of Russian messianism, with an absolute lack of understanding of the messianic idea and an aversion to it... Nationalism can come to represent a purely Westernised, Europeanised Russia, a phenomenon particularistic in its spirit, without containing any great idea concerning Russia, ignorant of Russia, as something of the great East. And conversely, the total denial of nationalism can be a phenomenon deeply Russian, an ignorance of the Western world, inspired by the universal idea concerning Russia, by its sacrificial messianic calling. The messianism, passing over into a denial of every nationalism, desires that the Russian people should sacrificially devote itself in service to the deed of the deliverance of all peoples, so that Russian man should manifest his all-human image. Characteristic to the Russian soul is a religious, and not an "international", denial of nationalism. And this aspect -- is Russian, characteristically national, behind which stands the image of all humankind, and which resolutely needs to be distinguished from the guise of the cosmopolitan.

IV.

But the Russian soul is lacking in a masculine consciousness, and is not aware, does not enlighten, is much confused. The Russian apocalypsis has been experienced passively, as a transfixing of the Russian soul by mystical currents, as the quivering of its subtlest texture. This passive, receptive, feminine-like apocalyptic aspect of the Russian soul ought to be combined with the masculine, the active and creative spirit. Russia has need of a masculine national consciousness. There is needful the creative work of thought, which will make for a difference, to shed light upon the Russian darkness. The apocalyptic experiences in the life of the Russian people, immersed in darkness, have led to self-immolation and the eradication of all existence. There is always this tendency in the Russian thirst for the absolute, in the Russian denial of everything relative, of everything historical. Likewise immersed in the darkness is the consciousness of the Russian revolutionary intelligentsia, so often denying the national within Russia, and yet very national, very Russian in its element. The Russian element remains dark, lacking for form from the masculine consciousness. The Russian soul often experiences an unconscious, dark messianism. This was the case with Bakunin, in his own way confessing a Slavic messianism. This was the case with certain of the Russian anarchists and revolutionaries, believing in a world conflagration, out of which miraculously would be born a new life, and seeing in the Russian people that messiah, which should set alight this conflagration and bring the world this new life. With our nationalists of the official mold, both of the old form and of the more recent Western form, there is in any case already less of the Russian messianic spirit, than with certain of the sectarians or certain of the anarchists, people dark in their consciousness, but truly Russian in their composition. In the oddest and most varied forms the Russian soul tends to express its old inherited idea concerning world liberation from evil and woe, and about the birth of a new life for all mankind. This idea, truly a messianic idea, was alike held by both Bakunin and N. F. Fedorov, by both Russian socialists and by Dostoevsky, by both Russian sectarians and by Vl. Solov'ev. But this Russian messianic consciousness is not pervaded by the light of consciousness, not given form by the masculine will. We ought to be aware, that Russian messianism cannot be pretentious and self-assertive, it can only be a sacrificial blazing of spirit, only a great spiritual impulse toward new life for all the world. The messianism does not mean, that we are better than others or can pretend to more, but signifies rather, that we ought to do more and forsake harmful means. But every messianic service ought to be preceeded by a positive national effort, a spiritual and material cleansing, by a strengthening and developing of our national existence. Messianism cannot be a programme, the programme ought to be creatively national. Messianism however is at the eisoteric depths of a pure, healthy and positive nationalism, it is an unmediated spiritual creative impulse.

Nationalism and Imperialism[1]

I.

The problem of nationalism and the problem of imperialism have become quite acute amidst the present worldwide struggle of peoples. In the sphere of thought, one of the fruitions of the current war might be a philosophy of nationalism and a philosophy of imperialism. But the work of construction in this direction may also be fruitful for practical tasks, for all the currents of our internal and world politics. Our nationalism at present is situated at a very low level of consciousness. Our national impulses of will have not been enlightened. And Russian imperialism, as a world historical fact, has been a matter still not sufficiently thought over nor been posited in conjunction with the so-called nationalistic politics. Among the wide circles of the Russian intelligentsia these problems have generated little interest and were even viewed as rather "reactionary". A national feeling was inspired only by the war and at an elemental level it compelled the forming of a national awareness. Otherwise unbothered, and without extreme necessity, we were in this regard quite careless.

The world war can be viewed from various perspectives. In one of these aspects of the world war there has to be acknowledged the inevitable and fateful momentum in the coursing and dialectic of imperialism. It is the result of the clash of imperialistic wills for world might and world dominion. The existence of certain world pretensions could not but beget a world war. The world imperialistic pretensions of Germany came too late within history, when the earthly orb was already in the grip of the greatest sea power, and Russia -- the greatest dry-land power. But the world war is connected not only with the heightened tension of the imperialistic politics of the great powers, -- it likewise very sharply posits the question concerning the fate of all the nationalities, right down to the very least. All the national organisms seek to arrange for their own matters in the world,

---

[1] NATSIONALIZM I IMPERIALIZM. Originally published separately as a pamphlet, Moscow, G. A. Leman & S. N. Sakharov, 1917, (Klepinina № 11).

to have their own national borders. The war involves also and wears down the weak nationalities, yet together with this it inspires in them the will towards an autonomous existence. The enormous imperialistic organisms are spread out and strive towards the forming of a worldwide kingdom. Yet parallel to this the smallest national organisms strive for independence, relying upon the bloodshed of the great powers. Imperialism and nationalism -- are different principles, and behind them stand hidden different motifs, and it is proper to clearly distinguish this point.

Within the history of modern mankind there is occurring twofold a process -- a process of universalisation and a process of individualisation, of an uniting into large bodies and of a differentiation into small bodies. Nationalism is a principle for individualisation, imperialism -- a principle for universalisation. At the same time as nationalism tends towards particularity, imperialism seeks to enter out upon a world scale. These principles differ qualitatively, but they do not exclude each other, they co-exist. Imperialism by its nature goes out beyond the borders devolving upon its national existence, the imperialistic will is always a will for a world-scale existence. Through struggle and through discord imperialism all the moreso enables the unification of mankind. The imperialistic will has spilled much blood within human history, but behind it stood hidden the idea of the world unity of mankind, surmounting every national particularism, every provincialism. In the ancient Roman empire there was nationality no longer, it strove to be universal. The idea of a world empire extends throughout the whole of history and reaches down to the XX Century, when it loses its sacral character (the Holy Roman empire) and discovers its basis to a remarkable degree to consist in mercantile interests. The economic aspect of our century has set its seal also upon the idea of a world empire. England showed itself to be the first mighty model of the new imperialism. And it mustneeds be said, that in its imperialistic policies great success befell its lot and bloodlessly rendered it the master of the seas and oceans. All the great powers strive towards imperialistic expansion and conduct an imperialistic politics. This -- is the fated lot of every great power. At the time, when there blazed forth a world war unprecedented in all history, it became apparent, that there are three great powers, which can make pretense to world domination -- England, Russia and Germany. The co-existence of these three imperialistic wills is impossible. A clash and choice was inevitable. And very naive is that philosophy of history, which would tend to believe, that it is possible to preclude movement along this path of a world imperialistic struggle, desiring to see in it not the tragic fate of all mankind, but merely the evil will of this or that class, of these or some other governments.

II.

It is impossible to posit the problem of imperialism upon the subjectively moral grounds of our sympathy or lack of sympathy for imperialistic politics. It is possible entirely to be lacking of an imperialistic pathos and even to react with repugnance towards the many ugly sides of imperialistic politics and to acknowledge everything as being of an objective inevitability and an objective meaning to imperialism. It is possible to react with indignation to certain sides of colonial politics and yet entirely admit, that it allows for a world unity of culture. Imperialism makes for division and causes a world war. But it also unites mankind, leads it to unity. the formation of large imperialistic bodies was completely inevitable, something through which mankind has to pass. This is one of the irreversible aspects of the historical process. Mankind moves towards unity through struggle, strife and war. This -- is pitiful, this can evoke our indignation, this -- is an indication of the great darkness, in which the very roots of human life are immersed, but this is so. Humanitarian pacifism proclaims exceedingly fine moral truths, but it does not obviate the paths, by which is wrought the historical fate of mankind. This fate is accomplished through very tragic contradictions, and not along direct morally clear paths. The historical paths of mankind, full of contradictions, contain within them great dangers, the possibilities of inward collapse and being thrown backwards, to the beastly instincts, but it is necessary to bravely go forward, guarding the utmost image of mankind. The objective meaning of imperialism is deeper and broader than what is superficially termed imperialistic politics. Imperialism, though often its motifs be vile and its objects ugly, yet all the same leads out beyond the borders of a closed-in national existence, it leads out beyond the borders of Europe into the wide world, out beyond the seas and the oceans, it unites East and West. The pathos of all the wide world lives also in mercantile-interests imperialism.

But imperialism with its worldwide pretensions does not at all mean the certain oppressing and exterminating of lesser nationalities. Imperialism is not the unfailing expansion of one particular nationality, exterminating every other nationality. The German type of imperialism is not the sole type of imperialism. There is even moreso a basis to think, that Germany has no imperialistic vocation and that its imperialism is but a nationalism given to a conceit beyond all measure. It is characteristic, that the greatest statesman of Germany -- Bismarck, was still lacking of an imperialistic mindset, and his politics were but national. Too conceited and too inflated a nationalism bears with it an oppressing of all the national individualities. Nationalism has to know its limits. Beyond these limits, there starts already not nationalism, but rather imperialism. England realised this. And here we come nigh to a very important question for Russia, concerning the correlation of imperialism and nationalism. Russia -- is the greatest dry-land empire in the world, a whole tremendous world, encompassing endless variety, a great East-West, surpassing the delimited concept of individuality. And insofar as there stand before Russia world imperialistic tasks, they surpass the tasks purely national. Thus it was in antiquity in the Roman empire, and thus also in modern times stands the question in the empire of Great Britain. A great empire ought to be a great unifier, its universalism ought giftedly to encompass every individuality. Every great empire, historically fit for life, ought to have an innate national core, from which and around which is wrought its world historical work. The Great Russian ethnos comprises also such a core for Russian imperialism, and it has created the enormity of Russia. The Russian empire includes within it a very complex national composition, it unites a multitude of nationalities. But it cannot be viewed as a mechanical medley of peoples -- it is Russian at its basis and task in the world. Russia is a particular organism within the world, having its own specific calling, its own singular visage.

III.

Russian imperialism, to which so much by nature is given, does not resemble the imperialism of the English or the German, it is altogether unique, and more contradictory in its nature. Russian imperialism possesses a national basis, but in its purposes it exceeds all the purely national purposes, and before it stand tasks of wide unification, perhaps as the yet invisible unifier of West and East, of Europe and Asia. But have we risen to the occasion of these tasks befallen our lot? This leads us to the question concerning our nationalistic politics. Russia will only then rise to the occasion of its world imperialistic tasks, when it overcomes its own old nationalistic politics, essentially discordant with the spirit of the Russian people, and enters upon a new path. If the world war ultimately leads Russia out onto the world stage, onto the path of its realisation of its world vocation, then first of all there ought to be changed the politics in regard to all the peoples settled within it. The all-human and generous spirit of the Rsusian people should prevail over the spirit of provincial exclusiveness and self-assertion. Our politics will firstly be rendered truly national, when it ceases to be coercive and exclusively nationalistic. Such a nationalistic politics is completely at variance with the idea of a great world empire. Such a sort of nationalism is an indicator of weakness, it is incompatible with a sense of strength. It is possible only among peoples, liberated from slavery, or with lesser and weak peoples, afraid of falling into slavery. A great world empire, at the basis of which lies strength, rather than weakenss at the governing national core, cannot conduct a nationalistic politics inlaid with animosity towards those nationalities which it encompasses, inspiring in all no love for it and a thirst for liberation. Such a politics in the final end is against the interests of the state and will lead to the disintegration and diminishing of Great Russia. Russian politics can only be imperialistic, and not nationalistic, and our imperialism, as regards our position in the world, ought to be magnanimous, and not that of a rapacious robber. The national core of a great empire, encompassing a multitude of peoples, ought to be able to inspire love for itself, ought to attract towards itself, ought to be endowed with a gift for fascination, ought to convey for its peoples both light and freedom. And it can be said, that the people's Russia does inspire such a love for it seeking to draw all to it. Our non-Russian elements are under the charm of a genuine Russian culture. The official Russia, however, assiduously makes itself repulsive and therein seeks to erode this love and this attraction. It seeks to disunite inwardly, to shove down as much as possible and enchain by constraint and force. But Russian imperialism then only will have a right to existence, if it be gifted with plenteous abundance, and in this would be the sign of its might. Russia should be providentially imperialistic, but bereft of the imperialistic pathos, and in this would be its uniqueness. The old nationalistic politics was cowardly and sterile, it acted violently out of fear and at its basis was a lack of belief in the Great Russian ethnos. But if within the Great Russian ethnos there be not a genuine strength and a genuine spirit, then it cannot have any pretense to world significance.

Force is no substitute for strength. The absence of this gift cannot be compensated for by any sort of intimidation. It is striking, the extent to which our nationalists have always been non-believers in Russia. Their gestures have been the gestures of the powerless.

It is in Russian imperialism namely that there ought to be the all-human in scope with an acknowledgement of every individual people, an assiduous and generous attitude towards every people. An understanding of the souls of the various peoples -- is a point of pride of the Russian genius. At the basis of the Russian idea lies the consciousness of Russian man, as an every-man. And if Russian imperialism fails to express this spirit of the Russian people, then it will begin to fall apart and lead to the collapse of Russia. A great empire, believing in its own strength and its calling, cannot transform its own citizens into disenfranchised outcasts, as has happened for us with the Jews. This leads to a disintegration of the imperialistic unity. Only free citizens can be the proper supports of empire. A great quantity of the disenfrancised, oppressed and everyway disdained, presents a danger. With us officially has been chosen the ugliest method of preserving the national visage, a method actually distorting this visage, and not safeguarding it. Russian imperialism has enough with its expanses, and with it there ought not to be cultivations of brigandage.

The outward tasks of Russian imperialism are in the gaining of outlets leading to the seas. Other tasks are in the liberation of oppressed peoples. But this fine mission can be fulfilled only in that instance, wherein Russia does not exert oppression with its own, only if it inwardly be also a liberator of oppressed peoples. Russia ought first of all as a liberator seek to resolve the Polish Question, as being a worldwide question in scope. And otherwise, but in all the same spirit as liberator there ought to be resolved the questions -- of the Jews, of the Finns, the Armenians etc. Our Galitsia politics has not enabled the strengthening of Great Russia and its prestige. It has enabled only the intensification of the Ukrainian separatist intents. If Russia has not the wherewithal to inspire love for itself, then it will lose the grounds for its great position in the world. Its imperialism cannot be aggressive. And its nationalism ought to give expression to the all-human character of the Russian people.

The End of Europe[1]

I.

The visionary dream about world unity and world dominion -- is an age-old dream of mankind. The Roman Empire was the greatest attempt at such unity and such dominion. And every universalism is bound up even at present with Rome, as a concept spiritual, and not geographic. The present-day world war, which is spreading all over and threatens to engulf all lands and peoples, would seem deeply contrary to this old dream about world unity, about a single world governance. Such a terrible war, it would seem, is destroying the unity of mankind. But this is so only for the superficial glance. From a perspective at greater depth the world war to the ultimate degree has brought into sharp focus the question concerning world order upon the earthly globe, about the expanse of culture upon all the surface of the earth. The present historical period has similarity to the era of the great transmigration of peoples. There is the feeling, that mankind is entering upon a new historical and even cosmic period, amidst some sort of great inevitability, completely unforeseen by any of the scientific prognoses, meanwhile toppling down all the doctrines and teachings. And it demonstrates first of all, that the ancient, the irrational and indeed primitive instincts are stronger than all the modern social interests and humanitarian feelings. These instincts, rooted within the obscure wellsprings of life, win out over the feeling of bourgeois self-preservation. That, which seemed to the consciousness of the second half of the XIX Century to be the solely essential things within the life of mankind, has proven all to be merely at the surface level of life. The world war tears away this surface skin of the civilisation of the XIX and XX Centuries and reveals the deeper layers of human life, it sets loose the chaotically irrational within human nature, covered over only outwardly, but nowise changed within modern man. The social question, the struggle of classes, the humanitarian-cosmopolitanist socialism etc, etc, all that which not so long ago seemed still singularly important, and in which they saw the only

---

[1] KONETS EVROPY. Article first published in the literary gazette "Birzhevye vedomosti", 12 June 1915, № 14900. (Klepinina № 195).

possible future, now fades into the background, gives way to deeper interests and instincts. Into the foreground move questions of nation and ethnos, the struggle for dominance of various imperialisms, all that, which had seemed overcome and left behind by cosmopolitanism, by pacifism, by the humanitarian and socialistic teachings. The eternal bourgeois and socialistic world has proven phantasmic, a mere abstraction. Within the fires of this terrible war have been burnt up all the doctrinalisings and there has been melted away all the fetters, latched upon life by the teachings and theories. The instincts of nation and ethnos in the XX Century have proven to be mightier than instincts social and of class. The irrational has proven stronger than the rational within the most bourgeois and well-organised of cultures. The struggle of ethnos, the struggle of national dignities, the struggle of great empires for might and dominion is essentially supra-national. Here the dark will for the expansion of the supra-personal life wins out over all personal interests and plans, it capsizes all the individual perspectives on life. How many individually unrewarded go the sacrifices that are demanded by imperialistic politics or the struggle for national worth. And in our epoch there is the displacing of instincts by still stronger instincts, upon which stand the imperialistic and national struggle. The instincts particular to life, of the egoistic family, the philistine, are won out over by interests of national life, of historical and world life, by instincts of the glory of peoples and states.

II.

The national consciousness and nationalism -- are phenomena of the XIX Century. After the Napoleonic wars, inspired by the idea of a world empire, there began the wars of national liberation. And national self-awareness grew. National states crystalised into shape. Lesser peoples even wanted to assert their national visage, and to possess an independent life. The national movements of the XIX Century are profoundly contrary to the universal spirit of the Middle Ages, which was under the sway of ideas of world theocracy and world empire and which did not know nationalism. The intense national energies within the XIX and XX Centuries act alongside energies that were cosmopolitan, socialistic, humanitarian-pacifist. The XIX Century -- was the most cosmopolitan and yet the most nationalistic of centuries. The bourgeois European life was also both very cosmopolitan and very nationalistic. But in it the spirit of universality would be difficult to find. The nationalisation of human life has involved also its individualisation. And the striving towards individualisation always involves new appearances. The national states, the national individualities are fully definable only for the XIX Century. And quite parallel to the growth of the national manifold was a lessening of the remoteness of states and nations, it weakened the provincial isolation. It might be said, that mankind moves towards unity through a national individualisation. Parallel to the individualisation in national existence is an universalisation, a developement in breadth. And it can likewise be said, that mankind at present moves towards oneness and unification through a worldwide discord of war, through prolonged misfortune, into the period we are now entering. History -- is paradoxical and antinomic, and its processes -- are twofold. Nothing within history is realised alongside a straight line, by peaceful growth, without detours and without sacrifices, without evil, accompanying the good, without a shadowing of the light. Races and peoples are locked in a bloody struggle. Within the war there is an outlet for the particularistic and isolated existence of peoples.

The most compelling feeling, evoked by the world war, might be expressed thus: this is the end of Europe, as a monopoly on culture, as a closed-in province of the earthly sphere, with its pretensions to be universal. The world war pulls into the cycle of world life all the races, all the parts of the earthly orb. It brings East and West into so close a contact, as never yet known within history. The world war poses the question about an emergence onto world expanses, about the extension of culture across all the surface of the earthly globe. It sharpens to the final extreme all the questions, connected with imperialistic and colonial politics, connected with the relations of the European states to other parts of the world, to Asia and Africa. One such aspect already is this, that the present-day war with a fateful inevitability posits the question about the existence of Turkey, about the dividing up of its holdings, which leads us beyond the borders of European horizons. The semi-phantasmic existence of Turkey, which for a long time was sustained by European diplomacy, kept Europe within its closed-in condition, forestalling the too acute and catastrophic setting of questions, connected with movement towards the East. In Turkey all was tied up in a knot, the undoing upon which depends the character of the existence of Europe, since the end of Turkey represents the emergence of culture eastwards, beyond the bounds of Europe. And besides the question concerning Turkey the war posits still many other questions, connected with the world-historical theme: East and West. And the world war demands resolution of all the questions.

III.

The great powers conduct world politics, and make pretense of spreading their civilising influence beyond the borders of Europe, to all parts of the world and to all peoples, upon over all the surface of the earth. This -- is imperialistic politics, which always contains within it universalistic pretensions and which ought to be distinguished from nationalistic politics. Nationalism is particularism; imperialism is universalism. On the strength of some almost biological law, a law of biological sociology, the great, or in the terminology of N. B. Struve, the greatest powers strive towards a swallowing up of all the weak and the small, towards a worldwide dominion, they want on their own terms to civilise all the surface of the earthly sphere.

The talented and original English imperialist Cramb sees the significance of English imperialism in this, that it "should inspire all peoples, living within the bounds of the British empire, with the English world-outlook".[1] In this he sees the striving of the race for immortality. Imperialism with its colonial politics is a modern, a bourgeois method of spreading of the universalisation of culture, of spreading civilisation beyond the bounds of Europe, beyond the seas and oceans. Modern imperialism -- is a phenomenon purely European, but it bears with it an energy, the ultimate revealing of which spells the end of Europe. In the dialectics of imperialism is a self-negation. The endless expansion and might of the British empire spells the end of England, as a national state, as the individually particularistic existence of a people. For the British empire, as in every empire, within its own bounds is the world, the earthly orb. In modern imperialism, which I term "bourgeois" in distinction to the "sacred" imperialism of former ages,[2] there is the same striving for world

---

[1] Vide Cramb. "Germany and England".

[2] Vide my article: "Imperializm svyaschennyi i imperializm burzhuaznyi" ["Sacred Imperialism and Bourgeois Imperialism".] (This article of N. Berdyaev was published in the "Birzhevye vedomosti" gazette, 5 November 1914, and in the present anthology is not included. --

dominion, as was also in the Roman empire, and which is impossible to investigate, as mere national existence. This -- is the tantalising torment of the great powers, unquenchable in their thirst. Only small peoples and states are content with a purely national existence, making no pretense to be all the whole world. But how distinct are the methods of modern bourgeois imperialism from the methods of the old sacral imperialism. Both the ideology and the practice are altogether different. Now everything possesses, foremost, an economic undertone. Modern imperialists no longer speak about a world theocracy, nor about a sacred world empire. Colonial politics, the struggle for dominion on the sea, the struggle for markets -- this is what concerns modern imperialism, here are its methods and means of world might. Imperialistic politics indeed does lead out beyond the bounds of the closed-in existence of Europe and indeed does serve towards the universalisation of culture. But this is accomplished by crooked and negative paths. In a straight-forward intent of imperialism to spread culture it is impossible to believe. We know only too well, how the European great powers peddle their culture over all the earthly sphere, how rough and ugly their contacts are towards races of other parts of the world, their civilising of old cultures and savages. The cultural role of the English in India, an ancient land of great religious revealings of wisdom, which even now could help the peoples of Europe deepen their religious consciousness, is all too well known, for it to be possible to sustain the lie of the cultural ideology of imperialism. The world outlook of modern Englishmen is more superficial, than the world outlook of Indians, and they can convey to India but an outward civilisation. The England of the XIX Century would nowise be capable to beget a Ramakrishna, who was born in India. In the contacts of modern European civilisation with the ancient races and ancient cultures there is always something of the sacrilegious. And the conceited European, bourgeois and scientific, civilising consciousness -- is a phenomenon so pitiful and trite, that it spiritually can be looked at only as a symptom of the ensuing end of Europe -- the monopolist of world culture. It is the nightfall of Europe -- here is a feeling, impossible to be rid of. Barbarisation in part threatens Europe. Yet all the same it is impossible to deny the significance of imperialism, as an emergence beyond the borders of Europe and purely of

compiler's notation.) [Translator note: "compiler's notation" is part of the Russian text footnote; the article referred to is Klepinina № 180].

the European civilisation, it is impossible to deny its external, material, geographic mission. All the surface of the earthly orb has inevitably to be civilised, all the races have to be drawn into the coursings of world history. This worldwide task stands now more acutely before mankind, than the tasks of the inward life of the crystalised European states and cultures.

IV.

The British empire was the first to appear within the type of modern imperialism. The last attempt at a sacred imperialism was the world empire of Napoleon, all still constructed under the spell of the Roman idea. In the era of Napoleon however it ultimately vanished, transformed into a phantasm, the Holy Roman empire. Hereafter an empire, all still making pretense to world domination, would be built upon different foundations and would have a different ideology. Imperialism is closely interwoven with the economics of the capitalist era. England presents the example of a classical land of building the growth of empire. The instincts of the Anglo-Saxon race have proven fully suitable for the creation of a world empire on the new model. The British empire is strewn throughout all parts of the world, and to it belongs a fifth part of the earthly orb. The English have the calling for this, to spread their might beyond the seas. The English imperialism -- is peaceful, non-militaristic, culturo-economic, sea-mercantile. It is impossible to deny the imperialistic talent and the imperialistic vocation of the English people. It might also be said, that England has a geographic-imperialistic mission. This mission consists not in the sphere of an higher spiritual life, but it is necessary in the fulfillment of the historical fates of mankind. Both as regards their geographic position and innate to their race, the English -- are the most imperialistic, and perhaps, the solely imperialistic people in the modern sense of the word. The English -- are great successes at imperialistic politics. It is impossible to say this for the Germans. Both an unfavourable geographic position, and the military-force instincts of the Germanic race make the German imperialism onerous, coercive and intolerable for other lands and peoples. The Germanic imperialism has to be aggressive and grabbing by force. In German imperialism, capitalism on the modern model is closely interwoven with militarism. This imperialism is purely militaristic, and the militarism -- is modernly capitalistic, futuristic. The German empire, striving for world domination through force, always produces the impression of being an upstart, and it tends to obsess the unbearable conceit of the parvenue. It is characteristic, that Bismarck still was not an imperialist: he was more than careful in regards to colonial politics. He created a national empire, he completed the unification of the German people. The imperialism here is the child of the most recent generation of the German bourgeoise and German Junkerism. Modern Germany with its bourgeois feelers stretches into Russia, into Italy and other lands, and it tries to Germanise everything. But Germany is not an imperialistic land as regards vocation. Its imperialism -- is fatal for it itself and for all Europe. To the censuring namely of German imperialism would be the fact upon exposure, that the imperialism inevitably leads not only to war, but also to a world war. The world war -- is the result of imperialistic politics. The seeds of war were lodged in the original grounds of quite peaceful an imperialism. But no people is fated by a peaceful imperialistic politics to spread its might over the surface of the world. Every imperialism in fatal manner crashes into a stormy clash with another imperialism. The existence of several worldwide pretensions foreshadows a world war. The clash of the rather older English imperialism with the more recent Germanic was fatally predestined. Several years before the war, Cramb spoke about this with great enthusiasm in his lectures, "Germany and England", although it would be difficult to agree with his idealisation of German imperialism. Imperialism does not have as its aim the spreading of civilisation over all the earth, the increase of world community, but leads rather to discord and war. In the materialistic imperialism ensues the nightfall of Europe. But the dawn after this night can only be a worldwide dawning.

The world war presents the XX Century the task of the emergence of culture beyond Europe and into the world expanses over all the surface of the earthly sphere. Through the terror of the war and the evil of colonial politics, through the struggle of races and nationalities will be accomplished the unification of mankind and the civilising of all the earthly sphere. In facing this worldwide task, questions provincially European for a certain while will be relegated to the secondary plane. Sooner or later there has to begin the movement of culture towards its ancient sources, to the ancient races, to the East, to Asia and Africa, which anew need to be drawn into the course of world history. Egypt, India, Palestine are not forever fallen away from world history. And with its tormentive problem China still has to be taken into account. The disappearance of a purely European culture will be a dawning of the sun in the East. The enigmatic expression of the faces of the ancient peoples of the East, which are so striking for us as Europeans, ought for once to find solutions at some high points of history. To this enigmatic glance of the ancient races Europe has not succeeded in determining, whither to go. Europe ought not only to convey its culture to Asia and Africa, but it ought also to receive something in return from the ancient cradles of culture. Imperialism with its colonial politics has been but an external, a bourgeois expression of that inevitable worldwide historical movement, which we foresee. Inwardly, this historical turnabout is being readied by the spiritual crisis of European culture, the crashing of the positivism and materialism of the contemporary European consciousness, the disenchantment in life, the thirst for new faith and new wisdom. The centre of gravity for Western Europe, in all actuality, is shifting still more to the West, to America, the might of which will grow quite much after the finish of the war. And indeed the Americanisation of modern civilisation will extend Europe all the way to America. The East -- is one exit beyond the bounds of European culture, America -- is another exit. Europe is ceasing to be at the centre of world history, the sole bearer of an higher culture. If Europe had wanted to remain a monopolist and dwell in its European self-smugness, it should have refrained from the world war. But long ago already European life had been transformed into a fiery volcano. Now Europe faces fully a basic theme of world history -- the unification of East and West. And the task is in this, that the end of Europe and the critical point in history has to be experienced by man at spiritual depth and with a religious light.

V.

Great roles in this worldwide movement of culture should fall to the allotted portion of Russia and England. The mission of the English is rather more external. The mission of Russia -- is more inward. Russia stands at the centre of East and West, it -- is an East and West. Russia -- is the largest empire. But that is namely because foreign to it is the imperialism in the English or German sense of the word. With us, as Russians, there are no great-empire strivings, since a great empire -- is already a given for us, and not a goal. Russia is too greatly large, to have pathos over expansion and domination. And indeed the temperament of the Slavic race -- is not an imperialistic temperament. Russia does not aspire after colonies, since that in it itself there are vast Asiatic colonies, which present it much work. The mission of Russia -- is in the defense and liberation of lesser peoples. Russia has still to be the bulwark against the dangers of the Mongol East. But for this, it first of all has to be liberated from everything of the Mongol-East within itself. The sole essential pretension of Russia appears to be Constantinople and egress through the water-courseways to the seas. A Russian Constantinople ought to be one of the centres of the unification of East and West. Material power and the material greatness of Russia -- are initial givens for us. We have no need to conquer with difficulty every jot of earth, in order to be great. And we have all the basis to suppose that the world mission of Russia is in its spiritual life, in its spiritual, and not material universalism, in its prophetic presentiments of new life, which Russian great literature was full of, just as with Russian thought and the religious life of the people. And if there approaches also the end of the provincially shut-in life of Europe, then all the more there approaches also the end of the provincially shut-in life of Russia. Russia has to emerge onto the world stage. The end of Europe will be with the emergence of Russia and the Slavic race into the arena of world history, as determined by its spiritual power. The strong cosmic gusts batter all the lands, and peoples and cultures. In order to withstand this gale, there is needed a strong spiritual concentration and depth, there is needed a religious experiencing of the historical catastrophes.

The Tasks of Creative Historical Thought[1]

I.

One of the saddest things, made evident during the time of the war, is something that brings little attention upon itself. I have in view the almost complete absence among us of creative historical thought. The traditional character of our thinking is very poorly adapted to the positing of creative historical tasks, to world perspectives. Our national thought is all still stuck entirely in its provincialism, and its direction chiefly is in reporting negative accounts. Russia has been too inwardly torn apart and absorbed with trifling political disputes, with party considerations, with social group antagonisms, obscuring moreso all the world historical perspectives. The unempowered Russian society cannot feel a sense of responsibility for deciding the world destiny of Russia. The world war, essentially, ought to have directed national thought to world tasks. It would seem, that there ought to have been made attempts to ponder about the war, to define the place of Russia in world life, to conceive of its vocation. A genuine national self-consciousness should set the existence of nation into the perspective of world history, it should surmount the provincialism of national life and national interests. An insightful national awareness is likewise a consciousness that is all the world historical. The naked and unenlightened egoism of nationalism or imperialism is no justification, and upon it cannot be conceived the spiritual existence of peoples.

Does Russia exist, as a certain unity, deeper, than all the separate interests of its human composite, is there in the world an unique visage of Russia and what does the expression of this visage mean for the world? Does Russia have its own unique calling in the world, ought it to have its say in world history? What sort of concrete tasks face Russia from the world war? All these questions, which relate to a new day in world history, demand tremendous efforts of creative thought. No sort of the ready and traditional categories of thought are suitable for the resolving of these

---

[1] ZADACHI TVORCHESKOI ISTORICHESKOI MYSLI. First published in literary gazette "Birzhevye vedomosti", 22 December 1915, № 15285. (Klepinina № 218).

questions. There needs to be wrought a totally independent and new reworking of thought, an extension of the creative spirit. But our national thought tends to think very little about this or it thinks in accord with the old models, with the customary categories. The tasks of the war for us have not all still been genuinely thought out. The prevailing justifications of the war are sufficiently alike banal. It is impossible to be satisfied merely thinking that Russia is repulsing the evil of German militarism. The problem, posed by the war, goes much deeper. It is impossible likewise to rest easy upon the old Slavophil self-praise, -- for in this is expressed a laziness of thought, an inclination spiritually to live in any event. The Slavophil thought indeed is all still an assertion of the self-smug provincial existence of Russia, and not its worldwide existence. Slavophilism worked great services in the matter of national self-consciousness, but it was an initial and childish stage of this self-consciousness, not corresponding to the current historical stature.

Neither in our "right" nor in our "left" camps is there as yet transpiring any creative historical thought. They are too absorbed by their matters of the "right" or of the "left", i.e. by all the still national and not world tasks. The historical mindset is almost absent among us. We are accustomed to operate exclusively by moral or sociological categories, not by the concrete, but by the abstract. Our consciousness moves predominantly along the negative, and not the creative path. The "rightists" are absorbed by completely negative badgerings about the nationalities, the intelligentsia, the rosy "leftist" dangers and the quest for the exterminating all the manifestations of a free society. The "leftists" in contrast are concentrated upon exposing the "bourgeoise", on the utilising of negative facts for agitational purposes, and overly dividing Russia into two camps. And Russia still cannot at all conceive of itself as one, still cannot creatively define its world historical tasks. The process of applying abstract sociological categories divides, and does not unite, the ill-will with moral suspicions and moral judgement ultimately disunites and leads to a splintering, as it were, into two different races. Only a resolute turning of our consciousness to the depths of national existence and towards the wide expanse of world historical existence will set before us the pressing creative problems. Creative historical thought ought ultimately to surmount both our negative nationalism and our negative cosmopolitism.

II.

For anyone, who looks at the world war from the point of view of the philosophy of history, it ought to be clear, that at present there is being played out one of the acts of the world historical drama of East and West. The world war leads to an exceptional coming into contact of the world of the West and the world of the East, it unites through division, and it leads out beyond the borders of European culture and European history. The problem of East and West has in essence always been a basic theme of world history, its axis point. The European equilibrium has always been a conditional arrangement. Beyond the bounds of the self-enclosed world of Europe there has been a wide world, stretching far off into the East. Unsettling for the state and cultural life of the peoples of Europe always have been the world expanses, the unknown and unexperienced East and South. The imperialistic politics of the great powers of Europe have occasioned the spreading of imperialistic might and cultural influence beyond the seas and oceans, towards the surmounting of the isolation of a purely European existence. The unknown extents of the earthly orb exerts an attractive pull. Glances were turned towards Asia and Africa, towards the ancient cradles of culture. The reverse movement from West to East, evidently, reflects an inner inevitability of the dialectics of European culture. In the shut-in and self-satisfied European culture there is a fatal tendency towards a limited satisfaction, towards desiccation, towards decline. And it inevitably has to search for stimulation beyond its borders, in the far and yon. Imperialism with its colonial politics is one of the outward expressions of this irresistible movement of history. But still deeper lies the cultural and spiritual challenge of the re-uniting of East and West. The nightfall for Europe has begun.

It was not by chance, that the conflagration of the world war began with the Balkans, and from thence always has come the threat to the European world. It is not by chance, that now also the central interest of the war again turns to the Balkans. The Balkans -- are the path from the West to the East. Constantinople -- is that gateway, through which the culture of Western Europe can pass through to the East, in Asia and in Africa. At Constantinople -- is the point of intersection of East and West. The destruction of the Turkish empire would be a reverse coursing of the West to the East. The peoples of Europe are afraid of this prospect, sensing themselves unprepared for it, and the fact of the continued existence of

Turkey with Constantinople as the entryway of the West to the East has been an expression of the spiritual immaturity of the European peoples. How dissimilar in this is the modern Europe from the medieval Europe, given over to the impulsive visionary-dreams of the Crusades! But now Europe as it were is itself fighting for the defense of Turkey. And Europe is even moreso afraid of the enormous and mysterious Russia, seeming always so foreign and unfriendly. The European politics of the XVIII and XIX Centuries was to a remarkable degree directed to the object of keeping Russia from Constantinople, keeping it from access to the seas and oceans. Europe was interested in forcibly keeping Russia going in circles, not allowing it to enter onto the world stage, impeding the world role of Russia. Such Russian national ideologies, as Slavophilism, sought to justify the provincially isolated, the non-worldly extent, of the existence of Russia. Russia set itself all in opposition to Europe, to Europe as an unified whole. Both the Slavophil, and also the Westerniser consciousness alike believed in the existence of Europe, as being of one spirit, of one single type of culture. Slavophilism set Russia in contrast to Europe, with Russia being of an higher spiritual type, and Westernism dreamed about Europe, as the ideal for Russia, as the singular type of world culture. But herewith exploded the world war and it destroyed the illusion of an united Europe, of a single European culture, of a single spiritual European type. Europe can no longer hold a monopoly on culture. Europe -- is a study in instability. Within Europe itself lie concealed quite contrary principles, quite hostile elements, quite mutually exclusive spiritual types. Germany has proven to be more terrible to many of the peoples of Europe, than was Russia, more foreign, than was the East. The war ought on the one hand to move Europe towards the East, and on the other towards the extreme West. In the final results of the war it cannot but bolster America and it cannot but posit questions about the historical vocation of the Slavic race. Europe long ago already has aspired to surmount itself, to emerge beyond its bounds. Europe is not some ideal culture all in general. Europe itself is provincial. In Europe long ago already there is a secret inner tugging towards the East, which on the surface of history has received various explanations. Such phenomena, diverse in character, as imperialism in politics and theosophy in spiritual life, alike are symptomatic in the gravitation for an outlet beyond the borders of European culture, for the movement from West to East. And while the great tasks of the Crusades have gone inward, they yet have remained for Europe. What sort of position, however, ought Russia to occupy in this world historical movement?

III.

Russia can conceive of itself and its vocation in the world only in light of the problem of East and West. It stands at the centre of the Eastern and Western worlds and can be defined, as an East-West. It was neither in vain nor by chance that Russian thought throughout the course of the XIX Century centred round the disputes of Slavophilism and Westernism. In suchlike a direction of Russian thought there was the same truth, which for the Russian consciousness was a basic theme -- the theme concerning East and West, about this, whether Western culture appears to be singular and universal, and whether or not it be perhaps a different and higher type of culture? In the actual ideologies of Slavophilism and Westernism there was a limitedness and immaturity. But the theme itself of the Russian thinkers was profound, and for Russia fundamental. This theme has remained all still ideological, little connected with practical perspectives. Russian intellectual society was indeed quite irresponsible, and its thought thus could remain quite irresponsible. But the world war has dragged Russia into the vital setting concerning the theme of East and West. At present the pondering on this theme can no longer be so abstract and irresponsible. But it has so happened, that for this critical moment of our history that the level of our national thinking has gone downwards, the themes of the eternal ponderings of our intelligentsia have diminished quite downwards. And before us stands the task -- to raise the level of national thought and connect it with the vital tasks, posed by world events. Russia has been so deeply sucked into the very muck of world life, that no sort of Russian lethargy and inertia can still spare it from resolving the basic tasks of its history. Should the war happen to end, whatever might be its immediate political consequences, -- the spiritual consequences of this war can be foreseen.

The world war ought to lead Russia out of its isolated provincial existence into the wide world of life. The potential strengths of Russia have to be discovered, and its genuine visage, which up til now has been all still twofold, -- has to be shown the world. This, in any case, ought to happen, if not by way of victorious power and direct growth of might, then by way of sacrificial suffering and even humiliation. There is mystery in many a path, so likewise in the fate of peoples, which we rationally never will resolve. The most terrible sacrifices are perhaps necessary for a people, and through the great sacrifices become possible achievements, which would have been impossible for the self-contented and happy mere vegetative existence. A spiritual result of the world war will likewise be an overcoming of the one-sidedness and aloofness of the so-called European culture, its emergence onto the world stage. And this means, that the world war will bring Russia and Europe face to face with the age-old theme of East and West in a new concrete form. Before Europe and before Russia, with an unprecedented acuteness and concreteness, will be set not only the external, but also the inward spiritual questions about Turkey and PanSlavism, about Palestine, about Egypt, about India and Buddhism, about China and PanMongolism. Europe has been too shut-in within its own self-smugness. The old East and South have interested it, chiefly, on the side of colonial politics and the grabbing of markets. Russia however still has not risen up to the setting of the worldwide questions, with which is connected its position in the world. Russia has been too inwardly in disarray, too much of the elementary has yet to be resolved in it. Vl. Solov'ev attempted to turn our attention to these world-historical themes, but he was not always successful. Yet in any case, he represented a great step forward in comparison with the Slavophils and the Westernisers.

IV.

Russia ought to manifest a type of East-West culture, to overcome the one-sidedness of Western European culture with its positivism and materialism, the self-smugness of its limited horizons. Our Russian provincialism and isolatedness cannot be overcome by the European provincialism and isolatedness. We have to cross over onto the world stage. And in this expanse there ought to be seen the ancient religious cultural sources. The East ought anew to counter-balance the West. In a certain sense the Europeanising of Russia is necessary and irreversible. Russia ought to become for Europe an inner, not an external power, a power creatively transfigurative. And for this Russia has to be culturally transformed into European. The backwardness of Russia is not the uniqueness of Russia. The unique moreso ought to be discovered at the higher, and not the lower, stages of developement. Russia has to conquer in itself the dark East, held in the grip of its elemental stages. But the

Westernism is a mistake of childish immaturity, and it runs counter to the world tasks of Russia. The patterns of Westernising thought are just as ill-suited for comprehending the meaning of world events, as are the patterns of Slavophil thought. The historical epoch, into which we are entering, demands an organic combining of a national consciousness with a consciousness universal, i.e. defining the world vocation of nationality. Afront our thinking stands quite concretely the task of being aware of the world role of Russia, of England and Germany and their interrelation. It is necessary to speak about this some other time, but I think, that in the world the dominant position has to belong either to Russia and England or to Germany. The prevailing of Russia and England ought to lead to a closeness of East and West and to a deciding of the problem of East and West. The prevailing of Germany would lead to an attempt to create a new world empire, making pretense to world domination and essentially incapable of bringing together and uniting anything, since it would be incapable of admitting the worth in itself of anything.

The orientation towards creative historical tasks would heal us of our inward provincial disputes, from the trite hostility. We are spiritually obligated to perceive the place of Russia within the worldwide struggle. It would be shameful to define oneself only negatively through the will of the enemy. Russia has its own independent tasks, quite apart from the ill-will of Germany. Russia should not only defend itself, but should also decide its own independent tasks. Yet over these independent tasks our thought has been too little at work. It is necessary to appeal to the independent creative national thought, to lead us out into the free air, at the surface. But creative historical thought presupposes acknowledging the history of independent initiative, of an especial metaphysical reality. Such a turning to history has amongst us up to the present been almost non-existent, and we have not seized upon responsible categories for thinking over history and its tasks. But in such a turnabout of consciousness there would be for us something liberating.

Slavophilism and the Slavic Idea[1]

I.

The war has set fully before the Russian consciousness and the Russian will all the painful Slavic questions -- the Polish, the Czech, the Serbian, and it has led to momentum and has forced tormentive pondering over the fate of the Slavic world within the Balkan peninsula and within Austria Hungary. Everything is ailing within Slavism at the present time. And sometimes it seems almost impossible to reconcile the old disputes of the Slavs amongst themselves. The worldwide clash of the Slavic race with the Germanic race, which the whole of history has led to and which was not unforeseen, cannot, it would seem, but lead to a Slavic self-awareness. The Slavic idea had to be conceived in facing the threatening danger of Germanism. But the feuds in the Slavic family all continue. The Balkan peninsula is demoralised by disputes amongst its Slavs. Poland is in tatters, and in it brother is compelled to fight against brother. The mutual mistrust and suspicion are truly frightening. But is our Russian societal consciousness prepared to be the bearer and expresser of the Slavic idea? Has this idea come to maturity? Is it so popular, as to be strong and transformative of life? The Slavic idea among us is in a very sad position, it -- is as though caught in the jaws of a vise and cannot be freely expressed. I believe, that subconsciously the Slavic idea is alive at the core of the soul of the Russian people, it exists, as an instinct, all still obscured and not having found itself authentic expression. But a genuine Slavic consciousness, a genuine Slavic idea we do not have.

The Russian national self-consciousness and the AllSlavic self-consciousness was born for us within the disputes of Slavophilism and Westernism. The Slavic idea could be sought for only in Slavophilism, in Westernism there were no traces of this idea. But in our classical Slavophilism, with Kireevsky, Khomyakov, the Aksakovs, Samarin, it is

---

[1] SLAVYANOPHIL'STVO I SLAVYANSKAYA IDEYA. First published in literary gazette "Birzhevye vedomosti", 3 August 1915, № 15003, under alternate title "*Slavyanophil'stvo y vlasti*", or else possibly reworked from, per Klepinina Bibliographie. (Klepinina № 202).

difficult to find a pure expression of the Slavic idea. Slavophilism more accurately might be called Russophilism. Slavophilism affirmed first of all the unique type of Russian culture upon the soil of Eastern Orthodoxy and contrasted it to the Western cultural type and its Catholicism. In Slavophilism there was still much of the provincial isolation. The Slavophils were all still good Russian landowners, very intelligent, talented, educated, loving their native-land and captivated by its unique soul. But their consciousness did not contain world perspectives. The Slavophil ideology was moreso disuniting, than unifying. This was still a childish consciousness of the Russian people, the first national awakening from sleep, a first attempt at self-definition. But the Slavophil ideology cannot yet correspond to a mature historical existence for the Russian people. The Slavophil outlooks matured during a time of servitude, in them is felt a sense of surrender, they are ill-suited for a free and broadly historical life. The old Slavophil ideals first of all were ideals of the private, of the familial, the customary mode of life of Russian man, who was not given to emerge into the breadth of historical existence, and which failed to mature even for a talented existence.[1] The lack of freedom rendered the Slavophils irresponsible. They did not appeal for the realisation of their ideas, and their ideas often were but the fine feelings of Russian man. The weak sides of the Slavophil ideology, being out of touch with life, its hothouse effect with the old-style landowners, were all insufficiently apparent namely because that Slavophilism did not possess any real power in life, and actually was made to assume an oppositional posture. Power was held only by the official state nationalism, and it had no need for the suspect services of the Slavophils, it had no need for any such ideologies. The Slavophils sensed something in the Russian national soul, in their own way they were the first to express this Russian sense of self, and in this was their enormous service. But any attempt at the realisation of the Slavophil programme of ideas revealed either its utopian aspect and artificiality of life, or else its falling into line with the official political powers. And Slavophilism subsequently and in a fatal manner deteriorated prior to its identification with the official state nationalism. There was formed an official state Slavophilism, for which the Slavic idea and Slavic politics were transformed into a rhetorical terminology and to

---

[1] I am not referring here to the churchly ideas of Khomyakov, which are very profound and which are of an enduring significance.

which no one still gives credence, whether in Russia, or abroad. Slavophilism thus was rendered powerless for influencing the ruling powers in any direction of creative Slavic politics. What prevailed was not a Slavic, but rather a German inspiration, and by it was poisoned the very descendants of the Slavophils themself.

II.

Only with the Slavophils had there been a national idea, only they acknowledged the reality of the soul of the people. For the Westernisers there did not exist a soul of the people. Our Westernising thought did not deal with work over the issue of a national consciousness. But the attitude of the Slavophils towards the most painful and most important Slavic question for us as Russians -- the Polish question -- was at its root false and not Slavic. The Slavophils never felt in their relation to the Polish people any Slavic unity, a Slavic brotherhood. For the Slavophils the Slavic world in its spirit ought first of all to be Orthodox. They felt the non-Orthodox Slav to be a traitor to Slavic matters. And they could not forgive the Polish people its Catholicism. They could not understand and love the Polish soul, because they could not understand and love the Catholic soul. But everything unique to Polish culture is defined by this, that in it Catholicism is focused within the Slavic soul. Thus it was forged out of the Polish national visage, an altogether unique Slavic-Catholic visage, distinct also from the visage of the Romance Catholic peoples, and from the visage of the Slavic Orthodox peoples. For the Slavophils, Poland was that West within the Slavic world, to which they always set in opposition the Russian Orthodox East, the bearer of an higher spiritual type and the fullness of religious truth. The Polish seemed first of all to be Latins, and it was almost forgotten, that they were Slavs. Polonism represented the Catholic danger. In their repugnance towards Catholicism the Slavophils went so far, that they preferred Protestant Germany over Catholic lands and peoples. The Lutherans in Russia occupied a privileged position in comparison with the Catholics, and they often stood at the helm of government. The intellectual Slavophilism was also bereft of any idea of the power of rule and it concurred in this. In an even more extreme form with Dostoevsky was expressed the hostility towards Catholicism and towards Poland. He saw within Catholicism the spirit of the Anti-Christ and together with Protestant Germany he wanted to crush Catholicism.

There was formed a quite strong Slavophil-conservative tradition, which was accepted by our ruling authorities and led in practise to this, that our politics came to be always dependent upon Germany. The hostility towards Poland and friendship with Germany -- were two sides of one and the same matter for us. Indeed not only the Polish -- are Catholics within the Slavic world. And the old-Slavophil attitude towards Catholicism has made impossible a sincere Slavic unity. The hostility towards the Polish people, before which we ought to atone for our own historical guilt, has rendered our Slavophilism hypocritical. Rightfully it has been pointed out, that the Russians ought first of all to liberate their own oppressed Slavs, before moving on to liberate the foreign Slavs. The Slavic idea and Slavic unity are impossible, if the Russian and Orthodox type of Slavism be taken as the full and exclusively true, needing no other sort of complementation nor the existence of other types of Slavic culture. There would then remain only the politics of Russification and forceful conversion to Orthodoxy. But such a politics is incompatible with the Slavic idea. The Russian soul remains forever a Slavic soul, having accepted the engrafting of Orthodoxy into it. The Orthodox engrafting is to be discerned also in the moral stance of the Russian Intelligentsia-atheists and the reviling of Orthodoxy by L. Tolstoy. But this Russian soul can in a brotherly way co-exist with other Slavic souls, such as have accepted an other spiritual engrafting and represent a different cultural type. The soul of Russia can love the soul of Poland, another great Slavic people, and from this be still moreso itself. From such an unity of different souls and Slavs, the Slavic world can only benefit. The attitude towards the Balkan Slavs amongst the Slavophils was different and it was better, than towards the Polish. But here also the Slavophils were too much exclusively the Russophile, to allow for brotherly and equal relations. Certainly, small Serbia cannot pretend to an equal significance with Russia. And it is indisputable, that Russia should play a foremost role in the Slavic world. The question is altogether not in this. The question rather is in this, that Russia should ultimately renounce the frightful and repulsive idea, that "the Slavic branches should themselves flow together into a Russia sea", i.e. it should admit the eternal rights of every national individuality and relate to such, as something of value in itself. And such an attitude would fully accord with the soul of the Russian people, magnanimous, unselfish and patient, giving, and not taking, which the Slavs all do not realise, since it is concealed from them by our state politics which is not of the people.

Slavophilism frightens off, be it the Polish, or the Slavs, or the progressive elements of Russian society. In Slavophilism there was a true kernel of a Slavic idea, but it was enveloped by a decrepit and decaying covering, too ingrown with Russian officialdom. Vl. Solov'ev represents already an enormous step forward in comparison with the old Slavophils. He transcends the provincial nationalism of the Slavophils. The messianic consciousness of Vl. Solov'ev, just as with Dostoevsky -- was worldwide. The horizons are expansive. And in Vl. Solov'ev there was already an altogether different attitude towards Catholicism. He sees in Catholicism a righteous truth, with which the Orthodox world ought to be united. And therefore he relates to the Polish question otherwise, than did the old Slavophils. With a brotherly love love he turned his gaze towards the Polish people and bestowed it a great positive significance for the fate itself of the Russian people. But the Slavic feeling, the Slavic consciousness was weakly expressed in Vl. Solov'ev, and it is impossible to call him an herald of the Slavic idea. Dostoevsky and Vl. Solov'ev because of the universal character of their messianic consciousness could be set alongside the great Polish messianists: with [Adam] Mickiewicz, [Juiliusz] Slowacki, [Zygmunt] Krasinski, [Andrzej] Towianski, [August] Cieszkowski, [Jozef Hoene-Wronski] Wronski. We know shamefully little of the Polish messianists and we ought now to recourse to the study of them. Polish messianism is more pure and more sacrificial, than the Russian messianism, which is not free of idealisation of the sense of our state power. In the messianic consciousness of Dostoevsky it is impossible to find that pure sense of sacrifice, which has inspired the messianic consciousness of the Poles. Dostoevsky got himself too tied up with the aggressiveness of the Russian ruling authorities. It is impossible indeed to call the Slavophils messianists in any strict sense of the word, they were moreso nationalists, and as regards their consciousness they stand many heads lower than the Polish messianists, who have to be acknowledged as the foremost proclaimers of the Slavic idea. Regretably, the ultimate tragic fate of Poland has led to the supplanting of the Slavic messianism by an exclusionary Polish nationalism. Among the Polish messianists there is one, most reknown, -- Wronski, who has confessed a Russian, and not Polish messianism. Wronski long ago predicted the world war in almost suchlike a form, as now at present is occurring, the clash of the Slavic world with the German and the inevitability of the uniting of Poland with Russia in its struggle with Germany (vide his "Le destin de la France, de l'Allemagne et de la Russie comme Prolegomenes du Messianisme"). Wronski considers the Russian people a God-bearing people. But about Wronski we have heard almost nothing.

III.

Westernism has not at all acknowledged the value of nationality, and the Slavic idea has been foreign to both the Russian liberals and the Russian revolutionaries. In the Westerniser leftist camp, nationality is acknowledged only as something negative, and only insofar as it is persecuted and in need of liberation. They consider it necessary to take the oppressed nationalities under their wing, but this is always inspired by the cosmopolitan idea, and they do not admit of creative national tasks. Our leftist currents are prepared to admit the right to existence of the Polish nationality or the Gruzinian-Georgian, insofar as they are oppressed, but they do not consent to acknowledge the Russian nationality, since it dominates the state. But a foreign national soul can be sensed and recognised only by one, who senses and knows his own national soul. In the Russian liberal and radical circles only during the time of war has there begun to awaken the national consciousness. Thinking has begun to mull over the national self-definition and the national acknowledgement of Russia with a push towards the Slavic idea. Some elements of Slavophilism have to be assimilated also by that part of society, which has always conceived itself as Westernisers. The tragic fate of the tearing apart of Poland and Serbia forces us to turn our will and our attention to the Slavs and the Slavic idea. But we have to recognise, that Slavic unity is impossible upon the soil of the traditional Slavophilism and traditional Westernism, and it presupposes a new consciousness, new ideas. It is impossible to assert the AllSlavic idea upon the grounds of acknowledging Eastern Orthodoxy as the sole and complete source of an higher spiritual culture, since by this is cut off from spiritual interaction all the Polish and Catholic Slavs. It is clear, that the spiritual basis of the Slavic idea ought to be broad and encompass within itself some several religious types. And this presupposes a surmounting of the Russian religious nationalism.

At the basis of the Slavic idea, just as in general at the basis of the Russian messianic idea, there can be posited only the Russian spiritual universalism, the Russian all-humaness, the Russian search for the City of God, and not the Russian national limitedness and self-conceit, not the

Russian provincialism. It is necessary to love the soul of Russia and intimately know it, in order that there should be visible the Russian supra-nationalism and Russian unselfishness, unknown to other peoples. I think, that even the Slavophils have not expressed this depth of the Russian soul. They did not yet lift themself to the level of all-humaness, they had not yet overcome the greedy national self-assertion. There is necessary a new Slavic and a new Russian idea, a creative idea, oriented forward, and not backward. At present we are entering into a new period of Russian and world history, and the old, the traditional ideas have already become ill-suited for the world's new tasks, which face us in life. We have experienced too much, we have re-evaluated too much, and for us there is no return to the old ideologies. We are already neither Slavophils nor Westernisers, since we are living in an unprecedented course of events in the world, and there is being demanded of us incomparably more, than from our fathers and grandfathers. All the slumbering powers of the Russian people have to be brought into action, in order to deal with the tasks in front of us. We have to inspire confidence in ourself, in the strength of our national will, in the purity of our national consciousness, to push the vision of our "idea", which we convey to the world, whilst consigning to oblivion and forgiving the historical sins of our ruling authorities. Our depths are not known, but all too well known is the heavy hand of our state. And every Slavic idea, which is tied in with this heavy hand, frightens off and evokes horror. Slavic unity has to proceed along a completely new path. Our national thought ought creatively to rework a new Slavic idea, since that hour of world history has struck, when the Slavic ethnos ought to have its own say in the arena of world history. It will lead to a replacing of the dominance of the German ethnos and conceive its own unity and its idea in the bloody struggle with Germanism. The idea of Slavic unity, is first of all a Russo-Polish unity, and it ought not to be externally political, a matter of mere utility for the state, -- it ought first of all to be spiritual, a transforming of inner life. The fate of the Slavic idea cannot stand in a servile dependence upon the unsteady elements of the world, shifting military successes, the cunning of international diplomacy, politicised calculations. Just as with any profound idea, connected with the spiritual fundaments of life, it cannot perish under external failures, for it counts upon more distant perspectives. There has to begin among the people and in society a spiritual-cultural AllSlavic movement, and in the final end this movement will exert an influence also on our politics, having inherited so grievous a legacy from the past. But from the onstart everything ought not to be out of external, politically useful alliances and combinations, rather instead from a sincere and deep seeking for unity. We are weary of the lies of the politicians and we want to breathe in the free air of truth. Such truth is in the nature of Russian man. And it is such a truth that both we and the other Slavs expect.

The Cosmic and the Sociological World-Sense[1]

I.

The World War conveys within it a profound spiritual crisis for humanity, which can be judged about from different sides. The consequences of such an unprecedented war are incalculable and cannot completely be anticipated. There is much a basis to think, that we are entering upon a new historical epoch. And if we cast our glance at the changes in the external aspect, the international, the political and the economic, then the inward and spiritual changes tend to proceed unnoticed. This is always a subliminal process. Our foresight into the future ought to be totally free of the customary optimism or pessimism, free from estimates in accord with the criteria of happiness. It would be shallow-minded to think of life for oneself after such an exhaustive war in any especially cheerful and happy light. One might the sooner consider, that the world is entering upon a period of prolonged woe and that its tempo of developement will be catastrophic. But the values, discovered by man in the worldwide struggle, are not to be defined by any increase or diminishing of happiness.

Comparatively much is spoken and written about the economic and political consequences of the war. Less so is there thought about the spiritual consequences, upon its influence on all our world-outlook. It is about one such little foreseen consequence that I want to speak. During the XIX Century the world-sense and the world-consciousness of the progressive elements of mankind had become tinged in a vividly social light. It has been pointed out more than once already, that sociology had replaced theology, that the religious feeling of mankind's lost faith was redirected to the social. The orientation of life was rendered social predominantly, and to it were subordinated all other values. All values

---

[1] KOSMICHESKOE I SOTSIOLOGICHESKOE MIROOSCHU-SCHENIE. Published first in the newspaper "Birzhevye vedomosti", August 1916, №. 15706. (Klepinina № 235).

were posited in the social perspective. The human social aspect has been rendered isolated from cosmic life, from the whole of the world, and it has come to feel itself as a closed-in and self-sufficing whole. Man has tended finally to settle down into a closed-in social territory, in it he wanted to be lord, he forgot about all the rest of the world and about other worlds, in which extend not his power and domain. The conquests of man within a delimited and closed-in social territory brought about a weakening of memory, a forgetting of infinity. And perhaps it was necessary for man to experience the period of this isolated world-feeling, in order to intensify and strengthen his social energy. Every sort of limitation reflects pragmatic needs during certain periods of human evolution. But the limitedness of this sociological world-sense cannot be continued for too long. This limitedness has hidden within it the possibility too much of unanticipated catastrophes. The endless ocean of world life plies its waves upon the locked-in and defenseless human social realm, set out upon a not large territory of the earth. The World War is also thuslike a world Great War, ninefold so. It reveals for everyone, even the most blind, that all the social utopias, constructed in the isolation of the social aspect as separate from cosmic life – are all superficial and unenduring. Under the shock of the worldwide war have fallen the utopias of humanism, of pacifism, of international socialism, international anarchism, etc., etc. This finds its explanation not by some theory, but by life itself, that social humanism possessed too limited and too superficial a basis. It has been overlooked, that there exist the deep loins of the earth and the unbounded worldly expanse and starry worlds even. Much of the darkly irrational, always bearing the unexpected, lies within these loins and the unbounded expanse. The human shut-in and limited social mindset with its exclusively sociological world-outlook reminds one of the proverbial ostrich, hiding its head in its feathers. There is too much that is overlooked in the social utopias, always based as they are upon simplifications and artificial isolation. Or similarly, just as with the unenduring and insubstantial aspect of the existence of an oasis – is a community in the spirit of the Tolstoyans or utopian socialism, just as unenduring and insubstantial also is the existence of all the human social-outlook within the complexity and infinitude of cosmic life. Social utopianism is always rooted in this isolation of social-mindset apart from cosmic life and apart from those cosmic powers, which are irrational in regard to the social mindset. This always -- is a concealing of complexity through one's limitedness. Social utopianism is a faith in the possibility of a final and unceasing rationalisation of the social aspect, independent of whether all nature is rationalistic and whether there is some sort of cosmic harmony. Utopianism has no desire to know of any connection of social evil with cosmic evil, it does not see the social as belonging to the whole cycle of the natural order or natural disorder. And such catastrophes, as the World War, cause one to open one's eyes, they force a broadening of the horizon. There is discerned the bankruptcy of such rational utopias, as that of eternal peace in this evil natural world, or that of a stateless anarchistic freedom in this world of necessity, or of worldwide social brotherhood and equality in this world of discord and hostility. Oh, certainly the great value of peace, of freedom, of social brotherhood remains immutable. But these values are unattainable in that superficial and limited sphere, in which they are presupposed to be attainable. The attainment of these values presupposes an infinitely great depth and expanse, i.e. the still very complex and prolonged catastrophic process in human life, it presupposes the transition from an exclusively sociological world-sense over to a world-sense which is cosmic.

II.

A deepened consciousness ought to move forward with the idea of a cosmic social mindset, i.e. a social mindset, pondering and entering into unity with the world whole, with the world energies. There has always existed an endosmosis and exosmosis between the human social aspect and cosmic life, but this has not been sufficiently perceived by man, and he craftily surrounded himself within his boundaries, thus having saved himself from the infinitude. But on a deeper level there ought to be posited the truth, whereof the greatest attainments of human social life are connected with the creative power of man over nature, i.e. are connected with a creatively active orientation towards cosmic life, both in concept, and also in action. And this presupposes an immensely great self-discipline on the part of man, moreso than that which is in him at present, an higher degree of mastery over himself, of his own proper elements. Only the one, who has mastery over himself, can aspire to mastery in the world. The tasks of the social aspect - are first of all cosmic-productive tasks. With this is connected both the personal morals and societal self-discipline. And this mindset is directly contrary to that, upon which rests our populism in all its shades and with all its distributive morality.

Creative toiling over nature, extended to a cosmic dimension, ought to be set as the cornerstone. This toil ought not to be a servile attachment to the earth, towards its limited expanse, it ought always to have worldwide perspectives. The XX Century is advancing along with cosmic tasks in the sphere of creative work with nature, and in the areas of production and technology, about which the XIX Century with all its discoveries could not even dream, let alone suspect. And it is striking that Marxism, which so advocated the productive instances, the growth of the productive powers in social life and by this providing a counterbalance over the instances of distribution, it is striking that it was completely bereft of any cosmic world-sense and showed itself an extreme form of sociological utopianism, locking man in within a limited and superficial social outlook. Marxism has believed, that it is possible to rationalise all completely societal life and bring it to an outward perfection, not taking into account those energies, which in the infinitude of the world are over and around man. Marxism – is a most extreme form of sociological rationalism, and therefore also of sociological utopianism. All the social teachings of the XIX Century lacked the awareness, that man – is a cosmic being, and not the inhabitant of an ephemeral social aspect merely on the surface of the earth, it lacked the awareness that he is actually in communion with the depths of the world and the heights of the world. Man -- is not an ant, and human society -- is not an ant-hill. The ideal of a perfectly constructed ant-hill has been demolished and with no turning back. But a deeper consciousness is possible only upon a religious basis. The world catastrophe ought to enable a religious deepening of life.

That spiritual turnabout, which I characterise as the transition from the sociological world-sense to a world-sense that is cosmic, would have also quite purely political consequences and expressions. There would be overcome the socio-political provincialism. Facing the social and political consciousness would be the world's expanse, the problem of mastering and directing all the surface of the earthly orb, the problem of bringing together East and West, the meeting of all types and cultures, the unification of mankind through struggle, the interaction and communion of all races. The vital settings of all these problems would make politics more cosmic, less shut-in, would bring to mind the cosmic expanse and the historical process itself. Truly the problems, connected with India, with China or the

Musselman world, with the oceans and continents, are all more cosmic in nature, than the isolated problems of the struggles of parties and social groups. Ultimately the ever more acute question about the relationship of every individual national being to the oneness and unification of mankind has to be resolved, as a question of cosmic dimensions. The orientation towards the depths of national life involves together with this a turning to the broad expanse of historical life throughout all the world. Within imperialistic politics there were already objectively cosmic proportions and cosmic tasks. But the consciousness of the ideologues of imperialism was limited. This ideology was a bourgeois ideology, it rarely went deeper or farther than the purely surface economic and political tasks. And in the paths of imperialistic politics there was much evil, begotten of the limited incapacity to engage the souls of those cultures and races, into which the imperialistic expansion had spread, it was blind to the external tasks of mankind. But the significance of imperialism, as an inevitable phase in the developement of modern societies for the uniting of mankind over all the surface of the earth and for the building of a cosmic social awareness, can be acknowledged as irresponsible for the positive pathos of imperialism. The World War is a catastrophic moment in the dialectics of imperialistic expansion.

III.

In order to shed light on the darkness flooding the world, there is necessary a cosmic deepening of consciousness. If we remain but at the surface of the light, then the darkness will engulf us. The European peoples, the European cultures are entering upon a period of exhaustion. These shut-in cultures are headed towards decline, they are decaying. The long and destructive World War is sapping the powers of Europe, and for the peoples of Europe it is difficult to seek the sources of new energy in the great depth and great extent of the world expanses. The old purely sociological orientations and values of life are unsuited for the measures of the events that occur, for both their complexity and their novelty. Abstract sociologism, as a cohesive world-outlook, is discovering its unsuitableness in all regards, it reaches its end and ought to yield place to deeper and broader points of view. The catastrophe of this war is very bitterly dividing people and not at all per those categories, by which they are wont to be divided. They have proven to be quite spiritually unprepared for this catastrophe, it has burst out upon them as a greatly unanticipated happening, forcing them out of all their reinforced positions. And it is in such a position that a large part of the people of a purely sociological world-outlook now find themselves. They had been quick to adapt their old points of view to current events, but these despondent people have sensed, that they had been left behind. Many have come to feel themselves thrown overboard by history. Yet others are spiritually ready for the world catastrophe, there was in it for them nothing unanticipated, nothing relating to life from their point of view. Such people, who earlier had more cosmic a feel of life, had broader horizons. They know, that the war is a great evil and a chastisement for the sins of mankind, but they see the meaning of world events and they enter upon the new historical period without that sense of despondency and shipwreck, which the people of the former type feel, those who espy within it no inner meaning. The cosmic world-outlook is less so the happy, less so the rationalistically optimistic, and more untranquil, than is the sociological world-outlook, -- it foresees that there are great unanticipated events and is prepared to enter into a realm unseen and unknown. The deeper and broader world-outlook and consciousness does not permit of those rationalistic illusions, for which the future world is definable only by powers, set at the very surface of a delimited bit of the earth. There are active powers that are deeper, still unknown, with energies pouring forth from remote worlds. Bravery is necessary to go forth to meet the unknown day, to go into the darkness towards a new dawn. The World War is totally meaningless for every rationalistic optimism, for every sociological utopianism. For people of this spirit it cannot provide any sort of lesson, they have no desire to pass over to new life through death. But the World War possesses a symbolic meaning for those, who always have foreseen the actively concealed cosmic powers, not subject to rationalisation. The nature of war -- is not creative, it is negative, and destructive; but war can rouse creative powers, it can enable a deepening of life. Before mankind stand ever newer and newer creative tasks, tasks of a creative transformation of energy, issuing from the dark and primordial depths of being into a new life and a new consciousness. The developement of mankind, the ascent of mankind, never occurs along a direct line, by way of the growth of one-sided positive elements. This -- is a process to an utmost degree antinomic and tragic. The onrush of darkness is that barbarity of existence, without which in human life would ensue the drying up of energy, a desiccation. The World War serves a purpose for

European culture, with its being submerged in its barbarism and dark power. In this darkness much ought to perish and much be born, just as with the incursion of the barbarians upon the culture of antiquity. But this barbarian power -- is inward, and not outward. We can draw a conclusion. The people of the old sort, though regarding themselves as at the vanguard of the sociological world-sense, have been left behind. They -- are conservators of the yesterday and the day before. The people of a cosmic world-sense are spiritually prepared to go forth towards the unknown future with a creative impulse.

III. THE SOULS
OF VARIOUS PEOPLES
(Parallels)

The Fate of Paris[1]

I.

When the Germans advanced on Paris and Paris feverishly prepared itself for a defense, many an heart upon the earth experienced an acute agitation and disquiet. There was readied a blow not only at the heart of France, but also at the heart of modern mankind. And from the wound, inflicted upon Paris, there flowed the blood as it were not of France alone, but of all cultural mankind. Paris -- is a world city, a world city of modern Europe and of all the modern European mankind. The same acute distress would be experienced, if danger were to threaten Rome. Rome -- is a world city of the old mankind and a sacred memorial for modern mankind. The endangering and even destruction of Berlin, Vienna, London and other capitals of Europe would not so acutely agitate every cultural soul. The wound, inflicted upon these capitals of various states, would be first of all on the order of a national misfortune. And only a wound, inflicted upon Rome and Paris, would be a misfortune all-European and for all mankind. I believe, that even the finest of the Germans, the most refined of them, have experienced a moment of apprehension for the fate of Paris. We as Russians are under the inspiration of a great and just war, but we have not yet experienced the direct fear for the fate of the fatherland, with us there is not yet any feeling, that the fatherland is in peril. No one would grant the possibility of the approach of the Germans to the heart of Russia -- Moscow. Russia in this threatening hour of world history has sensed itself strong, and not weak, and summoned to assist others. Worldwide tasks face Russia, and world perspectives have opened up. This war is altogether differently being experienced in France. There actually have been moments there, when direct danger has threatened the fatherland and Frenchmen have experienced fear for the fate of their native-land. In modern France there is a sense of fragility and fatigue from its great history, in which there was quite much of the great and heroic, and there is a sense of exhaustion.

---

[1] SUD'BA PARIZHA. First published in the literary gazette "Birzhevye vedomosti", 22 November 1914, № 14510. (Klepinina № 181).

The modern Frenchman is also too cultivated, and too sunken in philistine satisfaction, enslaved to the thirst for pleasure and love for women. France is not at all a militaristic land. The military spirit in it has long since been extinguished. It has experienced its own heroic military spirit, it dominated Europe but now is no longer a threatening military power. And however bad it would be for Paris, it would be terrible for France. Many Russians have felt an affinity for France and have thirsted to aid it with their power, to sustain it. The saving of France -- is one of the great and world tasks of Russia. Certainly, France -- is not Belgium, not Serbia, France -- is a great power, and it renders us great aid, as our ally. But the predominance of power is on our side. And the direct danger for Paris has diminished to a large degree thanks to our victories. The Franco-Russian alliance, both diplomatic and of state, is now experienced by us as heartfelt, emotionally, popularly. In our alliance with France there is something deeper, than a mere consideration of international politics.

II.

Paris -- represents a world effort of modern mankind, the home of great beginnings and bold experiments. Paris -- reflects the free expression of human powers, their free interplay. The life of the world city is the life of man at freedom, a life autonomous, independent of sacred authority, secularised. Modern mankind has associated together with Paris the honeymoon of a free life and free thought; the great Revolution, socialism, aestheticism, the final fruits of bourgeois atheism and philistinism. The image of Paris is for us twofold and evokes a sense of contradictions. We know the charm of Paris, the singular magic inherent in this city, the unique beauty of the very old and the very new combined within it.

Paris -- is a living being, and this being is something higher and more attractive than the modern bourgeois French. The visage of its soul possesses an "uncommon" expression, not that, which usually is found with the great cities of Europe. This -- is a singularly modern, a new city, in which there is the beauty and charm of the new and the modern. How lacking in beauty, how disturbing is everything new and modern at Rome, how formless and obnoxious it is at Berlin. Our unarchitectural epoch, lacking in plasticity, creates only ugly houses and ugly clothing, the streets it makes are repulsive for the aesthetically refined man and recourses us to an aesthetic living off the old. In the City of Paris alone there is the beauty of the present day, a beauty twofold, perhaps illusory and revolting, but all the same it is beauty. Paris -- is a magical City, -- within it is concentrated all the magic of the modern great City, with all its attractiveness and all its evil. The magic of Paris -- a city in a very concentrated and ultimate sense -- the magic of it wraps about every refined and susceptible man. Any another of the great cities of Europe -- is already but a second or third rate Paris, not pure embodiments of the idea of the modern City, only but an half-fast and watered-down provincialism. Only Paris -- is the City of streets, a world City, the modern City of modern mankind. Berlin -- is a well-built barracks, technically perfected, with all the conveniences, but tasteless and lacking all the magic of the City, all its demonic power. Paris, not even a well-built city, is technically backwards as compared to Berlin, but its magic, the right to be the City preeminently and a world-class City is not rooted in this external technical process. In Paris there is the irrational mystery of the City, a power that is magical, and not technical. Paris is a place demagnetised by the currents, given to the free play of human powers. And in it there is a flash and a sparkle, a levity, inconceivable in the onerous bourgeois life of the modern city, a gaiety, terrible afront so tortuous a struggle for existence. Upon all of Paris lies the imprint of an exceptional acuity of mind, of the national genius of the French people, which knows how to die well-spoken. In Paris -- is an ultimate refinement of culture, of the great and worldwide Latin culture, before the face of which the culture of Germany is but barbarity, and in this selfsame Paris -- is the extreme evil of modern culture, of the modern free life of mankind -- a kingdom of the philistine and the bourgeoise. The free play of human powers, free of any sanctity, has led to a reinforced kingdom of the philistine. The bourgeois slavery of the human spirit -- is one of the results of the formal freedom of man, of his immersion within himself. Suchlike is the antinomy of being. The philistinism -- is another face of Paris, a face frightful and repulsive. Paris -- is an enormous experiment of modern mankind, and within it are hidden all kinds of contradictions.

It is namely within the talented, the mentally acute, the gay, free and bold Paris that the philistinism has found it end-point, its aesthetically completed expression, its limit. The whole period of the Third Republic was a perpetual developing of the philistine life, the fruition of an irreligious and atheistic spirit. The French had grown weary from their catastrophes, their revolutions, wars, their explorations, and they wanted a tranquil and satisfied life, shut-in within its philistinism, shut-out from every spiritual stirring. They love to call Paris the new Babylon, a city of debauchery. And actually in Paris there are the appearances of an ingenious and inventive debauchery. The debauchery -- is the fate of the modern City. But this selfsame Paris -- is a city of the shut-in philistine family, very strongly and well barricaded. Paris -- is a city of philistine morals and philistine virtues; useful for succeeding in life.

III.

The self-satisfied philistine family -- is an isolated cell, in which personal egoism is multiplied into a familial egoism, flourishing not among us as Russians, nor amongst the Slavs, but namely amongst the Parisians, who otherwise are known to the world only on the side of their reputation for debauchery. The philistinism is the flip side of the unrestrained thirst for pleasure. The philistine norms -- are the fruit of unbelief in the auspicious self-restraint of man. And a genuine existential freedom, a freedom from false conventions and hypocritical norms is only in the Russians. With Russians there is an openness of spirit. Nowhere is there such a pursuit of profit, of a successful life, such a cult of wealth and scorn for poverty, as among the Parisians. The French are misers, they make an economy and are full of a philistine fear in facing an unsuccessful and unfavourable position. Philistine France has exalted personal and familial egoism into a virtue. This France is nowise so casual, as might seem with the superficial acquaintance with it. We Russians namely are the ones casual in worldly matters. Hertsen discerned this victorious march of the kingdom of philistinism and he shuddered with horror, he sought salvation from it in Russia, in the Russian peasantry.[1] Not in vain did there appear in France that great exposer of philistinism, Leon Bloy, writing a fiery expose of "both sides" of the philistine wisdom, -- he was an indigent knight within philistine Paris. Philistinism -- is a metaphysical, and not social category. But socialism is pervaded by the spirit of philistinism. The nature of philistinism -- is atheistic, irreligious. The philistine life is a life of the superficial aspects of life, substitutes for the core, the depth and essence of life. In the philistine life there have begun to perish the national virtues of the French people, their capacity for heroism and magnanimity, their love

---

[1] The selfsame Hertsen prophetically predicted the kingdom of Prussian militarism and the inevitability of the clash with it.

of freedom and fecklessness afront death. In philistine France, rich, orderly and self-satisfied, it is impossible any longer to recognise the land of Joan of Arc and of Napoleon, of a great Revolution and of great searches for freedom. The thirst for wealth has passed over into dishonesty and corruption. The political forms have ultimately vanished. Everything has reached the limit, beyond which is but still -- disintegration and death. The philistinism gradually has killed the soul. And it was said to the Christian world, that there is a greater need to fear the killing of the soul, than the killing of the body. Now they have begun to kill the body, -- the outward man, but perhaps the soul, the core of man, will be reborn from this. For the deadened soul sits up to its knees in philistine life, rather than up to its knees in water in the trenches. The philistine life in Paris has become so stuffy, so murderous for the soul, that only great catastrophes and great tribulations can cleanse and free man from the philistinism. The smug and shut-in philistine life has begun already to believe in its own earthly immortality, in its own enduring endlessness. But to let man remain in this faith in the unshakable stability of the philistine realm would mean the ruination of Paris, the death of his soul. There are in the world higher powers, which will not permit this. And inevitably it had to be revealed to the world, that in the very depths of bourgeois life there lay already the seeds of a great war, of a great catastrophe. It is impossible eternally to live by the worldly bourgeois life of saeity; for the very goals of bourgeois life it becomes necessary to make war with great sacrifices and sufferings. In this there is an inner dialectic, exposing the falsehood in life. The principles, having begotten too peaceful the bourgeois life, have begotten also war. The mysterious dialectic is especially to be felt in Paris, in France, in a land nowise military. The bourgeois and gay Paris is summoned at present to make an effort and it does make efforts. It is covered with blood. Through great tribulations and shocks there is awakened anew the heroic in the French, forsaking the too self-satisfied philistine life.

IV.

It does not become man to remain at the heights of the too peaceful, too satisfied, too felicitous a life. For philistine France there was necessary the threat, and inevitable was the misfortune and suffering. But everything in time will have passed. The world catastrophe, so immediately a threat for France, will be a crisis and a finish for the philistine ideals of life, confined within an earthly satisfaction. Read a letter from Paris. Paris has become serious, capable of sacrifices, the philistine cells within it are shaken open. There has awakened the finest sides of the French people -- the love of native-land, the sense of citizenship, enthusiasm, magnanimity, fearlessness in the face of death. France once again faces something worldwide and it has forced back the philistine part. Deliberate judgements of the love for native-land and for world justice have won out in the hearts of the French over the love for women, for pleasure and for saeity. The world war -- is a great exposer of the lie of the carefree philistine life. There are wars, which are sent by Providence, in order to compel the peoples to start thinking, to deepen, to stand up. The inevitability of the present-day war was lodged already within an inner sickness of mankind, in its bourgeois aspect, in that philistine smugness and limitedness, which could not but lead to mutual slaughter. The philistine isolatedness has shaken loose in the blood, the politics in the war. And in the nervously susceptible refined culture of France this is felt more acutely, than where it had not been so. And the fate of France, as a great land, is first of all the fate of Paris, its heart and the heart of Europe. There is distress for Paris and the desire to aid it. The world City cannot be allowed to perish, it is needed by the world, in it are the nerves of the new free mankind with its good and its evil, with its truth and its untruth, in it pulses the blood of Europe, and it will sicken the blood, if Paris suffers the blow. Inevitable was the end of the philistine atheism and the bourgeois hostility towards religion. And Paris is being reborn for a new life. The symptoms of a religious rebirth were there already prior to the war. The fate of Paris -- is the fate of the new man and fate of the new City.

The Russian and the Polish Soul[1]

I.

The old quarrel within the Slavic family, the quarrel of the Russians with the Polish, cannot be explained merely by the external forces of history and the external political reasons. The sources of the age-old historical dispute of Russia and Poland lie deeper. And at present it is especially important for us to be aware of the spiritual causes of this hostility and antagonism, which divides the Slavic world. This is a dispute first of all between two Slavic souls, kindred by blood and by language, with traits of ethnos common to all the Slavs yet so very different, almost opposites, compatible but with difficulty, incapable of understanding each the other. Peoples that are kindred and close tend less so to be capable of understanding each other and are moreso antagonistic towards each other, than those remote and foreign. The kindred tongue sounds odd and seems a corruption of one's own language. In family life also it is possible to observe this antagonism between the close and the impossibility of understanding one another. For outsiders, much is forgiven, but for one's own there is no desire to forgive anything... And no one seems so foreign and unpleasant, as one's own and near.

The Russians and the Polish have fought not only over territory and their different feel towards life. Outwardly -- the Russians historically have come out on top in this age-old struggle, they not only warded off the danger of the polonisation of the Russian people, but they also aggressively set upon the Polish people and made attempts at its russification. The Polish state was broken apart and divided, but the Polish soul was preserved, and with a still greater intensity the Polish national visage was expressed. The great spiritual upsurge, voiced in Polish messianism, came

---

[1] RUSSKAYA I POL'SKAYA DUSHA. First published in the newspaper "Birzhevye vedomosti", 10 October 1914, № 14610-14424, under the original title "Rossiya i Pol'sha" ["Russia and Poland"]. (Klepinina № 178).

155

about already after the destruction of the Polish state. The Polish people, so little capable at building a state, was endowed though with features individualistic and anarchistic, and proved spiritually strong and indestructible. And there is no other people in the world, endowed with so intense a national feeling. The Polish are completely not given to assimilation. And it is with the Polish namely that the idea of a national messianism has reached its highest upsurge and intensity. The Polish have conveyed into the world the idea of a sacrificial messianism. And the Russian messianism always has to seem to the Polish as something non-sacrificial, greedy, with pretensions to seizing territory. After the war, much has to change in the external, the state fortunes of Poland, and it is already impossible to return to the old repression of it. The outward relationships of Russia and Poland will tend to fundamentally change. Russia is aware, that it has to redeem its historical guilt regarding Poland. But the Russian and the Polish souls all still remain the opposite of each other, as terribly foreign, infinitely different, incomprehensible each for the other. The Polish-Russian question is posited by both the Polish and the Russians too externally, on the political plane, and its resolution vacillates depending upon the fluctuations of political intents and military successes. The liberation of Poland would make possible a genuine communion between Poland and Russia, a genuine rapport between the Polish and the Russians, which up til now the repression of Poland has impeded. But what inwardly has to be done for such a communion and rapport? To outward promises the Polish relate suspiciously. At present these historical suspicions are baseless, but psychologically the Polish have quite much basis for them. Spiritually however very little is done for any rapport with the Polish. But I should want to draw special attention to this, that in Polish-Russian relations there is a deeper, a spiritual side. Only a genuine understanding can be liberating, it frees one from any initial negative feelings, and tends to familiarise both us, as Russians, and the Polish, as to why it is always so difficult for the Russian soul to be fond of the Polish soul, and why the Polish soul relates with such suspiciousness towards the Russian soul? Why so foreign and so incomprehensible to each other are these two Slavic souls? Inside the Slavic world has occurred the clash of East and West. The Slavic West has felt itself more civilised, a bearer of unified European culture. And the Slavic East has opposed to the West its own particular spiritual type of culture and life.

II.

I have always thought, that the dispute of Russia and Poland is, first of all, a dispute of the Orthodox soul and the Catholic soul. And within the Slavic world this clash between the Orthodox and Catholic souls has assumed an especial acuteness. Russia historically has been wont to preserve its Orthodox soul and its unique spiritual inheritance against the Western side. In the past, polonisation and latinisation of the Russian people would have been to the ruin of its spiritual self-existence, its national visage. Poland descended upon the Russian East with a sense of its own cultural superiourity. The Russian spiritual type seemed to the Polish not some other spiritual type, but simply a lower and non-cultural condition. The historical struggle of Russia with Poland had a positive significance, and the spiritual uniqueness of the Russian people was affirmed in it forever. The memory of this struggle has left in the souls of both peoples traces so deep, that at present it is difficult to be free of it. Russia grew into a colossus, both as a state, and likewise spiritually, and long since already the fomenting of passions over the Polish danger, just like the Catholic danger, has become shameful and insulting to the dignity of the Russian people. It ill becomes a strong offender to shout about the danger posed by the weaker, the already crushed. At present Russia has facing it tasks creative, and not of oppressive preservation. Russian politics regarding Poland long since already has become historical a relic, connected with the remote past and presenting no opportunity to create for the future. In this mindless politics the guilty one ought not to be forgiving the one, before whom he is guilty. This is something within the realm of external state politics. In the sphere however of the inwardly spiritual there is still hindrance for the Russian soul in approaching the Polish soul by a feeling of foreignness and hostility, evoked by the Latin Catholic engrafting onto the Slavic soul, constituting the Polish national visage. To the self-absorbed Russian soul, having received its own powerful Orthodox engrafting, much is not only foreign and incomprehensible in the Polish, but disagreeable, repelling and arousing of hostility. And even Russian people having fallen away from Orthodoxy remain Orthodox as regards their spiritual type, and it is all the more difficult for them to understand Catholic culture and the spiritual type, nurtured upon its soil. German Protestantism has been less repellant for Russian man, and this has been a genuine misfortune for the fate of Russia.

Nicholas Berdyaev

In the typical Russian soul there is much simplicity, directness and a lack of cunning, foreign to it is every affectation, every overwrought pathos, every aristocratic ambition, all the gesturing. This soul -- readily falls and sins, yet repenting even to the point of morbidity it remains conscious of its own insignificance before the face of God. Within it there is some sort of an especial, altogether non-Western democratism upon religious grounds, a thirst for the salvation of all the people. Everything remains in the depths for the Russian people, and it is not wont to express itself in a plastically facile manner. In Russian man there is so little a sense of discipline, an orderly soul, a tempering of person, he is not extended out upwards, in the stuff of his soul there is nothing of the Gothic. Russian man expects, that God Himself will set order to his soul and arrange his life. In its utmost manifestations the Russian soul -- is a wanderer, seeking for the City not here present and awaiting its descent from Heaven. The Russian people in its lower aspects is immersed in the chaotic, still pagan earthly element. But at its summits it lives in apocalyptic expectations, it thirsts for the absolute and is not ready to settle for anything relative. Altogether different is the Polish soul. The Polish soul -- is aristocratic and individualistic to the point of morbidity, in it so powerful is not only the sense of honour, connected with the knight-chivalrant culture unknown to Russia, but also an obdurate ambition. This is the most refined and elegant soul within Slavdom, drowning in its own suffering fate. Pathetic to the point of affectation. The mannerisms of the Polish soul always strike Russians as artificially elegant and sweet, lacking in simplicity and directness, and repelling in its sense of superiourity and suspiciousness, of which the Polish are not free. The Polish have always seemed lacking in a sense of the equality of human souls before God, of brotherhood in Christ, as connected with the acknowledging of the infinite value of each human soul. The unique spiritual aspect of the Polish nobility has poisoned Polish life and played a fateful role in its state destiny. Russian man is little capable of such scorn, he does not love to give another man the feeling, that he is lower than him. Russian man is proud in his humility. The Polish soul however draws upward. This -- is the Catholic spiritual type. The Russian soul prostrates itself stretched down before God. This -- is the Orthodox spiritual type. With the Polish there is a love for affectation. With the Russians however there is altogether no affectation. In the Polish soul there is an experiencing of the path of Christ, the sufferings of Christ, and the sacrifice on Golgotha. At the summits of the Polish spiritual life the fate of the Polish people is experienced, as the fate of the Lamb, offered in sacrifice for the sins of the world. Suchlike is Polish messianism, first of all sacrificial, not connected with state power, nor with success and dominance in the world... Hence there is born in the Polish soul the pathos of suffering and sacrifice. Everything is different in the Russian soul. The Russian soul is connected moreso with the intercession of the Mother of God, than with the path of Christ's sufferings, with the experience of the Golgotha sacrifice. In the Russian soul there is a genuine humility, but little of the sacrificial victim. The Russian soul devotes itself to a churchly collectivism, always connected for it with the Russian earth. In the Polish soul there is sensed a cramped oppositeness in the person, a capacity for suffering and an incapacity for humility. In the Polish soul there is always the venom of sufferings. The Dionysianism of the Russian soul is altogether different, not so bloody. In the Polish soul there is a terrible jealousy over women, a jealousy, often assuming repulsive a form, spasmodic and convulsive. This power of women, the slavishness of sex is sensed very powerfully in the contemporary Polish writers, Przybyszewski [Stanislaw Feliks, 1868-1927], Zeromski [alt. Zheromski, Stefan, 1864-1925], et al. In the Russian soul there is no such sort a slavery over women. Love plays less a role in Russian life and Russian literature than with the Polish. And Russian sensuality, with genius expressed by Dostoevsky, is altogether different, than with the Polish. The problem of women for the Polish is posited altogether differently than it is with the French -- this is a problem of suffering, and not of delight.

III.

In the soul of each people there are its strong and its weak sides, its qualities and its insufficiencies. But it is mutually necessary to love the qualities in the souls of the peoples and to forgive the deficiencies. Only then is possible a true interaction. Within the great Slavic world there ought to be both the Russian element and the Polish element. The historical quarrel is outmoded and finished, and there is beginning an era of reconciliation and unity. Many a contrary feature can be pointed out in the soul of the Polish people. But there can also show forth features in common to the Slavs, indicators of belonging to the selfsame ethnos. This common affinity is to be sensed at the summits of the spiritual life of the Russian and the Polish people, in the messianic consciousness. Both the

159

Russian and the Polish messianic consciousness are bound up with Christianity, and alike it is filled with apocalyptic presentiments and expectations. The thirst for the kingdom of Christ upon earth, for the revelation of the Holy Spirit, is a Slavic thirst, a Russian and Polish thirst. Mickiewicz [Adam, 1798-1855] and Dostoevsky, Towianski [Andrzej Tomasz, 1799-1878] and Vl. Solov'ev tend to intersect on this. And justice demands the acknowledging, that Polish messianism is moreso pure and sacrificial, than is Russian messianism. There was many a sin in the old Polish nobility, but these sins are redeemed by the sacrificial fate of the Polish people, by the Golgotha experienced by them. Polish messianism -- represents the blossoming of Polish spiritual culture -- it overcomes the Polish deficiencies and defects, it consumes them within the sacrificial fire. The old frivolous Poland with the magnate feasts, with the mazurka and the oppressed common people has found its rebirth in the suffering of Poland. But if the Polish messianic consciousness can be posited as higher than the Russian messianic consciousness, I still believe, that within the Russian people itself there is a more intense and pure thirsting for the truth of Christ and the kingdom of Christ upon earth, than there is in the Polish people. The national feeling has been crippled for us, as Russians, by our inward slavery, and for the Polish -- by their outward slavery. The Russian people ought to atone its guilt afront the Polish people, to understand for it the strange of soul Poland and not regard as bad the dissimilar to its own spiritual sort. The Polish people however ought to get a sense of and understand the soul of Russia, to free itself of the false and ugly contempt, whereby an other spiritual sort seems lower and uncultured. The Russian soul will remain Orthodox in the fundamentals of its type of soul, just as the Polish soul will remain Catholic. This is deeper and broader than Orthodoxy and Catholicism being mere faith-confessions, this -- is an uniqueness of the sense of life and uniqueness of the stuff of soul. But these differing souls of peoples are capable not only of understanding and loving each other, but can also sense their belonging to the same ethnic soul conceiving of its Slavic mission to the world.

The Religion of Germanism[1]

I.

We tend to reflect too simplistically on our enemy, we but poorly know and understand his soul, his feeling for life, his world-outlook, his faith. And A. Bely has quite justly said, that the soul of a people during a time of war is what holds the rear, upon which much depends (vide his article, "The Modern Germans" in the "Birzhevye vedomosti" gazette). We customarily tend however, to either altogether separate spirit and matter in Germanism, or else falsely and simplistically see them as combined. For some, there does not exit any sort of connection between the old Germania, -- the Germany of great thinkers, the mystics, poets, musicians, -- and the new Germania, -- the Germany materialistic, militaristic, industrialistic, imperialistic. The connection between the German -- romantic and visionary dreamer, and the German -- violent and aggressive, remains misconceived. For yet others, German Idealism ultimately had to beget in practice the thirst for world might and dominion, -- so that from Kant there runs a direct line to Krupp. The second point of view renders a slanted deduction, unaffected by the complexity of life, and creates a simplistic polemical schema, but in principle it is the more correct. One mustneeds establish the connection between the German spirit and German matter. Everything material is wrought by the spiritual, it symbolises the spiritual and cannot be investigated separately, as an independent reality. Materialism is but a trending of spirit. That, what we term as German materialism, -- their technology and manufacturing, their military power, their imperialistic thirst for might -- is a manifestation of spirit, of the German spirit. This -- is the embodied German will. The Germans are least of all materialists, if by materialism there be understood the acceptance of the world on the outside, as materiality regarding its objectively real composite. The whole of German philosophy possesses

---

[1] RELIGIYA GERMANIZMA. First published in the gazette "Birzhevye vedomosti", 9 June 1916, № 15608. (Klepinina № 232).

idealistic a trend, and the materialism in it can but be a capricious and unremarkable phenomenon.

The German -- is neither a dogmatist nor a skeptic, he is a criticist. He begins from this, that he rejects the world, he does not accept the outward state of being objectively given him, as an uncritically questioned reality. The German physically and metaphysically -- is a Northerner, and to him the objectively outward world does not get illumined with the solar light the same, as it does for the peoples of the South, the Romance peoples. The primal feel of being for the German is, first of all, the primary feeling of his own will, his own thought. He is a voluntarist and an idealist. He -- is musically gifted but in matters of plasticity giftless. The music is still the subjective spirit, an inward condition of spirit. Plasticity involves already objective spirit, embodied. But in the sphere of the objective, the embodied spirit of the German, they have proven capable of creating only an extraordinary technology, manufacturing, militarisitic weaponry, and not beauty.The tastelessness of the Germans, even in the grandest of them, even in Goethe, is connected with the transfer of the centre of gravity into an inner exertion of will and thought. On the side of sensuality, as an aesthetic category, the Germans are nowise adept nor conducive. In the life of the sensual they can but be sentimentalists.

The genuinely profound German always seeks, in having rejected the world as something dogmatically fixed and critically unexamined, he always seeks to recreate it for himself, from his own spirit, from his own will and sensings. Such a direction of the German spirit was operative already back in the mysticism of Eckhardt, it was there in Luther and Protestantism, and with great force it is discerned and rooted in the great German Idealism, with Kante and Fichte, and otherwise in Hegel and E. Hartmann. It would be a mistake to term this direction of the German spirit as phenomenalism. This -- is an unique ontologism, an ontologism of a vividly voluntaristic hue. The German by nature is a metaphysician, and with his physical tools he creates with a metaphysical pathos, he never becomes a naive realist. And the German gnosseologism is a special sort of metaphysics. The German has striven such, that his ideal mental tools could be transformed into real tools for struggle.

Faust passed over from the idealistic searchings, from magic, metaphysics and poetry, to the real and earthly deed. "Im Anfang war die

Tat!"[1] In the beginning was the act of will, the act of the German, calling into being all the world from the depths of his spirit. Everything is born from the darkness, from the chaos of formless experiences through an act of will, through an act of thought. And the German is inclined to accept nothing prior to the Tat/Act wrought by him. Within him there is no passively-feminine acceptance of the world, of other peoples, there is no sort of brotherly and erotic feelings towards a cosmic hierarchy of living beings. All has to proceed through the German's activity and organisation. The German by his nature is not erotic and is disinclined towards nuptual union.

II.

The German senses darkness and chaos in the primordial. He strongly feels the irrational in the givenness of the world. This is discerned within German mysticism. But he will not tolerate having chaos, the darkness and irrationality, after the rendering of his will and act of thought. Where being is touched by the hand of the German, there everything has to become rational and organised. The world initially faces the German as dark and chaotic, and he accepts none of it, he relates to nothing and to no one with brotherly a feeling. But after the Tat/Act wrought by him, after the act of his thought and will, everything is changed, wherein there first appears the authentic world, a world rational and well-ordered, in which everything is put in its place, a place, set by the German spirit. The reverse side of this age-old Germanic primordial sense of the irrational, the subconsciously chaotic as reflected in German mysticism and philosophy, appears to be the demand, that everything should become organised, disciplined, given form and rationalised. Facing the German consciousness is the categorical imperative, that everything should be put in order. The German himself has to put a stop to the world disorders, and to the German all and everything appears disorderly.

The world's chaos has to become well-ordered for the German, everything in life has to be disciplined by him from within. Hence are begotten the immeasurable pretensions,which are experienced by the German as a duty, as a formal, categorical imperative. The Germans exert

---

[1] "In the beginning was the deed!" -- a quote from Goethe's "Faust" (compiler's note).

their force over being with a moral pathos.The German consciousness is always normative. The German does not commune with the mysteries of being, he sets before himself a task, as obligatory. He transfixes in his gaze all the world with his sense of duty and with his resolve to fulfill it. The German never senses other peoples as brotherly, as equal before God, accepting of their souls, he always senses them, as disorderly, chaos, darkness, and only senses himself as a German, as the singular source of order, organisation and light, of culture for these misfortunate peoples. Hence -- the organic Kulturkampf of the Germans. In the state and in philosophy, order and organisation can come only from the Germans. The rest of mankind is situated in a condition of disarray, not knowing how to assign everything its place.

The German is wont to admit, that at the basis of being lies not reason, but rather a subconscious, Divine madness (pessimism, E. Hartmann, A. Drews). But through the German this subconsciousness arrives at consciousness, the madness of being is abolished, and there arises conscious being, rational being. For Hegel within German philosophy and at its summit, in the philosophy of Hegel himself, God ultimately become self-aware. In this, very akin with Hegelian optimism is Hartmann's pessimism, for which likewise the progress of the self-consciousness of God occurs within the German spirit. The same process occurs also with the Neo-Kantians, although it is also expressed otherwise. For them the transcendental normative consciousness sets in order and organises the givenness of the world. And there are the greatest of grounds to presuppose, that this transcendental consciousness is a German consciousness, that behind it stands a purely Germanic will. They usually term such a consciousness immanentism. But this, certainly, -- is not the sole possible form of immanentism. This consciousness is very strait-laced, always disciplined and organised within, from its own depths, in which is lodged the German will, the strong will. Such a consciousness is imposing, but aesthetically not attracting. And it mustneeds be said, that the tragedy of Germanism is, first of all, a tragedy of the primordial will, too pretensive, too exertive, acknowledging nothing outside itself, too exclusively masculine, the tragedy of an inwardly non-nuptual German spirit. This -- is a tragedy, the opposite of the Russian soul. The German people -- is a remarkable people, a mighty people, but a people, bereft of charm.

III.

The German people has spent a long time in gathering its energy, exerting its thought and will, in order so as then to show the world a manifestation of its material power. The German senses himself an organiser from within, bringing order and discipline into the chaos of the world. Thus in the sphere of thought, of philosophy, and so also in practical life, in statecraft, in manufacturing, in military technology the German always is inspired by the categorical imperative, and he esteems himself alone capable of fulfilling duty. In the categorical imperative, in his duty the German believes moreso, than he does in being, than he does in God. Upon this point stand Kant and Fichte and many of the great Germans. And this renders the very virtues of the Germans difficult to bear. For us, as Russians, it is quite the opposite of this German formalistic pathos, this desire to set and arrange everything in order.

The German, first of all, believes in his own will, in his own thought, and by his inwardly posited categorical imperative, in his own organising mission in the world, both spiritual and material. He likewise well-organises everything the same in gnosseology and in methodology, just like in technology and manufacturing. And here has ensued the moment, when the German spirit matured and inwardly prepared itself, when the German thought and will had to direct itself upon the outer world, upon its organisation and regulation, upon all the world, which to the German presented itself as disorderly and chaotic. The will to power over the world was begotten upon spiritual grounds, it appeared as a result of the German assumption of the world as disorderly, and the German himself, as the bearer of order and organisation. Kant constructed a spiritual barracks. Contemporary Germans intend to build material barracks. German gnosseology has the same drill-discipline, that there is in German imperialism. The German senses himself free only in the barracks. In the free air he senses the oppression of a chaotic necessity. In his understanding of freedom we could never agree with the Germans. The German has submerged himself into matter, into material organisation and material domination as the grounds of his spiritualism. From his spirit he has become a materialist, he has created a mighty material world, and his spirit has gone out into matter. The might of Germanic matter threatening all the world is an emanation of the Germanic spirit, and the German spirit has exhausted itself in this emanation, it has diminished itself in this exertion outwards. In the German spirit there is not an unboundedness, this rather in its own sort is a great and profound spirit, but still a limited and measured spirit, in it there is not the Slavic immeasurable boundlessness. The spirit of Dostoevsky -- is inexhaustible.

The grandest manifestations of the German spirit, such as Boehme, Angelus Silesius, Fr. Baader or Goethe, E. Hoffman, Novalis, all managed to transcend the bounds of this "German idea", which I have attempted to characterise...

In a complex relationship to the "German idea" stands Nietzsche, who in both his spirit and his blood was not a pure German. The German spirit, a very powerful spirit, desires in the final end to give birth to an unique German religion of Germanism, which would enter into antagonism towards Christianity. In this religion is not the spirit of Christ. Artur Drews is a very characteristic expression of this religion of Germanism, and likewise is H. S. Chamberlain. R. Wagner was its prophet. This -- is a pirely Aryan, anti-Semitic religion, the religion of a smooth and insipid monism, without maddening antinomy, without an apocalypse. In this German religion there is no repentance and no sacrifice. The German is least of all capable of repentance. And he can be virtuous, moral, accomplished, venerable, but scarcely can he be a saint. Repentance is replaced by pessimism. German religion relates the source of evil into the subconscious of the Divinity, to the primordial chaos, but never to man, not to the German himself. The German religion is a purest monophysitism, with the acknowledging of one only nature -- the Divine, and not of two natures -- the Divine and the human, as it is in the Christian religion. Therefore, howsoever lofty, this German religion on the evidence has not exalted man, rather, in the final end and in a deepest sense it denies man, as an autonomous religious principle.

In such a purely monistic, monophysite religious consciousness there cannot be the prophecies concerning a new life, a new world epoch, a new earth and a new heaven, there is no searching for the new city, so characteristic of Slavdom. The German monistic sense of organisation, the German order, does not permit of apocalyptic experiences, is not tolerant of the onset of the end of the old world, and they fetter down this world in a bad infinity. The Germans ascribe apocalypse entirely to the Russian chaos, so scorned by them. We however scorn this eternal German sense for order.

IV.

The German world is also Central Europe predominantly. The German ideologues conceive of the Germans as creators and preservers of Central European culture. They consider France, England, Italy and Russia as the borderlands of Europe. The fate of Germanism is presented as the fate of Europe, and the victory of Germanism -- as the victory of European culture. The religion of Germanism conceives of the German people as that sole pure Aryan race, which is called to affirm the European spiritual culture not only by exertions of spirit, but likewise by blood and iron. Germanism seeks as though to secure the world primacy of Central Europe, it aspires to spread its influence to the East, to Turkey and China, but indeed it impedes the genuine emergence beyond the borders of Europe of the ingrown European culture. Germanism, everywhere obsessed with the idea of its own exclusive cultural mission, conveys its own ingrown European and ingrown German culture, by nothing enriched, of nothing and no one in the world acknowledging... And these pretensions of a Germanic European centralism prove a great impediment to the paths of uniting East and West, i.e. the resolution of a fundamental task of world history.

These exclusionary pretensions of the German spirit are intolerant of all the rest of the world. The German ideologues even have a racial anthropological theory concerning the exlusive excellence of the high-foreheaded and blond-haired, and have transformed it into something of a sort of religious German messianism. In place of "Aryan" they introduced into use the term "Indo-Germanic". The spirit of Teutonic pride feeds off the whole of German science and philosophy. The Germans are not satisfied with an instinctive contempt for other races and peoples, they desire to contemn upon a scientific basis, to contemn in a well-ordered, organised and disciplined way. The German self-assurance is always pedantic and methodological at its basis. We, as Russians, can least of all put up with the pretensive arrogance of the religion of Germanism. We have to oppose its spirit, its reliigon, its expectations. This does not hinder us from appreciating the great manifestations of the German spirit, to be nourished by them, just as with everything great in the world. But the pride of the German will ought to be opposed by our religious will. World domination cannot belong to Germanic Central Europe, its idea -- is not a world idea. Within the Russian soul is lodged a great Christian universalism, a great acknowledgement of all and everything in the world.

IV. THE PSYCHOLOGY OF WAR
AND
THE MEANING OF WAR

Thoughts about the Nature of War[1]

I.

It is not about the present war that I want to speak, but about every war. Why is there war? How philosophically to make sense of war? At the superficial glance, war is a moving about and clash of material masses, physical violence, killing, maiming, the working of monstrous mechanical weapons. It would seem, that war is an exceptional submersion into matter and has no sort of relation to spirit. People of spirit sometimes readily avert their attention from war, as from something materially external, as a remote evil, bound up with force, from which one can and ought to withdraw into the higher spheres of spiritual life.

Some reject war out of a dualistic point of view, according to which there exists a completely independent material sphere, external, given to violence, separate from and opposed to the spiritual, the inward and free. But everything material is however only a symbol and sign of spiritual activity, everything external is but a manifestation of the internal, everything coercive and by force is a falsely directed freedom. To inwardly make sense of war is possible only with a monistic, and not dualistic point of view, i.e. seeing in it the symbolics of what transpires within spiritual activity. It can be said, that war happens in the heavens, within other planes of being, within the depths of spirit, and upon the flat surface of the material are seen but external signs of what is transpiring in the depths. Physical violence, the committing of murder, is not something in itself substantial, as an independent reality, -- it is a sign of spiritual violence, committing evil within the spiritual activity. The nature of war, as a material violence, is purely reflective, a sign, symptomatic, not something independent. War is not the source of evil, but rather a reflection in evil, the sign of the existence of inner evil and sickness. The nature of war -- is symbolic. Suchlike is the form of every material form of violence, -- it is

---

[1] MYSLI O PRIRODE VOINY. First published in literary gazette "Birzhevye vedomosti", 26 June 1915, № 14928. (Klepinina № 197).

171

always secondary, and not primary. The particular condition of spiritual activity, wherein mankind dwells, inevitably has to make use of material signs, as implements, without which spiritual life could not realise itself. Man in the expression of his spiritual life has to move his hands, his feet, the tongue, i.e. to recourse to material signs, without which it is impossible to express love or hate, without which it is impossible to realise his strivings of will. And war is a complicated complex of material moving about of feet and hands, and of various implements, conducive to movement by the human will. On principle one can grant the possibility of spiritual life without material signs and tools, but this presupposes some other level of spiritual activity, at present unattained by mankind and the world.

There occur sicknesses, which are accompanied by a rash upon the face. This rash is but a sign of an inward sickness. The outward removal of the rash only drives the sickness inward. It might even make matters worse from the sickness. It is necessary to treat the inner sickness itself. The evil of war is a sign of an inner sickness of mankind. The material acts of violence and the terrors of war are but the rash upon the body of mankind, from which it is impossible to be healed externally and mechanically. We are all culpable in this sickness of mankind, which breaks out with war. When an ulcer with puss is discovered, then in this discovery of the ulcer itself it is impossible to see the evil. Sometimes this discovery is necessary to do something forceful for the saving of life.

Long since already within the depths of spiritual activity there was begun the World War, the world hostility, the hatred and mutual destruction. And this war, which began at the end of July 1914, is but a material sign of a spiritual war transpiring in the depths, a grievous spiritual infirmity of mankind. In this spiritual infirmity and spiritual war there is a mutual responsibility of all, and no one can be excused the consequences of the inner evil, of the inward murder, in which we all have lived. The war has not created the evil, it has just made apparent the evil. All of modern mankind has lived by hatred and hostility. The inner war has been veiled over only by the surface veil of world bourgeois life, and the falsehood of this bourgeois world, which to many seemed eternal, was bound to be exposed. The destruction of human life, as it occurs in world bourgeois life, is no less terrible, than that, which is happening in the war.

II.

In the Gospel it is said, that it is necessary more to fear those killing the soul, than those killing the body. Physical death is less terrible, than spiritual death. And prior to the war, in peacetime life human souls were killed, the human spirit was extinguished, and this became so customary, that they ceased to note any terror in this killing. In the war they destroy the physical outward part of man, but the core of the man, his soul can remain not only undestroyed, but can even be reborn. It is very characteristic, that those who most of all are afraid of the war and the killing in the war -- are the positivists, for whom the chief thing is in order that man should live well upon the earth, and for whom the totality of life consists in the empirically given. For those, who believe in the infinitude of spiritual life and in values, transcending all earthly blessings, those such the terrors of war and physical death do not so frighten. This explains why pacifists on principle are to be met with more often amongst the humanist-positivists, than amongst Christians. The religious outlook on life sees more profoundly the tragedy of death, than the outlook that is shallowly positivist. The war is a terrible evil and a profound tragedy, but the evil and tragedy are not merely in the outwardly assumed fact of physical violence and destruction, but rather quite deeper. And at this depth the evil and tragedy always obtain already prior to the war and its violence.

The war but manifests forth the evil, it thrusts it outwards. The external fact of the physical violence and the physical killing is impossible to look at, independently of the evil, as the source of the evil. The spiritual violence and the spiritual killing lie deeper. And the capacity for spiritual violence is very subtle and grasped but with difficulty. Some emotional stirrings and currents, some words, some feelings and actions, having no apparent signs of physical violence, are more murderous and death-bearing, than the crude physical violence and mayhem.

The responsibility of man has to be broadened and deepened. And indeed, man oftener becomes violent and a killer, than he himself suspects or is suspected of him. It is impossible to see the violence and killing only in war. All our peacetime life rests upon violence and killing. And prior to the start of the present-day world war we committed violence and killed in the very depths of life no less, than in the time of war. The war but made apparent and projected out onto the material plane our old acts of violence and killing, our hatred and hostility. In the depths of life there is a dark and irrational wellspring. And from it are begotten the most profound and tragic contradictions. Mankind, not having enlightened within itself with the Divine light this dark archaic element, inevitably passes through a cross-like terror and death in war. In war there is an immanent redemption of the ancient guilt. It is not given to man, remaining in the old evil and ancient darkness, to avert the immanent consequences in the form of the terrors of war. In the abstract intents of pacifism to avoid the war, while leaving mankind in its former condition, there is something ugly. This -- is a desire to run away from responsibility. War is an immanent chastisement and an immanent redemption. In war hatred is smelted into love, and love into hatred. In war there intersect the limits of the extreme, and the diabolical darkness is interwoven with Divine light. War is a material manifesting forth of the age-old contradictions of existence, the discerning of the irrationality of life. Pacifism is a rationalistic denial of the darkly irrational within life. And it is impossible to believe in an eternal rational world. Not in vain does the Apocalypse prophesy about wars. And Christianity does not foresee a peaceful and painless finish to world history. In the below is reflected the same, that is above, upon the earth the same, that is in the heavens. And above, in the heavens, the angels of God contend with the angels of Satan. In all the spheres of the cosmos there storms the fiery and raging element and it brings war. And upon the earth Christ has brought not peace, but the sword [Mt. 10: 34]. In this is a profound antinomy of Christianity: Christianity cannot answer evil with evil, cannot resist evil by force, and yet Christianity is a war, the destruction of the world, the experiencing prior to the end of the redemption of the Cross in darkness and evil.

Christianity is full of contradictions. And the Christian attitude towards war in a fatal manner is contradictory. A Christian war is impossible, impossible just as is a Christian state, or Christian violence and killing. But all the terror of life is experienced by the Christian, as a cross and a redemption of guilt. The war is guilt, but it is likewise a redemption of guilt. In it the unrighteous, sinful, evil life is lifted up upon the Cross.

III.

We are all guilty in the war, all are responsible for it and cannot escape the mutual responsibility. The evil, living in each of us, is made apparent in the war, and the war for none of us is something external, from which we can run away. It is necessary to assume upon oneself responsibility before the end. And we constantly are mistaken, in thinking that we can take off from ourselves the responsibility or not accept it at all. It is impossible in crudely an external way to understand participation in war and responsibility for it. We all in some way or other are participants in the war. Already in that I accept the state, accept nationality, the sense of mutual responsibility of all the people, or that I desire Russian victories, -- I therein participate in the war and bear responsibility for it. When I desire victories for the Russian army, I spiritually participate in killing and take upon myself responsibility for the killing, I accept the guilt. It would be base to impose upon others the blame of killing, which is needful also on my behalf, and myself hold the view, that in this killing I do not participate. Those, who eat meat, participate in the killing of animals and are bound to admit their responsibility for this killing. It would be hypocritical to hold the view, that we ourselves never do violence nor kill and are incapable of violence and killing, that it is others that bear the responsibility for this. Each of us benefits having the police, it is something needful, and it would be hypocritical to hold the view, that the police are not there for me. Everyone who sincerely wants the Germans to be squeezed back beyond the borders of Russia spiritually is responsible for the killing no less, than the soldiers, who go forth in bayonnet attack. The killing -- is in this case not physical, but rather a moral phenomenon, and it first of all is done spiritually. The soldier doing the shooting and slaughtering is less responsible for the killing, than that one, in whom there is the guiding will to victory over the enemy, and who nowise directly strikes the physical blow. Such an one morally blameworthy may want to be full clean and free of the guilt over the violence and the killing, and at the same time may want for oneself and for those near and dear, for one's native land, that it be at the price of violence and killing. There is a redemption in the very act of accepting of guilt in oneself. Being guilty becomes morally higher than being pure. This -- is a moral paradox, which it is proper to think upon deeply. The exclusive striving towards one's own purity, towards the guarding of one's own white garb is not the highest moral condition. Morally higher -- is to impose upon oneself the responsibility for those near and dear, accepting the common guilt. I think, that at the basis of all culture lies the selfsame guilt, which is at the basis of war, since it all is begotten and developes in violence. But the evil, created by culture, just like the evil, created by war, -- is secondary, and not primary, it -- is a response to the primordial evil, to the darkness, encompassing the primal bases of life.

IV.

It is impossible to approach war in a doctrinal and rational manner. Absolutism in evaluating life always proves bereft of life, coercive, always it is a pharisaical exalting of the Sabbath higher than man. But man is higher than the Sabbath, and the Sabbath ought not to serve as the absolute principle in life. There is both possible and desirable but a vital plasticity of morals, for which everything in the world is an individually creative task. The absolute is inapplicable to the sphere of the relative. In the historical corporeal world there is nothing of the absolute. Absolute life is possible, but it is impossible to apply the absolute to relative life. Absolute life is life in love. In absolute life there cannot be war, the violence and killing. The killing, violence and war is a sign of life that is relative, historically-corporeal, not of the Divine. Within the historical body, within the material limitedness, the absolute Divine life is impossible. We live by force, insofar as we live in the physical body. The laws of the material world -- are the laws of force. The absolute negation of violence and war is possible only as a phenomenon profoundly individual, and not as a norm and law. This presupposes an in-spiritising, a conquering of the "world" and its fatal law, the enlightening of the human body by the light from elsewhere. But for life within this material world it is impossible to apply the absolute, as a law and norm. The Gospel is not a law of life. The absolute is not applicable, but it is attainable. Absolute life lies within the life of grace, and is not life, filled with laws and norms. The legalistic application of the absolute to the relative is also the Sabbath-extolling, disdained by Christ.

The absolute truth about the non-resistance to evil by force is not a law of life in this chaotic and dark world, submerged as it is in the material relativeness, inwardly pervaded by discord and enmity. And grant that this world should pass over into absolute life in love. One can only but wish for this and strive towards this. Yet this would be accomplished mysteriously and unseen, just like it is that unseen cometh the Kingdom of God. But there is no sort of inward meaning to desire the external world and yet deny all external force, leaving the inner world in its former chaos, darkness, evil and enmity. This signifies but nothing. The binding of absolute law to the relative life is a doctrinalising, bereft of all inward meaning. One can but desire the inward health, and not the outward guise of health amidst inward sickness. It is impossible to stress strongly enough, that Christ's absolute love is a new life in the grace of the spirit, and not a law for the relative material life. And herein is why infinitely complex is the problem of the relationship of Christianity to war.

War can be conceived of only as tragic and suffering. The attitude towards war can only be but antinomic. This -- is an experiencing of the inner darkness of world life, of inner evil, the acceptance of guilt and redemption. A sweetly optimistic and exclusively happy attitude towards war -- is impermissible and immoral. We both accept and yet reject war. We accept the war in the name of its rejection. Militarism and pacifism -- are alike a lie. Both within the one and within the other -- is the external attitude towards life. The acceptance of war is an acceptance of the tragic terror of life. And if in war there is brutality and the loss of the human visage, then in it also there is a great love, focused into the darkness.

Concerning the Cruelty and Anguish[1]

I.

    Much is spoken of the cruelty of our days in our era, about the impossibility to bear all the assortments of anguish, having fallen the lot of our generation. Many even suggest that our time has become more cruel, than the past historical times. This -- is an illusion and self-deception. We have become too susceptible to the cruelty of life, in general, we have become too accustomed to the ills of everyday life. And exceptional outward manifestations of cruelty have been needed, to wound our soul and jolt our imagination. Prior to the war and its terrors we each day committed many a cruelty and suffered many a cruel ill. The process of all life -- involves cruelty and sickness. But our susceptibility has become dulled, our hides have grown thick. But we have become terrified by the cruelties of the war, and in our sympathetic pathos there is a modicum of subconscious hypocrisy. The growth of life always involves pain. When we seek to deal with life, we commit many a cruelty and many a cruelty is committed over us. We kill not only then, when we slaughter with the bayonette and shoot with a gun. Essentially anyone, who accepts the world process, historical developement, likewise accepts the cruelty and the pain and justifies them. There is cruelty and sickness in every process of developement, in every emergence from a condition of calm and immobility, in every upward ascent. The heroic principle -- is a principle of cruelty. Even movement itself implies infirmity, a lack of stability. Very unfirm even is the elementary mechanical thrust, engendering motion. And thus it is all the way to the utmost manifestations of spiritual life. And whosoever desires the accomplishing of the historical fates of mankind, its developement upwards, that same one is bound to admit of cruelty and pain, and fasten the armour upon himself. One, who desires no sort of cruelty and pain, -- has no desire for the advancing of the world process, for movement and developement, and he desires rather, that existence

---

[1] O ZHESTOKOCSTI I BOLI. First published in literary gazette "Birzhevye vedomosti", 15 January 1916, № 15306. (Klepinina № 220).

should remain in a condition of primordial immobility and calm, so that nothing might occur. Suchlike is the inevitable metaphysical deduction.

II.

In the historical life of every movement forwards, it begins with a breaking loose from established systems of application and balance, with an always tormentive emergence out from the condition of relative harmony. It is painfully difficult to break loose from a customary structure of life, from that, which has seemed organically eternal. But it is necessary to pass through the moment of rupture and disharmony. And this is always painful. But this painfulness, this cruelness of the start of every moment has to be admitted by everyone, who seeks not eternal stagnation and calm, who seeks developement and new life. Fierce and painful is the transition from a patriarchal structure of life to another, a more complex structure, in which the personal principle is raised up, and which prior to this time did but slumber. Painful and cruel is the sundering of a primordial wholeness and organicity. Having awakened, having gotten itself up and become conscious of itself, the person always is harsh in relation to the mediocre surroundings and the system availed to in the governing of it, and it cannot but occasion pain. How much cruelty and pain exists amidst every rift of the person with the family, which has its own systems in place! How much cruelty and pain exists in every struggle for a value, which becomes an utmost good! Painful and tormentive was the replacement of a natural economy by the monetary, painful and tormentive has been the disintegration of the obschina, the peasant-commune, the disintegration of the old order of the family, painful and tormentive every break with the old conventions of life, with the old ideas, painful and tormentive every spiritual and intellectual crisis. The painless path would have left matters at calm and immobility. From the perspective of sympathy for people and the human race, out of the fear of pain and cruelty, it would be the better to remain in the old system of ways, to seek for nothing, to struggle for no values. Harshness accompanies every initiating of movement, every breaking loose, an antecedent to creativity.

An historical religion of sympathy, fearing all pain and suffering, as for example in Buddhism, is a religion of stagnant immobility, of calm. In Christianity this is not so, -- Christianity reckons inevitable the passage of life through suffering, and Christianity knows values higher, than calm and painlessness. Christianity believes in the redemptiveness of suffering and summons towards a voluntary Golgotha. And the fate of Christian peoples -- is dynamic, it is not static, as is the fate of the peoples of the East. Christian mankind creates history. The acknowledging of some highest good, whether it be happiness, good fortune, a painless condition for people, or the immediate interests of the given generation, -- tends to lead to stagnation, to a fear of creative movement and history. All creativity and all history is a love for the far remote, and not a love for only the near and dear, it is a love for value, and not for felicity. Creativity and history are not without moments of suffering and pain, without a sacrifice of welfare and immediate life. In every love for the far remote, the upward heights, the supra-human value, there is its own cruelty. The dry fire burns away the moistness of life and bears suffering to all, that is close, that is on the surface level. The painless and more sympathetic approach would not defend the remote and lofty values but would instead surrender them in the name of the welfare of the people, would fail to create history. In such a point of view, value per se is already cruelty and anguish. In the perspective of the good -- the painless calm, the means employed, there would suffice what already is, and for those that already are. But with such an attitude towards life it would be impossible to create a great history.

III.

Everything spoken above can be applied also to war. War is cruel and painful. there is no one that would assert, that war itself per se is a desirable good. Everyone readily would consciously admit the desirability of the cessation of all wars and the pacification of mankind in brotherly oneness. But such abstract truths little help getting beyond the actual difficulties of life. The whole question consists in this, are there to be defended in war some sort of values, higher, than human felicity, than the peace and contentment of the modern generation? Is there to be accomplished in this terrible and cruel war something important for the historically remote and upwards? In the ideological laudations of the war there is always something diagreeable and unseemly. War can be admitted only as tragic a source of suffering. But this war that has descended upon us, being perhaps more terrible than any of the former wars, is in any case a tribulation of suffering for modern mankind, with its destruction of bourgeois happiness and tranquility, the loss of the possibility of an externally peaceful life amidst the internal discord. The value of honour, both national and personal, is higher than felicity and peaceful contentment. The attaining to historical life, the deciding of world tasks, stands higher than the attainments of closed-in egoistic life, be it personal or familial. Without such an awareness there cannot be forged a people's character. If amongst the people there wins out the interests of the peacefully-contented life of the contemporary generation, then such a people would not possess an history, would not be able to fulfill any sort of mission in the world. The cruelty of war, the cruelty of our era is not simply the cruelty, the spitefulness of heartless people, of persons, though all this also can be an accompanying phenomena. This -- is the cruelty of historical fate, of historical movement, historical tribulation.

The cruelness of man -- is reflexive. What seems just for us arouses the cruelty of the Germans. We sense behind this the transforming of man into a mechanical tool for the aims of the state, the deadening of the soul in the modern mass discipline. Against the embittering of the heart, against the cruelty of temperament it is necessary to contend with all our powers. The war, certainly, bears with it the danger of barbarisation and callowness. It strips away the veils of culture and lays bare the old human nature. But there is another side in the moral and psychological problem of cruelty. Modern people, spoiled, coddled and grown soft with the bourgeois-tranquil life, will not put up with this cruelty of the human heart, -- their hearts are sufficiently callous already in the peaceful life, -- they will not put up with the cruel tribulations, the cruel movements, destructive of the calm, the cruelty of history and fate. They do not desire history with its great aims, they desire its cessation in a calm contentment and well-being. And herein this fear of cruelty and pain is not an indicator of spiritual loftiness.

The most loving, good, sincere man can fearlessly accept the torment of the transpiring history, the cruelty of the historical struggle. Goodness is not contrary to firmness, even severity, when life demands it. Love itself sometimes is bound to be firm and harsh, and to not fear the suffering, which bears with it the struggle for that which one loves. The question entails a more manly, no wise soft attitude towards life. And in the final end, the fearless acceptance of moments of inevitable cruelty would lead to this, that many a suffering would be averted. Indeed it could be the necessity of an operation, to deliver from a deadly illness, to preclude still more terrible sufferings. This harshness and painfulness of the operation would have to be morally justified even in historical life. One would set mankind incomparably greater sufferings, in fearfully shutting one's eyes to the necessity of such operations, and out of goodness and softness of heart fore-ordain mankind to perish from festering ulcers.

With us, as Russians, there is a fear of power, there is an eternal suspicion, that all power is from the devil. Russians -- are non-resisters in spirit. Power is always represented by violence and cruelty. It may be, that the Russians have become such, since in their history they have suffered so much violence by the powers set over them. We have not been accustomed to look at power from a moral point of view, as a discipline of spirit, as a pledge of character. The Russian people out of an instinct of self-preservation are accustomed to submit themself under an external power, in order not to be destroyed by it, but inwardly it regards the condition of power not as something high, but rather a lower condition. Thus has the Russian people created its history. In the moral doubts, evoked by power, there is its own truth. The questionings of L. Tolstoy cannot be termed a misunderstanding. In them is sensed the great questionings of all the Russian people, its unique moral wont. But in the Russian non-resistance there is a dangerous, enfeebling tendency, a deviation from Christianity to Buddhism. To be strong of spirit, not to be afraid of the terrors and tribulations of life, to accept an inevitable and cleansing suffering, to struggle against evil -- remains the imperative of a truly Christian consciousness. Russians are most of all in need of a forging of character. Russian goodness often becomes a Russian lack of character, weakness of will, passivity, the fear of suffering. This passive goodness, always ready to pull back and give up every value, cannot be acknowledged as such high a quality. There is an active goodness, firm in the defense of values. Only for such a goodness is it necessary to appeal. And it is necessary to resist an enfeebling and withering terror in the face of the pain and cruelty of life.

Concerning Truth and Justice
in the Struggle of Peoples

I.

The most prevalent view in justifying the war by some of the people, -- is this, that truth and justice are on the side of our people. The enemy people however are seen as entirely dwelling in falsehood and injustice. This -- is purely a moral appraisal of the war, the transferring of the moral categories of personal life over to the historical life of peoples. Such an ascribing of exclusive moral uprightness to one's own people in the war, and to the enemy people an exclusive wrongness often becomes a covert form of pacifism, necessary to the justification of a given war. This noble point of view, which initially prevailed in Russia when the war broke out, is not only not accurate, but also dangerous. For the Russian generally it is very difficult to justify war. Among the wide circles of the Russian intelligentsia was dominant a mindset, quite negative about the war. The elementarily simplistic negativism on the war was based on various abstract teachings, such as humanitarian pacifism, international socialism, Tolstoyan non-resistance etc. The approach to the problem of war was always either abstractly-moralistic, abstractly-sociological or abstractly-religious. Among us, there had not occurred an independent working out of thought over the complex problem of the war. The war caught us morally unprepared. With a quick sleigh of hand was begun the building up of a justification for the war, employing a most elementary method -- transferring onto the worldwide struggle of peoples the customary categories of the moral life of the person. This has been done both by the leftist currents, deriving from a positivist world-view, and by the Slavophil and religious currents. The unique historical activity, endowed with its own independent values and appraisals, -- all these currents failed to acknowledge. Creative historical tasks disappeared from the field of view of their exclusive moralistic consciousness. As a result of our hasty justifications of the war, or more accurately, our self-justifications, there was indeed reached one conclusion: we are better than the Germans, the

185

moral uprightness is on our side, we defend ourself and are the defender, whereas the Germans in the moral regard are very bad, they -- are the aggressors, and in them -- is the spirit of the Anti-Christ. This conclusion is neither very elaborate nor very profound. But it is only on the strength of this moral judgement that we have deemed it possible to wage war. For some, the German people was considered the bearer of militarism and reactionism and therefore it was necessary to war on them, this -- was the progressive view. Even the anarchists of the Kropotkin sort have come to this point of view. For others, the German people have proved to be the bearer of anti-Christian principles, of a false spiritual culture, and therefore the war with them -- is a sacred war. But always it seems, that to make war is possible only because, that we are better. Hardly anyone has stood up for the point of view of a struggle of races.

I think, that such an exclusively moral appraisal of the war is false and in the final end is immoral. The elementary level of the moralising hinders getting at the moral significance of the war. Such an approach extinguishes the universal moral awareness of the guiltiness of all and everyone, of all the peoples and of all the human world, for the terror wrought by the war. It is morally more worthy to take upon oneself responsibility for the evil of the war, and not to blame it entirely on some other. It is a moral prejudice to consider oneself totally better than the other, to see a malefactor in the other and on this basis to justify one's struggle with him. In a duel there is needful a certain appreciation of the adversary, with whom there is no longer room in the world to live with. This should obtain also in the dueling of peoples. And it is indeed implausible, that we in all regards are better than the Germans, that our enemies should be but only such lowly evil-doers and their will consigned entirely to falsehood and evil. It does not exist thus. Even in our literature it has been pointed out, that the Germans have manifested not only fierceness and a will for domination and power, but also a sense of duty, patriotism, tremendous self-discipline, the capacity for self-sacrifice in the name of the state, and that the very evil which they do is from remaining faithful to the moral categorical imperative. Even moreso it has to be admitted, that in the spiritual life of the German people, in German mysticism, philosophy, music, poetry -- there have been great and world significant values, and not alone from the cult of power, not alone a phantasmic phenomenonalism, etc. And from the other side, with us there has proven to be many a moral defect, which can leap before the eyes with a painful shock. We are bitterly aware of many a Russian wrong. But ought this to impair our will for victory, our awareness of historical tasks, ought the whole justification for the war collapse because of this?

II.

All the shakiness of our moralistic grounds for war are apparent. Russian man, in doubting his own exclusive moral qualities and having admitted certain qualities in the enemy, has begun to think, that he cannot hold up in battle -- his will weakens, and he already lacks for the pathos of it. If indeed the Germans have their own claim to right and their own moral qualities, then to the Russian it begins to seem, that to war against the Germans is impossible, and neither good nor right. Upon the soil of such a moral reflection grows the mood of a passive defeatism, of an humanitarian pacifism and a simple withering away and indifferentism. But in order that we should get genuinely enthused, independent of considerations of the Germans, our consciousness has to be directed to quite different a side, we have to surmount the exclusive moralism in our estimations. The worldwide struggle of peoples within history is not determinable by moral prerogatives. This -- is a struggle for a worthwhile existence and historical tasks, for historical creativity. Justice is a great value, but it is not the sole value. And it is impossible to evaluate the historical struggle of peoples exclusively from the point of view of justice, -- there exist also other qualifications. National bodies within history take shape through a prolonged, tortuous and complex struggle. To have a worthy national existence is an historical task, and not simply an historical given. This task is realised by struggle. Historical struggle is a struggle for existence, and not for some straight-lined sort of justice, and it is realised by the aggregate of the spiritual powers of various peoples. This is a struggle for national existence -- not some utilitarian struggle, it is always a struggle for values, for creative power, and not for the elementary fact of life, nor for simple interests. One might say, that the struggle of peoples for historical existence has a profound moral and religious meaning, that it is necessary for the higher aims of the world process. But it is impossible to say, that in this struggle one people entirely represents the good, and another people entirely represents the evil. One people can be only but relatively more in the right than another. The struggle for the historical existence of each people possesses an inner justification. I can admit the rightfulness of my

187

own people in the world war, but this is not the rightfulness of exclusive moral superiourity, this -- is the rightfulness of created historical values and the beauty of selective an Eros.

And the world struggle of the Allies against Germany is a struggle for historical existence and historical values, not a struggle of exclusive moral qualities and prerogatives. I desire the prevailing of Russia and England in the world, and the weakening of the world significance of Germany. But it would be altogether inaccurate to say, that the setting of such an historical task and the struggle for such an historical value represents a demand of abstract justice and is determined by the exclusive moral superiourity of England and Russia in facing down Germany. The struggle, which Germany is waging so aggressively for world domination, can be for it no less justifiable and can serve to its own moral pathos. It mustneeds be acknowledged, that the war can alike be justified from both sides. This is a morally paradoxical assertion on the outside and it leads not to a moral indifferentism, but to a raising of moral consciousness. It would be morally a mistake and improper, for example, to base the great mission of Russia on the bringing low of other peoples. More worthy it is to fight for historical values against an antagonist, in whom be admitted certain values. The war is a clash of destinies, a duel, a recoursing to the Highest Judge. Suchlike is the nature of every clash of individualities in the world. In the duel, which is an appealing of the two to the Third, to Providence, the one can be more right than the other. But the meaning of the duel, and in every clash of individualities, is not at all in this, that the one possesses exclusive moral superiourity over the other. The question rests on this, that Germany began the war, that it is the chief culprit of the spread of the aggressive might of militarism over the world, that it has transgressed the norms of international law, and questions diplomatic and military -- are for our theme of secondary import. This point of view however does not get at the depths of the question, it remains at the surface. The matter involves the world spiritual prevailing of the Slavic ethnos. All the moral baggage of the German is diagreeable to me, I am opposed to his formalistic pathos of duty, his deification of the state, and I am inclined to think, that the Slavic soul albeit with difficulty can withstand the very moral qualities of the Germans, their moral idea on the arrangement of life. And I should want that there be the struggle against the Germans for our moral composite, for our spiritual type. But this least of all would signify, that the war is subject to assessment purely from the point of view of the moral prerogatives of the adversaries. The war represents not an appeal for moral justice, but to ontological power. The prevailing of the Slavic moral mindset over the German moral mindset is not at all a matter of justice. To the clash of individualities is not applicable the category of justice. This is rather moreso a matter of historical aesthetics.

III.

It is impossible to seek out justice in the formation of great empires, as for example Rome or Britain. It is possible to judge about the methods, which were employed in the formation of great empires, but the point of view of an abstract justice in the evaluating of great historical formations is completely sterile and fruitless. We admit, that the formation of the great Roman empire had enormous significance for the unification of mankind, for the unity of world history. But it is very doubtful, that in the formation of the Roman empire there was evidenced justice. For the purely moralistic perspective, transposing into historical activity the moral categories of personal life, there do not exist historical tasks and the values of historical life, as an independent sphere. Such a moralism leads to an affirmation of the status quo. Justice -- is static, and not dynamic. Every creative historical task presupposes the changing of the status quo and does not come about without a compelling re-distribution of historical bodies. Moralism, totally taken up with the single idea of an abstract justice, permits only of a defensive war, only negatively as self-defense. But the great war ought also to have creative historical tasks, ought to change something in the world for the better, to more valued an existence. For example, the struggle for coastal outlets is not a struggle for abstract justice, this -- is a struggle for historical existence, for an uplift of historical value. It would be difficult even to say, what would signify abstract justice as regards the Turkish problem. Would the defending of the Turkish empire be just, or would it be just, its destruction? I believe, that the world predominance of Russia and England would advance the value of the historical existence of mankind, would enable the unification of East and West and would clear the way for every individual historical existence. But the problem of East and West is not a problem of abstract justice, this -- is a problem of concrete being. For the abstract moralists, an evaluation of the historical struggle of East and West does not exist, it does not interest them.

For us, as Russians, there is needful a spiritual enthusiasm on the basis of an awareness of great historical tasks, the struggle for the heightening of the value of our existence in the world, for our spirit, and not on the basis of some outlook, that the Germans are evil-doers and immoral, whereas we are always in the right and morally higher than everyone else. The surmounting of the elementary moralism would lead to higher a moral consciousness. A just and gentlemanly attitude towards the devil can only intensify the struggle with evil. A more just attitude towards the enemy ought not to weaken, but rather to strengthen the will for victory. The will for victory ought to be posited as dependent upon our creative historical tasks, and not on the negative appraisals of the moral qualities of the Germans. We believe, that the final and ultimate victory in existence ought to relate to spiritual power, and not to material force. But spiritual power can come into the world through great tribulations and humiliations, through Golgoths. Triumphant power in the world can prove illusive. And however the external fates stack up, our task -- is to forge out the will towards higher an existence.

Mobility and Immobility in
the Life of Peoples[1]

I.

The historical life of peoples is full of struggles and movements. The accepting of history and an historical destiny entails also movement, with all its pain and torment. The struggle among peoples for advancement and growth cannot represent immobility. Yet amidst this, very widespread are the ideological outlooks, which would see justice in immobility, in the preservation of the status quo, while every struggle, the re-distribution of historical bodies, they consider unjust and a matter of violence. Many find very progressive, democratic and just a point of view which proclaims: unnecessary be any annexations, let all remain in their former borders. It is quite inconceivable, why the status quo, the preservation of the former borders of the existence of peoples is less a matter of violence, than a changing of borders, than a re-distribution of national bodies, than these or other annexations. Modern people are quite ready to consent to the results of an old violence, of an old struggle, of the old re-drawings and annexations. But they do not consent to themself assuming the responsibility for re-distributive movements, for the new agony of historical constructs. The national bodies were formed within history and determined their borders through struggle, and in this struggle there were elements of violence. But can it be said, that the great historical tasks are already completed and that there remains only the preservation of what has been established? There is a latent denial of all historical tasks in the modern ideologies, which appear very progressive. The worldwide task of mastering the surface of the earth and the settling of peoples upon it is presented as already completed. In their coordination, the peoples ought to cease any movements about, and immobility ensue. There remains only to

---

[1] DVIZHENIE I NEPODVIZHOST' V ZHIZBU NARODOV. First published in the literary gazette "Birzhevye vedomosti", 3 May 1916, № 15535. (Klepinina № 229).

happily set about building upon the justly assigned land. But happy construction -- is a static, and not dynamic idea. The abstractly humanitarian denial of all re-distributive and creative national movements is also the readiness to admit, that the war ought to be nullified and that there should be a return only to the *status quo ante bellum* (i.e. the state of things before the war), and is thus hostile to historical creativity.

The point of view of an abstract justice -- is static. This abstract justice but supports the world inter-balance, an ideal equilibrium. Historical dynamics presupoose a breaking of the equilibrium and that which already is too accustomed to be regarded as just, it presupposes a passing over through this, that it can point out the injustice, and admit of other values, than the value inhering in an abstract and restrictive justice. The pacifist theory of eternal peace is readily transformed into a theory of eternal calm, of an happy non-stirring, since consequently it would deny not only the anguish, committed with the movement of the war, but also the anguish, connected with every stirring, with every start of the historically creative. If it be asserted, that war itself per se is not a good thing, that it is connected with evil and terror, that there is to be desired such a condition of mankind under which wars would be impossible and unnecessary, then this is all very basic and indisputable. Mankind and all the world should pass over to an higher state of existence, and there would not be still the materially violent wars with all the terrors, bloodshed and killing. But then also even in this higher state there would still occur conflict, movements, historical creativty, the new re-distribution of bodies and spirits. The methods of struggle would change, everything would be rendered more refined, and inward, the quite coarse and external methods might be surmounted, but even then there would still be the anguish of movements and struggle, and even then the happy calm and immobility, the graceful equilibrium would not ensue. Even in heaven, in the hierarchy of the angels, there has been war. Wars can be spiritual, with the warrings of spirits. The good spirits contend against the evil spirits, but their weaponry is more refined and perfected. The creative tasks of the historical world process cannot be halted and there cannot ensue the static condition of an eternal happy calm. Mankind is called to ascend upwards, and not settle down on the flatlands. And an utmost human joy is a joy of movement, and not a joy of immobility, of stasis. Facing mankind there stand yet tremendous tasks of mastering the surface of the earthly orb and its regulation. The process of the formation and crystallisation of national bodies is still not yet finished. The missions of various peoples wthin history are still not fulfilled, and there exist peoples and races, which still have not yet had their say, have not fulfilled their deed, and periods of an upward ascent still stand before them.

II.

The formal principle of the denial of all annexations, the preserving of the old ordering of borders is unacceptable, consequently it neither includes nor makes pretense to an unconditional significance. Annexations can be abhorrent, but they can also be desirable. Try to apply this static point of view to Turkey and Austria, and at once its inconstancy is apparent. Why would it be just, preserving in the status quo a decaying and futureless Turkey or an artificial and unorganic Austria bereft of any independent mission? The instincts of historical creativity, the valuable historical tasks demand here the great changes and re-distributions. The new formations of the future are more of value, than the guarding of senile historical organisms. All the national and state formations have their own fate, their own periods of birth, blossoming and decline. All peoples are called to have their own say, to make their own contribution to world life, to attain the utmost blossoming of their existence. But the existence of peoples and states within history does not endure eternally, in immovable forms and bodies. There ensue movements of exhaustion and the loss of vitality. Greece created the grandest blossoming of world culture, it knew unprecedented and singular creative upsurges, but it too decayed and disappeared. The Hellenes, the Greeks exhausted their powers and had to yield place to the Romans, having an altogether different mission in the world. I believe, that ancient Hellas remains forever alive in the Divine world-order of things, but empirically it has ceased to exist. Spain was a great land, it knew great creative upsurges and flourishing. But it soon exhausted itself, it was pushed back and transformed into a second rate land. And scarcely does anyone think, that Spain can be reborn into a world role. All the peoples have their own times and seasons, they know their own hour. There is a changing shift in the mission of great peoples. One people will already have fulfilled or exhausted itself beforehand, in what it had to fulfill prior to its end. Another people goes to take its shift. And beforehand, the peoples store up their potential powers. And this shift in the missions of various peoples, is not subject to a judgement of justice. This -- is a matter of utmost destiny.

The struggle of peoples is a struggle of spiritual powers, foremost and foreordained, and not a struggle for living space nor elementary interests. Yet living space and the satisfaction of elementary interests is possible also amidst the pushing back of peoples and states onto the secondary plane of history. The humiliation of a people inflicts a wound first of all upon its spirit, and not its body, upon its calling, and not upon its interests. The spiritual and cultural blossoming of a people presupposes also a certain material mightiness, a symbol of its inner potential. But a people withers and perishes, when the material mightiness becomes transformed for it into an idol and wholly chokes its spirit. There are great grounds to think, that the German people, having its own great mission in the world, will in this war exhaust its powers. It has directed too much its powers in the creation of a material mightiness, and this has distorted its spirit. The Russian people however has hidden away its powers, has not revealed them totally within history. And it is possible to believe, that the hour of the replacement shift in history has struck. Much is in the process of being redrawn within historical bodies from the shift changes of historical vocations. But for this shift change in the callings of peoples, always altering so much on the face of the earth, the judgements of a static justice are altogether inapplicable. There exist lands and peoples, the enormous role of which within history is defined not by a positive, a creative calling, but the rather of that of chastisement, which they inflict upon other peoples for their sins. And most of all this can be said concerning Turkey. The extension of greater Turkey into Europe, its grip over Christian peoples -- was a punishment, from on high for the sins of Byzantium and the Christian peoples of Europe. Turkey, as a great empire, always was sustained by the mutual hatred and the disputes among the Christian peoples. The preserving of the status quo in Turkey was from a craven, cowardly and mutually-jealous politics on the part of the great European powers. With such an approach they hindered Russia from showing its might in the world and fulfilling its calling. And if the unprecedented war fails to decide the Eastern Question, then mankind will face the threat of terrible new wars. Not infrequently the preservation of the status quo means watching over a fiery volcano, which sooner or later will erupt with lava.

III.

The struggle between Russia and Germany is not a contest on the grounds of justice, nor is it likewise an elementary biological struggle for interests. In this struggle stand forth dynamic, creative tasks. Russia and Germany contend for their own place in world life and world history, for the prevailing of their spirit, for the creativity of their values, for their own stirring forth. Material interests place here a role, but subordinately. In such a struggle there has to be brought into motion all the totality of the spiritual powers of the peoples. But the positing of the historical tasks of whichever the great people presupposes a certain creative capriciousness, the free exertion of all the energies of the people. A creative task is not the fulfilling of a law, it is not a matter of a divine fate. It might be suggested, that God Himself sets before His peoples the freedom in the setting of dynamic historical tasks and in their fulfillment, not forcing them, when they struggle for the creativity of higher values. And the spiritual prevailing in the world of Russia, and not Germany, would be a matter of creative caprice, rather than of abstract justice. This is a matter of a free movement forward in the world, and not of a static equilibrium of balance.

The justification of Russia in the worldwide struggle, as also every land, can only be in this, that it should bring into the world greater values, higher qualities of a spiritual energy, than Germany, the pretension of which to world domination it is countering, and that by its unrepeatable individual spirit it lifts mankind to an higher degree of existence. This is not something from all ages forespoken and ontologically ordered, some already realised pre-eminence of Russia, this -- is a free creative task facing us ahead in life. The justification of every people, just as with every man in facing the utmost meaning of life, can only be dynamic, and not static. In creative motion, and not in age-old immobility, which would seem the just thing, it is necessary to seek higher qualities. The ideology of a static justice or eternally realised static being, -- is deadening and lifeless. Only a creative consciousness can provide justification in one's own eyes, and in the eyes of the world. We can however bring creative values into the world only in this instance, if we lift ourself up both in values and in the quality of our own existence. Every creative pretension has to be justified by creative action, by movement towards an higher quality. And a true national politics ought only be creative, and not protective, creating a better life, and not swaggering over its static life.

Concerning the Partial and the Historical Outlook upon Life[1]

I.

The attitude towards the war quite divides people into two types, difficult to get to concur. The one looks at the war, as also upon everything else in the world, from a partial point of view, from the perspective of personal or familial life, or the welfare and happiness of people or their sufferings and woes. Others look at the war from a supra-personal, historical, worldwide point of view, from the perspective of the value of nationality, of the state, of historical tasks, the historical destiny of peoples and all mankind. The partial perspective on life, having in view exclusively the welfare or woe of people -- of the Peters and the Ivans, -- is not a constantly everyday clueless sort of perspective, -- it can be very intelligent and compelling. For an intelligent consciousness, the happiness or suffering of Peter and Ivan can reflect the happiness or suffering of the people. It is very characteristic, that L. Tolstoy both then, when he wrote "War and Peace", and then, when he wrote his moral-religious tracts, was hopelessly locked within the circle of the partial perspective on life, wanting to know nothing except the individual life, its joys and sorrows, its perfections or imperfections. For Tolstoy, the feeling of life was really and essentially only the partial particular life of Ivan and Peter, a familial and moral life, their moral doubts and their search for moral perfection. Very indicative is the attitude of Levin towards the Russo-Turkish War and towards the Slavic Question. Life historical, national, the tasks of history, the conflict of peoples and kingdoms, the great historical figures -- all this seemed to L. Tolstoy as insubstantial, unreal, the deceptive and outer wrappings of life. In "War and Peace" not only does "Peace" win out over "War", but also in general the "partial" reality of life wins out over the

---

[1] O CHASTNOM I ISTORICHESKOM VZGLYADE NA ZHIZN'. First published in the literary gazette "Birzhevye vedomosti", 6 September 1916, № 15785. (Klepinina № 237).

197

"historical" illusion of life, and the childish diaper, soiled with green and yellow, is shown to be more substantial, than all the Napoleons and all the clashes of West and East. For Tolstoy the partial, the vegetatively organic life is always more real and more substantial, than is the spiritual life, than is the cultural creativity scorned by him, than is "science and art". Yet amidst this, with his "partial" perspective, Tolstoy fails to see the human person, every face for him fades into the impersonal. Tolstoy with such ease radically renounces history and everything historical, since he does not believe in its reality and he sees in it only an accidental and chaotic heap of rubbish. But history took its revenge on him. He ceased to see even the person, it sank away into the organic element. With Platon Karataev there is no person, just as there is none in Natasha. The person is shaded out by such "partial" things, as diapers and foot-wrappings. Within history however, in the supra-personal, in world history namely is seen the person, he manifests himself in a vivid individuality. The "historical" reveals the person, gives it motion, whereas the "partial", the domestic economic aspect, closes out the person and provides it no path.

There is another outlook on life, less consequential than that of L. Tolstoy, which likewise renounces the historical and affirms the "partial", -- that of a remarkable portion of the Russian intelligentsia in its traditional world-view. In distinction from the moralistic individualism of Tolstoy, the radical intelligentsia has held to a societal world-concept and societal valuations. But this sociality itself has been profoundly "partial", acknowledging as the sole value the welfare of the Ivans and the Peters, and in its orientation ignoring the historical values and tasks, the worldwide and supra-personal perspectives. For this societally-partial world concept of the intelligentsia there has not existed, for example, the autonomous value of nationality nor a concrete type of culture. This world-concept has been nominalistic in regard to all the historical organisms: national, state, churchly -- and realistic only in regard to social man and social classes. For this world-concept Russia has not existed, as an independent reality, having its own destiny and purpose in the world. Russia is not real, but rather only the people inhabiting it, for example, the peasants and workers, their welfare and their fate. With women generally is very weakly developed the sense of history, it is very difficult to bring them to a consciousness of historical tasks and historical values, their outlook on life -- is hopelessly and inexorably "partial". The feminine sympathy for the partialistic aspect can lead to an increase in the suffering, since it does not perceive the general perspectives of human life, it is taken up entirely with the momentary partial.

Such a feminine-partial and feminine-sympathetic attitude towards life always results with a decisive predominance of fellings over will. If the feminine principle were exclusively to govern in the world, then there would be no history, the world would remain in the "partial" condition, stuck within the "familial" circle. Least of all can it be said, that such a feminine-partial attitude towards life is a result of a strong sense of person. On the contrary, a strong sense of person resides in that masculine principle, which is the principle whereby history strives to attain its final end. Everything in the world transpires through a true co-relationship of the masculine and feminine principles and their mutual interaction. But in the attitude towards life with the Russian intelligentsia, and indeed in general of the Russian people, there is as it were a predominance of the feminine, the prevailing of the sense of feminine sympathy, of feminine "partial" appraisals, of a feminine repugnance to history, to the harshness and severity of everything historical, to the cold and fire of the upward ascent of spirit.

II.

This "partialistic" world-concept is the fruit of humanism. But this is not the humanism of the era of the Renaissance, this rather -- is the humanism, reaching the XIX Century and taken to its final conclusions, combined with positivism, spurning all values, except the welfare of man. In the final end, this humanism is anti-religious in its nature. This exclusive attention to the fate of the individual man proves illusory. In actuality, the nominalism of this world-concept goes farther, it decomposes man also, forces a spurning of the reality of the soul of man, the soul as it is connected always with the infinite depths of world being, and man is cast forth and left but at the surface. Man is rendered but a tool of a fictitious good. The humanitarian theory of progress brings every man into making sacrifice to his own small-idol and it cannot provide justification for the sufferings and sacrifices of the human person. There is thus the inevitable dialectic process: the positivist-humanitarian turning away from Divine values leads in the final end to a turning away from man, from the value of his soul, and to the exalting of this visible empirical life.

For this world-concept, the welfare of man and the absence of suffering stands higher than the value of man, higher than the integrity and worth of man. The societally-partial, the humanistic world-concept enfeebles man, takes away from him that depth, in which he always finds himself connected with everything "historical" and worldwide, makes of him an abstractly-empty man. Thus perishes mute the great truth of humanism. Truly every man is a concrete man, a man historical, national, belonging to this or another type of culture, and not an abstract machine, for the calculating of its good and misfortunes. Everything historical and worldwide in man assumes the form of deeply-individual instincts, of an individual love for one's nationality, for the national type of culture, for concrete historical tasks.

A more profound, a more religious outlook on man leads to an openness in him, in his depths of everything historical and worldwide, of all the supra-personal values. *The nationalness is my nationalness and it is within me, the realm -- is my realm and it is within me, the church -- is my church and it is within me, the culture -- is my culture and it is within me, all history is my history and it is within me. The historical destiny of peoples and all humankind us my destiny, I am within it and it is within me. I live in the past and in the future of the history of my people, of the history of mankind and the history of the world. And all the sacrifices of all the world history are rendered not only mine, but also for me, for my eternal life. The tiny tear of the child flows not only for the world, for the accomplishing of world fate, but also for the child itself, for the accomplishing of its fate. For all the world is the world of this child, he is within it and for it.* The child cannot recognise his all-worldness, just as many grown-up children -- the Peters and Ivans, do not recognise it. But this weakness and narrowness of the human consciousness, this throwing of man out onto the surface, cannot be refuted by that great truth, that each man -- encompasses all the world in his nature and that within him and for him is accomplished all history.

Only such a profound outlook can render me free, a citizen of my fatherland and universal a citizen. The "partial" outlook on life however, for which everything historical, the worldwide supra-personal -- is strange and foreign, makes for the slave, enables only the slave's revolt. The slave eternally senses violence against him from the outside, and for him everything outside -- is foreign. The free however sense everything as their own path, their tribulation, their fate. And thus I ought also to comprehend the war as an accomplishing of my fate -- I am culpable in it and it transpires within me, in each Ivan and Peter and for each Ivan and Peter. For truly each Ivan and Peter -- is a world being, in his depths having a commonness with everything historical and supra-personal. For the enormous masses of the Ivans and Peters this world process transpires for them within the unconscious or subconscious element. But the consciousness of these masses ought to be raised up to this worldwide awareness, and not merely to the slave's isolated awareness, for which everything worldwide seems from the outside and by force. Only upon this basis is there possible a resolution of the problem of Ivan Karamazov concerning the tiny tear of the tormented child. From the "partial" point of view this tear of the child cannot be justified. The tormented child -- is a meaningless sacrifice, evoking a protest against all the world, and in the final end, also against God. But sacrifices and sufferings can be justified, if there be seen that depth of every being, in which fate national, historical and worldwide, is his own particular fate.

III.

It is very characteristic, that the religiously deep outlook of life allows of sacrifices and sufferings, yet in much it is too difficult to glimpse the redemption and path to an higher life. The more superficial, the "partial" oulook on life, however, is afraid of sacrifices and sufferings, and every tear it reckons meaningless. That outlook on life, which I term historical only in opposiiton to the partial, and which essentially is religious, -- posits values of an higher good, it accepts sacrifices and sufferings in the name of utmost life, in the name of world ends, in the name of human ascent.

Everything heroic is begotten upon this basis. The prevailing of partial evaluations and partial points of view upon life do not enable a flourishing of the person. Upon such basis is begotten rather the meaningless revolts of slaves, but there are born no vividly creative individualities. Vividly creative individualities always are oriented towards the worldwide, towards the "historical", and not towards the "partial". For the historical outlook on life oriented towards world values, the command of Nietzsche remains in force: be stern, be firm. And yet another command resides at the basis of this sense of life: love the remote more than the immediate. The sternness is not altogether harshness, it is a spiritual trait, and not biological, -- a sacrifice by the lower conditions of spirit in the name of the highest conditions, a sacrifice upon the elementary goods in the name of the ascent and evolution of man. In accord with his own personal experience each man knows, that a fearful and timid postponement of certain sufferings and sacrifices leads only to this, that in the future these sufferings and sacrifices will be made all the greater. There is an inevitable harshness to the developement of life, and amidst the fulfilling of the commands of sternness and firmness this harshness can be diminished and abated. Thus with the war, in becoming too deplorably viewed by people, might lead to this, that there perish a still greater quantity of people. There is harshness within every state, it has the nature of a "cold monster". But without the state as regards mankind, at the level at which it finds itself, would be plunged into yet more cruel and beastly a condition. The destiny of harshness in the state is in the final end the fate of man, his struggle with the chaotic elements within and around him, with the primordial evil in nature, the ascent of man towards an ultimate being beyond the state. The state itself can wreak evil and destruction, it is always subject to the temptation of becoming a power unto itself. But this is already a question of fact, and not principle, this is a question in that the state has either to develope or perish. The state has to know its own place in the hierarchy of values. The kingdom of Caesar ought not to infringe upon the Kingdom of God and demand for Caesar what is God's.

Pushkin's "Bronze Horseman" depicts with genius the clash of the "partial" world-view with that of the "historical". The hero of the "Bronze Horseman" curses the wondrous builder Peter, doing so from his "partial" point of view, of a person's individual fate, opposing himself to a destiny that is historical, national and worldwide. The diminutive and partial life, feeling itself trampled upon, revolts against the great and historical life. But this revolt -- is a slave's revolt, it is begotten amidst a superficial awareness. Everything quite small can sense itself a co-participant of the great, the great becomes conscious of its ability and from this accomplishes greatness. Only the affirmation of the popular, immanently-human character of the state can lead to that utmost awareness, that the state -- is within each man and each man is responsible for it. In the various social ideologies, "partial" as regards their pathos, much is said about the "bourgeois" aspect of the state, of nationality, of the "bourgeois" aspect of all the historical organisms and historical cultures. But in actuality, it is these partial social world-views that are deeply "bourgeois", casting man out on the surface of things and impeding him in his interests, in his perspectives of well-being and the "partial" aspect of an earthly paradise. Quite "bourgeois" also is the humanitarian socialism, insofar as it acknowledges only hedonistic values and recoils from every sacrificial and suffering path of the human ascent towards utmost life, insofar as it confesses a religion of quantities, and not qualities. Man by sacrificial and suffering paths emerges onto the world expanse and into a world stature. The depths of man draws him to the heights. And "bourgeois" is everything, that leaves him out upon the surface and admits in him only the superficial. There is the "bourgeois" also in anarchism, combining fiercest destructions with a prettymost feeling of the idyllic. "Bourgeois" also is the familial and partial outlook on life, that too great and enslaving a love for the comfort of the partial life. Such a "bourgeois" aspect exists within the realm of the everyday ordinary, now experiencing a cruel drama. The non-love for the historically great -- is a "bourgeois" non-love. In the finest segments of the Russian intelligentsia there was an heroic principle, but it was inaccurately directed and resulted from a false consciousness. The world war -- is a greatest of tribulations for the humanitarian partial world-view, it has sent it rocking upon its foundations. The old, the glibly-superficial humanism did not want to know the depths within man himself. And only a deepening of world-view can lead the human person, so tragically facing the problems of the world, can lead to a consciousness of his own world historical, and not "partial" only, vocation.

V. THE PSYCHOLOGY OF POLITICS AND OF THE SOCIETAL ASPECT

On the Abstract and the Absolute in Politics[1]

I.

An SD representative has declared, that the Social Democrats are refusing participation in the military-naval commission and that they will not take upon themselves responsibility for the defense of the land, since in the defense ought to participate all the whole people. With equal success he might as well have said, that there ought to participate all mankind or even all the animal and vegetative world. And still more he might have said, that the Social Democrats will be in whatever way positive about participating, only when the end of the world ensues and the Kingdom of God transpires, since beforehand it is difficult to expect absolute justice upon the earth. This is a classic model of the modern abstractness and formal absoluteness in politics. In essence, this is a refusal for acting, on the grounds that the world is in too bad a shape for me to participate in its affairs. In the affairs of this world always what rules is the relative, and not the absolute, and in them everything is concrete, and not abstract. And a large portion of the declarations of the Social Democrats are distinguished by the extent of their abstraction and fictitious absoluteness. The Social Democrats do not believe in an absolute, -- in philosophy, in religion they are always for the relative. But their politics is a continuous application of the absolute to the relative, the absolutisation of the relative material matters of this world, using abstractive categories for a concrete activity. I speak about the Russian Social Democrats, who not infrequently remind one typically of Russian boys. The German Social Democrats long since already are involved in a real, concrete and relative politics, although they also earlier were absolutists. And everything that I am talking about is even moreso applicable to the Social Revolutionaries. Absoluteness and abstraction tend to distinguish the declarations of the political doctrinists, whose fine constructs on societal life in the sphere of thought become mistaken for real life. Such abstraction and absoluteness in politics in

---

[1] OB OTVLECHENNOM I ABSOLIUTNOM V POLITIKE. First published in the literary gazette "Birzhevye vedomosti", 8 August 1915, № 15034. (Klepinina № 205).

practice leads to this, that the interests of a particular party or social group are set higher than the interests of the country and the people, the interests of the part – are put higher than the interests of the whole. The part, the group senses itself detached from the life of all the people, the life in common of the nation and the state, so as to dwell itself in absolute truth and justice. It casts aside the burden of responsibility for the whole, for the fate of the land and all the entire people. That portion dwelling in their own absolute and abstract truth have no wish to participate in the mutual trust of national life, yea even of mankind in general. Such is the psychology of a sect, sensing itself saved and righteous in an endlessly surrounding sea of evil, darkness and perdition. And this is how every Social Democrat in the State Duma senses himself. The sectarian psychology carries over from the religious sphere into the political sphere. The sectarian psychology in religious life is also a deviation and leads to self-assertion and self-absorption, but in political life it has no rights to existence, since always it is a self-wrought idol from the relative things of the world, replacing the Absolute God with the relative world.

II.

A doctrinaire and abstract politics is always giftless – in it there is no intuition of concrete life, there is no historical instinct nor historical insight, no subtleness, no suppleness nor plasticity. It is like a man, who cannot turn his neck and is able to look only straight ahead at a single point. Herein all the complexity of life eludes the eyes. A living reaction to life is impossible. The abstractive doctrinalists in politics think, that they can see far off. But their "remote vision" is not a foreseeing of the remote future. They – are not prophets, and they see only their abstract doctrines, and not the real life ahead. And indeed even the "remote vision" represents an impaired condition of sight, which requires corrective spectacles, in order to see what is right under their very nose, to read and to write. The abstraction in politics is a frivolous and irresponsible proclaiming of trite commonplaces, irrelevant to the vital tasks arising and irrelevant for the historical moment. Wherefore, there tends to be no demand for any sort of creative work of thought over the complex tasks, no sort of sensitivity, no sort of penetration into what is happening. It suffices but to take out from the pocket the small catechism and recite from it some several paragraphs. The abstract and maximalist politics proves always to be a violation of life, its organic growth and flourishing. Such an abstraction denies, that politics is creativity and an art, that a genuine, moreso historically based politics demands special gifts, and not a mechanical application of trite commonplaces, a large potion of which are out of place. The simplistic denial of the complexity and concreteness of historical life, in which all the politics transpires, is an indicator of either a lack of giftedness amidst an elementary approach in this sphere, or else it is an absence of interest for this sphere, a lack of vocation for it. The aversion from the concrete complexity of societal political tasks occurs with us often as the result of a monomania, when a man comes wholly under the grip of a single idea, be it moral or religious or social, but unfailingly it is in the sense of the salvation of mankind by some sort of one method, by one path. This, in the final end, leads to a denial of the multiplicity of being and the asserting of one single whatever. But politics always has to deal with the given, with the concrete condition of the entire world, with the lower level of the human masses, with unregenerate souls, against the resistance of necessity. Abstract social and political teachings always err by their rationalism and their belief in the good fruits of outward force over the low level of developement of the human masses, and the needs begotten by this level. There is thus no rebirth in the texture of the soul of man and the soul of society. Politics always is immersed in the relative. It exists only for a society, in which are strong the swinish instincts. For a righteous society there would be no need of politics.

The direct straight-line application of the absolute values of spiritual life towards the relative historical life and the relative historical tasks is based upon a completely false mindset. The absolute can be in the soul of politics and in the soul of the people, within the subject of social creativity, but it is not in the politics itself, not in the social object. I can be inspired to social action by absolute values and absolute ends, and behind my activity can stand the absolute spirit. But the social deed itself is a turning towards the relative, it is complex, demanding subtleness and flexibility in interaction with the relative world, always infinitely complex. The transfer of absoluteness into the objective social and political life is an entrapment of spiritual life by the historico-relative and socio-material. Together with this, there is also an enslavement of all relative historical life in context of the absolute connections and abstract principles. And it was thus with all the theocratic currents, with pretensions to formally subject the society to a church. This always represents a lack of desire to admit the freedom of a multi-faceted relative life. There is a monistic coercion in both the right-theocratic and the left-socialist currents. Spiritual life per se with all its absolute values is fully concrete. But its direct straight-line conveyance over into the relativeness of the naturo-historical process transforms the spiritual life into abstract principles and doctrines, bereft of concrete vitality. Spirit, free in its inner experience, becomes instead obtrusive and coercive; it reveals itself to the relative external life not as a living experience, but as inwardly obligatory lifeless principles or norms. From a philosophic perspective, the relative historical life can be acknowledged as an independent sphere of absolute life itself, one of the manifestations of its drama being played out. And therefore the absolute ought not to be coercive, with an external and formal obligating for the relative by transcendent norms and principles, rather only can it be an immanent revealing of utmost life into the relative. The abstract and absolute politics of the Social Democrats is just as bad and enslaving a transcendentalism, as is the theocratic politics, as is Papocaesarism or Caesaropapism.

The denial of abstractness and absoluteness in politics should least of all be understood, as a lack of principle or want for ideas. All the societal and political activity ought to be inwardly moved and inspired by the utmost ends and absolute values, and behind them ought to stand a spiritual rebirth, the regeneration of the person and the people. But this spiritual tempering of the person and the people consists not at all in this, in the applying of abstract ideas to life. The spiritually regenerated man and people would make their politics otherwise, than with the proclaiming of external absolute principles and abstract norms. The moral pathos would not be weakened, but rather increased, it would carry over into another plane, would be made inward, not outward, with an heightening of spirit, and not the political hysterics and political fanaticism. Robespierre was very doctrinaire on principle and he loved abstract declarations, but he was a man of the old sort, not the reborn man, he was of the flesh from flesh and blood from blood of the Old Regime, an oppressor in the matter of freedom. There was only a change of attire. Our maximalists in the revolutionary years likewise were of the old sort unregenerated people, a poor human material for the deed of liberation, -- the makeup of their souls was not ready for the fulfilling of historical tasks. Freedom – is not an external principle in politics, but rather of an inwardly inspired origin.

III.

The question about having principles in politics is quite more complex, than the doctrinaire tend to think. It necessitates a recoursing to the question about spiritual renewal, about a transformation of the very fabric of the people and society, about a tempering of the character of the people. An outward and obligatory moralism in politics is out of place and unsupportable. But behind politics there ought to stand the moral energy of man, the moral tempering. However, with many of the moralists and radicals in politics, grounded in abstract principles, there is often absent all the moral tempering of the person. This too is to be discovered during moments of chaos and anarchy in society. And thus it was at the pitiful end of the Russian Revolution [of 1905]. In it we had individual heroes, capable of sacrifice, giving up their life for an idea, but in the revolutionary masses there was no moral character. And the important thing is not the abstract principle, but a live spirit, the renewed person. Having ideas in politics is bound up with the deepening of the person, with a nourishing of the soul of all the entire people, with a consciousness of great responsibility, and not with the simplification and schematisation of complex historical life. The moral principles in politics are affirmed from within, from the taproot of man, and not from the outside, not from the external principles of sociality. I repeat, the absolute in politics is impossible, impossible whether it be theocratic, or Social Democratic, or a Tolstoy's anarchistic absoluteness. But the absolute is possible within the well-springs of the human spirit, in the inward fidelity of man to the holy. Politics however is itself always concrete and relative, always complex, always it has to deal with historical tasks of a given time and place, all which are not abstract, nor absolute, nor monistic. Our standing on principle regarding abstract politics has been but a form of detachment from politics. In politics everything becomes "in part", nothing becomes "in general". In politics it is impossible to repeat anything automatically on the force of principle. What is fine at one historical time, becomes bad in another. Each day has its own unrepeatable and singular tasks and it demands skill.

Every sensitive man, non-doctrinaire, tends to understand, that the historic present day in Russia pushes into politics foremost the tasks of governance, the organisation of a responsible ruling power, and not tasks purely of legislative creativity and reform. But the day can quickly ensue, when the tasks will be altogether otherwise. At present all the forces have to be mobilised for the defense of Russia and for victory. This is an entirely concrete task, it is not dictated by any sort of abstract political principles. But the adherents of abstract political principles even now are making political declarations, which are completely lifeless and which bypass the most urgent tasks of the historical day. A spiritual upsurge, a moral power and inspiration is to be evidenced in a patriotic deed of service to the native land, in defending the native land to the point of death. These needs tend not to be foreseen by the principles of abstract politics; these tasks have arisen within a given historical day, and this moral energy is evident only now. Several years back there was not one of the politicians that foresaw, upon what it has become necessary to direct all his powers. And yet now for one who has to readjust his activity for the defense of the native land, there is hardly anyone who would call this opportunism. This -- is not opportunism, but the demand for action and responsibility. The war teaches concreteness in politics, and it tempers the spirit. It introduces tremendous changes in our moral judgements, it establishes an altogether different correlation between the moral and the political. The point of view, which we are defending, acts to liberate from the absolutisation of politics, from transforming it into an idol, into a god. We ought not to bestow to the relative, that which is proper to bestow only to the absolute, i.e. we ought to bestow to Caesar what is Caesar's, and to God – that which is God's. The spirit, strengthened in its absolute well-springs and regenerated, ought to turn itself to the manifold and complex concreteness of the world, with a living creative reaction and discover its creative gifts. Russia has need most of all of people with a talent for rule, and such people have to appear.

Words and Reality in Societal Life[1]

I.

Words possess an enormous power over our life, a magical power. We are under the enchanting spell of words and to a remarkable degree we live in their realm. Words tend to act, like independent powers, and independent of their content. We are accustomed to pronounce words and to hear words, not rendering for ourself an accounting of their real content and their real gravity. We take words on faith and provide them limitless credit. At present I propose to speak exclusively about the role of words in societal life. And in societal life it is a conditional phraseology, having become customary, that acquires sometimes a power almost absolute. Label-words -- possess a societal power all their own. The words themself per se can inspire and they can kill. Apparently it was Thackeray who said: "Men kill by deeds, and women -- with words". But men also can quite go the womanly route, -- and their words can kill. Behind the words follow the masses. Every agitation to a remarkable degree is based upon the power of words, upon the hypnotic spell of words. The customary phraseology is spliced together with the instincts of the masses. For one segment of the masses it is necessary to employ "leftist" phraseology, for another -- "rightist" phraseology. And demagogues well know, what words necessary are to be employed. Societal life gets weighed down with the routing of words. How impressively and how powerfully come across in effect such words as "the left", "the right", "radical", "reactionary", etc., etc. We become hypnotised by these words and are almost unable to think on society outside of these labels. And yet the real gravity of these words is not so great, and their real content gets to be all the more and more inverted. In the societal word useage it is a nominalism that reigns, and not realism. I might hear, how everyone says: this is a very "radical" fellow, vote for him. And this "radical" fellow -- is a lawyer, pulling down a tidy 20,000 rubles a year, neither believing in anything nor given to any values,

---

[1] SLOVA I REAL'NOSTI V OBSCHESTVENNOI ZHIZNI. First published in the literary gazette "Birzhevye vedomosti", 26 August 1915, № 15049. (Klepinina № 206).

and behind the radical phraseology is concealed a quite complete societal callousness and irresponsibility. The personal preparedness of a man for social action is relegated to the background in the face of conditional and routine phraseology. With us, the qualities of the person in general are little valued, and have no defining role in societal life. With us therefore there tends to be so many completely false a societal reputation, and there is many a name, created by the power of words, and not by the reality. The inertia and conditional aspect of words impedes the analysis of genuine character. In societal life, almost not at all does there occur a natural selection of persons of character. And in the life of the state clearly there occurs the selection of characters unfit and lacking in good qualities. With us, amidst the help of conditional phraseology, people profound of idea and with a moral tempering of character in a trice are made scoundrels of, while people bereft of idea and lack of moral tempering get to be highly exalted. Least of all tolerated are people of an independent and original frame of mind, unable to be crammed into any of the customary routine categories. With us, people often kill by means of affixing labels -- "reactionary", "conservative", "opportunist" etc., even though perhaps behind this be hidden a more complex and original phenomenon, undefinable by the customary categories. In the other camp they kill with the help of words of an opposite stamp. And everyone lives in terror of the words and labels.

The vast masses of the people live not by realities and not by the essentials, but by the outer trappings of things, they see only the cut of the clothes and only in accord with the cut of the clothes is anyone met. Broad segments of the Russian Intelligentsia within society live especially by fictional watch-words and illusional trappings. The power of inertia is truly frightening. If there tends to be the great power of inertia and habitually ingrained categories within the unsophisticated circles, then this is understandable and forgivable. But the Intelligentsia make pretense to be the heralds of thought and awareness, and it is more difficult to forgive this laziness and indolence of thought, this servility to the rote and obligatory and outward. It is difficult to live by the realities. For this there is necessary an independent working of spirit, an independent effort, an independent thought. It is easier to live by fictions, by words and the outer trappings of things. The vast masses of the people accept on faith words and categories, worked out by others, like a vampire it lives off the experience of some stranger. There is no sort of properly real experience bound up with the words, by which however, are defined all the values in life. The words were real content for those, whose own experience and whose own thought and spiritual life they were. But these selfsame words have become normal and without content for those, which live by inertia, by rote and by imitation. Thus also it happens in the religious life, where too many feed off the experience of a stranger and live purely by a literal dogmatics, and it is there too in societal life, where the memorised party slogans, the formulas and words are repeated without any independent act of will and thought. Upon this basis is worked out the political formalism, bereft of any desire to know the real content of human life. In the life of society everything indeed -- is in the strength, the energy of spirit, is in the character of the people and their society, in their will, in their creative thought, and not in abstract principles, formulas and words, all not worth the half-copeck. The indeed most important and essential thing -- is the people, the living souls, the interweaves of the societal fabric, and not the external forms, behind which can be hidden whatever the content one pleases or even the full absence of any content. A democratic republic, in which everything is set together upon fine formulas and words, can reflect a most abject slavery and violence. This long ago already became apparent with the bitter experience of life of European mankind, which ought to teach us to be mistrustful towards the purely outward forms and not be duped by the pretty phraseology of equality, brotherhood and freedom. How merely formal, how indeed nominal even people of a Socialist bent can prove to be. Here is why it is necessary to strive with one's will towards an essential freedom, towards a regeneration of the fabric of society, towards the realisation of values yet higher, those of the life within. This inward process would lead inevitably to an outward change of the societal order and societal system, but always in correlation with a real content and direction by the will of the people.

II.

Many think, that the chief woe of Russia is in this, that Russian society is insufficiently liberal or radical, and they expect much from a turnabout of our society leftwards in the traditional sense of this word. And in this opinion there is evoked for us the fatal power of words and formal concepts. Our society -- is liberal and of a leftist bent, but this liberalism and this leftism -- is powerless and is expressed primarily in an oppositional mindset or else indignation. The chief woe of Russia -- is not in any insufficiency of leftism, which can grow even without any essential changes for Russian society, but rather in a poor societal fabric, in an insufficiency of authentic people, with which such as history could summon forth for a real and genuinely radical transformation of Russia. It however is from the weakness of the Russian will, in the insufficiency of societal self-nourishment and self-discipline. For Russian society there is an insufficiency of character, of the ability to define oneself from within. The "means" too easily entangle Russian man, and he is too wont to emotional reactions upon everything outward. The "radicals" and the "leftists" might be completely unsuitable a material for a new, regenerated Russia. It is unseemly to get caught up in the illusions of word-play. The important and the essential thing, is of what sort is the man himself and of what sort is the people, and not the what sort are his word slogans and abstract political concepts.

Thus too, for example, our "rightists" have been poor material for a true conservatism. They have always been sooner the destroyers, rather than protectors of whatever the values. The patriotic, the national and state phraseology of the "rightists" -- is words, words and more words. Our rightist circles are bereft of a true state of national consciousness. Such an awareness is possible to be met with only in individual persons, but not in their societal segments and groups. The complete absence of a genuine conservatism -- is a fatal peculiarity of Russia. The Russia of the "right" had begun already to decompose, when the Russia of the "left" was still not yet fully matured. Everything happens for us too late. And we for too long have found ourselves in a transitory condition, in a sort of interregnum.

Russia needs, first of all, radical moral reform, a religious rebirth of the very wellsprings of life. But, alas, even a religious renewal can become merely nominal and formal. The great power of words exists even in the religious life. The labels -- "Orthodox", "sectarian", "the Christian of a new consciousness" etc., have assumed a significance nowise corresponding to their real gravity. The "Orthodox" nominalism has long since already poisoned the religious life in Russia. The religious phraseology of the rightist circles long since already has degenerated into an hideous hypocrisy and sanctimoniousness. But there is no help for us even having the assertion of whatever the "leftist" religious consciousness, applicable to the societal aspect externally and formally. In the depths of the fabric of the life of the people there has to happen a rebirth, occurring from within, and I believe, that it will happen, that the Russian people spiritually is alive and that a great future lies ahead of it. The troubled era will pass. Time will fling aside the outer trappings and discover the true essence of things, the true realties. Our greatest moral task -- is a passover from fictions to the realities, a surmounting of the hypnotic effect of words. Fearlessness in the face of words -- is a great virtue. And on the positive side of this fearlessness always there will be the love for righteous-truth. The pathos of the love for righteous-truth -- is a great pathos of the people. But around our words, our formulas and concepts, of the right, the left and the middle, there has accumulated too much of the conditional lie and rot. In truth, the singularly great revolution facing us to achieve, is a revolution of dethroning the false and the lie-laden, the empty and invented words, formulas and concepts. It is necessary to stop being afraid of labels, which they so love to stick on, in order literally to exalt or degrade people. It is necessary to catch sight of the realities beyond the words. And genuine insight involves also a scorn for much, which is insignificant and insubstantial. And thus ought to transpire the nurturing of the independence of the societal character, the maturing of autonomous societal thought.

III.

The tragedy of the war gives a primacy to deeds over words -- it manifests the realities and casts down the fictions. The rightist bureaucracy with its national state phraseology thus clearly has lived by fictions and empty words. This has become evident. The lie is toppled. Now already it is becoming more clear, who actually is the patriot, who it is that loves his native-land and is prepared to serve it. The words of the nationalists are being weighed on the scales of history. Last Winter among us here began to spread about a pseudo-patriotic mindset, intolerant of self-criticism in Russia, a mindset irresponsible and tending to self-praise. With some it found expression in the restoration of a religio-Slavophil phraseology, the more lofty option, and among others -- a state national phraseology, less lofty. But these frames of mind were swept off by events. And this Summer there has begun a genuine and healthy patriotic upsurge, there has grown a sense of societal responsibility, which always presupposes self-criticism. The words and fictions face opposite the realities. The unhealthy patriotism, fearful of the truth and given to expression to a literal idealisation of what actually is, is being replaced by an healthy patriotism, staring fearlessly into the eyes of the bitterest truth, as expressed in service to that, what ought to be. And to breathe it will become easier, though events be gloomy and onerous. One can speak the truth and appeal for the deeds of truth. In that stifling atmosphere, which one time formed, only false words could be dealt, only fictitious ideologies could flourish.

A freedom of words is necessary for the dethroning of the fictitious power of words.

In an atmosphere lacking in freedom it is the empty words that flourish, and they become irrefutable. The word itself per se betokens something Divine [trans. note: the Logos-Word of God underlying the logical, through the word], and the Divine signification of words can be revealed only in an atmosphere of freedom, where the realism of words wins out in struggle over the nominalism of words. A lack of freedom but encourages the empty phraseology of the "left" and the empty phraseology of the "right". The realities, such as stand behind the words, cannot be made apparent in this setting. The complete freedom of the word is a singularly real struggle against the misuse of words, against a degeneration of words. Only in freedom does the truth of words win out over the lie in words, the reality wins out over the nominalism. The freedom of words leads to a natural selection of words, to a survival process of words vital and genuine. The false and empty words will continue to be heard, but they will no longer have the halo, which is created for them by an atmosphere oppressive and stifling.

Render the word more powerful, and the power of words over societal life will cease; the word-realities will win out over the word-fictions. Freedom leads to responsibility. The lack of freedom makes everything all irresponsible. The restoration of the meaning of words, of a correct, real and fully-weighed use of words would lead to the awareness, that our society ought not to remake a mere change of clothes, howsoever very radical the costume should be, not merely replace the outward trappings, but actually instead it should be reborn and change its very fabric. The power of words has been an external power. And we ought to convert it into an inner one. The whole entirety of life has to begin to define itself from within, not from without, it has to be from the depths of freedom, and not from some superficial intermediation.

Democracy and the Person

I.

Among us at present there is little thought concerning the fundamentals of the societal aspect. Our awareness is directed to elementary needs, and these needs obscure the more remote perspectives. But there faces us the restructuring of our societal life, and we ought to be mentally prepared for it. Our societal movement is woefully poor in ideas, and there is too much accepted within it, as something rationally self-evident. Among the broad circles of the Russian intelligentsia and progressive Russian society, democratic ideas and ideologies are accepted, as a rationally self-evident truth. The idea of democracy has never been presented in all its complexity, has never been subjected to critique. The evil and falsehood obtaining in our societal and state life has rendered our thought simplistic and elementary. And everything the opposite of our oppressive actuality seems automatically good and bright. Every too complex a societal thought has seemed incomprehensible, irrelevant and regarded with suspicion. With us, there is the love for simple and straight-forward resolutions. In the West, the problem of democracy in its relation to the problem of the person long since already has become very complex. The vital historical process has led in the West to this complexity, it has made much problematic. Many a political form has been tried out there, and within political thought there is sensed exhaustion. We however, as Russians, have lived under great constraints and have had quite little experience in the sphere of political constructs. In thought, we have experienced quite extreme political and social teachings, and at times it has seemed to us, that we have passed through even anarchism already. But these extreme political and social teachings in Russia always are pondered over simplistically and on an elemental level. And such an elementalness and simplification has been there also in our comprehension of the idea of democracy. For many Russian people, accustomed to oppression and injustice, democracy presents itself as something defined and simple, something that has to convey great good, that has to liberate the person.

In the name of a certain indisputable truth of democracy, as a replacement for our age-old non-truth, we have been quite ready to forget, that the religion of democracy, as it was promulgated by Rousseau and realised by Robespierre, not only does not liberate the person and does not affirm its inalienable rights, but rather completely stifles the person and is lacking in any desire to know of its autonomous existence. State absolutism in democracies is just as possible, as it is in the most extreme monarchies. The people-power can deprive the person of its inalienable rights just the same, as where power is held by just one. And suchlike is bourgeois democracy with its formal absolutism of the priniciple of people-power. But the social democracy of Marx also likewise little liberates the person, and likewise does not take into account its autonomous existence. At one of the assemblies of the Social Democrats was expressed the opinion, that the proletariat could deprive the person of its seemingly inalienable rights, if this were in the essential interests of the proletariat. In this case the proletariat tend to think just the same as certain absolutists, that everything has to be surrendered for sacrifice. Everywhere we meet with the legacy of absolutism, be it state or societal, it lives not only where but one only rules, but also there, where a majority would rule. The instincts and habits of absolutism have passed over also into democracy, and they held sway in all the most democratic revolutions. In the West, long since already there has been disquiet over the question concerning the guarantee of the rights of the minority and the rights of the person in regard to the absolute pretensions of democracy, not delimiting itself in any absolute values of the personal spirit. The formal absolutism of the democratic idea cannot be something acceptable for us, it ought to be delimited by other ideas. The quantitative masses cannot hold complete sway over the fate of qualitative individualities, nor the fate of the person and the fate of the nation. The will of the people cannot be accepted formally and unconditionally, as the assertion of an absolute right of the will of the people, the will of the majority, the will of the quantitative masses to govern in whatever manner it pleases, to do whatever it pleases, to give and take as pleases it. In democracy there is its own right of an assertion by the free human element, of an immanent power itself of man and mankind. But democracy has to be inspired, has to have a connection with spiritual values and aims.

II.

The idea of democracy was conceptualised and formulated in an historical era, when the religious and philosophic consciousness of the progressive segments of European mankind was cast out onto the surface and severed off from the depths, from the spiritual wellsprings of man. Man was posited as dependent upon the external societal element. The societal element however had become something torn asunder from the human soul, torn away from the spiritual life of the person and from the soul of the world, from cosmic life. Man was acknowledged outwardly as a societal being, and completely definable by societal means. But since the human societal element had become isolated from the world in its entirety, from cosmic life, thereby allowing the societal element to assume an independent and exaggerated existence, there thus formed the rationalistic utopianism with its faith in an ultimately perfect rational arrangement of societal life, independent of the spiritual foundations of life for both man and the world. Democracy possessed no spiritual-religious foundation, it was rather the "Declaration of the Rights of Man and Citizen", which was born from the affirmation of a religious freedom of conscience in the communities of the Reformation. But the "Declaration of the Rights of Man and Citizen" in practice, in the democratic revolutions, in the mass societal movements, is very little followed out in life and tends to be supplanted by by societal-utilitarian interests. In Russia, the reception of the idea of democracy has transpired upon the basis of a positivist and materialist mindset and consciousness, sundered off from the idealistic idea of the rights of man and citizen. The pathos of social equality always has smothered out for us the pathos of freedom of person. The assertion however of the rights of the person both spiritual and moral was not connected with the assertion of the obligations of the person and the responsibility of the person. There has triumphed only the irresponsible theory of social means, begetting as it does only pretensions. The person is not recognised as a responsible creator by societal life. The new life is awaited exclusively from a change in the social means, from the external societal element, and not from creative changes in the person, not from a spiritual renewal of the people, of its will, of its consciousness. The character of the person and of the people is nowise taken into account in our democratic social teachings.

The idea of democracy in this linear straight and simplistic form, as accepted by us, has engendered a whole series of moral consequences. The abstract democratic societal ideology has snatched the responsibility away from the person, away from the human spirit, and therefore it has also deprived the person of autonomy and its inalienable rights. Only the responsible -- are free and only the free -- are responsible. In our democratic social ideologies, however, both all responsibility and all freedom has been handed over to the quantitative mechanism of the masses. The linear direct democratic metaphysics as it were does not demand any re-nurturing either personal or national, does not demand the fashioning of character, the disciplining of will either personal or societal, nor any inner spiritual work. Upon this basis is wrought but a moral pretentiousness, devolving upon societal means, a morality of expecting everything, of expecting that all the riches of life will come from the outside. All of life thus becomes oriented outward, and not inward. Such a type of democratic metaphysics will bestow a greater significance to mass excitements, to agitations, outward hype, without having any inner and substantial change of the human material of the societal element. And thus are created the phantasmic and totally external societal changes. This -- is a point of view of mere usefulness, nowise looking at anything essential. What becomes important is not the human developement of workers or peasants, not the raising of their human worthiness and qualitative ability, not the growth of their powers, which always indeed is a spiritual strength, but rather instead positing them in whatever the conditions, by utility needful. This is also a path of the moral degeneration of democracy. And it already has yielded its pitiful fruits. I have in view constantly here not the democratic programmes of demands and tasks, which do include a certain truth and justice, but rather that spirit of an abstractive democracy, that peculiar societal metaphysics and morals, in which prevails the outer over the inner, agitation over education, pretentiousness over responsibility, quantities over quality, the leveling mechanism of the masses over the creatively free spirit.

III.

An abstract and nowise delimited democracy readily comes into conflict wth the human spirit, with the spiritual nature of the person. And against this spirit of an abstractly-formal democracy, always oriented towards externals, there has to be decisively set in opposition another spirit, the true spirit of humanity, the spirit of the person and the spirit of the people. This spirit, nowise contrary to the truth of democratic programmes, demands first of all a personal and societal re-nurturing, of an inner work of the will and consciousness, it sets the fate of the societal element into dependence upon the inward life of the human person, the nation, humankind, the cosmos. This spirit strives for a true unification of people, and not merely to mechanically chain them together. Social creativity presupposes a creative spirit, it is impossible without a creative subject. The extreme democratic metaphysics is compelled to deny the creative spirit, it awaits everything from quantitative mechanisms, from an outward quantitative redistribution, and within it there is no admission of individual qualitativeness. Upon this path is denied the tremendous significance of spiritual selection amongst persons, of personal qualities and vocations, of personal fitness, and there is not proclaimed for the person all the enormous responsibility for the fate of the societal element. Quite the contrary, it is upon the external societal element, upon the social means entirely, is proclaimed responsibility for the fate of the person, for its fitness or lack thereof. But a true self-administering by the people as expressed by an organised human energy, as discerning the character of the people, presupposes the self-discipline and self-education of the person and of the people, a tempering of the will. A true self-direction by the people ought to impose a responsibility for the fate of the societal element upon man and his power, upon the people. But the people is not a mechanically formless mass, the people represents a certain organism, endowed with a character, with a discipline of awareness and a discipline of will, knowing, what it wants. Democracy, as a value, is already a formation of character of the people, the shaping of person, enabled to discover itself within natural life. Democracy is an organised and outwardly discerned potential of the human nature of the people, its attained capacity for self-direction and holding power. But mastery is possible only for one who has mastery over himself. The loss of personal and national self-mastery, the unfettering of chaos not only does not prepare the way for democracy, but rather makes it impossible, -- this always is the path to despotism. The task underlying the formation of a democracy is the task of the formation of a national character. The formation, however, of a national character presupposes the formation of a personal character. Societal awareness, the societal will ought to be directed to the working out of a forging of the person. This sense of direction is still lacking in us. Democracy too often tends to be understood wrong side out, not being posited as dependent upon an inward capacity for self-direction, as deriving from the character of the people and the person. And this -- presents a real danger for our future. The Russian people has to make the transition over to a true self-governance. But this transition depends upon the quality of the human material, the capacity for self-governance in all of us. This demands an exceptional respect for man, for the person, for its rights, for its spiritually self-governing nature. It is impossible to create the capacity for self-governance by any sort of artificial enthusiasms. A raging mob, gripped by greedy and wicked instincts, is incapable of governing either itself or others. Mobs and masses are not democracy. Democracy is an already transformed chaotic quantity into a certain self-disciplined quality. A man, first of all, just like a people, ought to have self-mastery. The defects of Russian democracy have been inherited from our slavery, and they ought to be corrected by the practice of self-discipline.

Suchlike an impetus of the personal, qualitative, spiritually creative principle, as a fundamental basis in societal life, least of all can be considered individualism. Through the inward action of the person and the nation, through the working out of the qualties of character is affirmed a spiritual social aspect. The matter constantly involves not only the soul of man, but likewise also the soul of society and the soul of the nation, aspects that the democratic mechanism so little takes into account. Democratism in the abstract is always formalism, it has no desire to know the content of the will of the people, the heart of the people, the mindset of the people, what is important to it rather is only the formal holding of power by the people. But the content of the will of the people is already something inward, already a spiritual content, a certain orientation of spirit. And against democratic formalism mustneeds be opposed the definitive content of the people's will and the people's consciousness, defining their inner spirit. Then only will the truth of democracy, the truth of human self-governance, be combined with the truth of spirit, with the spiritual values of the person and the people. We should ready ourself with all our powers, so as not to repeat the old mistakes, not to fall into some inescapable magic sort of circle, eternally begetting but reactions. Democracy cannot be, on principle,based upon an idea of delimited social and class privileges, on societally-external aristocracies, but the rather it has to be defined by the rights of the infinite spiritual nature of the human person and the nation, defined by a true qualitative selection. The spirit of a nation is deeper than democracy and ought to guide it. The wielding of authority cannot belong to all, to be a mechanical equality. The wielding of authority ought to belong to the finest, the select persons, upon whom is imposed great responsibility and who in turn impose upon themself a great sense of duty. But this wielding of power by the finest ought to be begotten of the very loins of the life of the people, ought to be immanent for the people, of its proper potentials, and not something connected externally, or set over it. The power of a democracy cannot be in an absolute and unlimited rule, it delimits it by its own qualities of impulse. The idea of democracy is strangely different from the idea of a self-governing nation.

Spirit and the Machine[1]

I.

Never yet has there been so acutely faced the question concerning the relationship of spirit and the machine, as obtains in our time. The world war has sharpened this theme all the more. Our disputes concerning Germanism revolve around this theme -- spirit and the machine. It is impossible to deny, that in Germany there has been much of spirit, and Germany has arrived also at quite perfected forms of mechanisation and machine production. The German machine, as though wrought from out of the bosom of the German spirit, goes forward, it sets the tone for life in peacetime, and now it sets the tone in the war. The Germans have become slaves to their own perfected machinery. There is transpiring a fateful process of the machinisation of life, the organic is replaced by the mechanical. This process frightens and terrifies many, accompanied as it is by monstrous appearances and the ruination of the old beauty. The triumph of the machine, replacing the organism by mechanism, represents a materialisation of life. But can it be said, that spirit perishes in this materialisation, that the machine banishes it from life? I tend to think, that this is too superficial a view. The meaning of the appearance of the machine and its victorious progress is not at all what it seems, at first glance. This meaning -- is actually spiritual, and not material. The machine itself is a manifestation of spirit, a moment upon its path. The reverse side of the mechanisation and materialisation of life is manifest as its dematerialisation and inspiritisation. The machine can be conceived of, as the path of spirit in the process of its liberation from the grip of materiality. The machine breaks apart spirit and matter, it brings fragmentation, it destroys the primordial organic integral wholeness, the welding together of spirit and flesh. And it mustneeds be said, that the machine is ruinous not so much for the spirit, as rather for the flesh. The machine aspect, the mechanical culture pulverises the flesh of the world, it kills organic matter, in it withers and perishes organic matter, engendering material life. The old

---

[1] DUKH I MASHINA. First published in the literary gazette "Birzhevye vedomosti", 12 October 1915, № 15143. (Klepinina № 210).

organic synthesis of the material and fleshly life reaches its end point in the machine. The growth of technology in the second half of the XIX Century -- is one of the greatest revolutions in the history of mankind. Something has shattered within the organic life of mankind, but something new has also started, all still not totally recognised and understood. After this war, perhaps, it will be better understood, with what is happening with mankind after the forcible entry of the machine into its life.

The problem of "spirit and the machine" has tremendous significance for the Russian consciousness, and it faces Russia, as the problem of its future. The disputes of Slavophilism and Westernism, of Populism and Marxism, can be transferred over into the spiritual sphere and deepened. And the point of view, that I want to defend, can be termed a "spiritual marxism". But this, certainly, is nothing more than an analogy. Russians love to contrast the uniqueness of the Russian spirit against the Western material culture, based upon its mechanisation and the machine. We tend to set our Russian organic integral wholeness in contrast to the Western mechanistic fragmentation. And in this grim hour of our history we try to oppose the German machine by the Russian spirit, and we try to consider this war, as a struggle of spirit versus machine. In this sense of the war there is some truth, but there is also a quite coarse confusion of various levels and planes. It is indeed necessary to admit, that the Slavophils and the Populists and the various Russian religious currents have not set spirit in opposition to the machine and material power, but still they have been in opposition to a more developed technology and ownership of technology and its economy -- contending against this with one less developed, and more backward and primitive. They thus seek a salvation against a more perfected matter via a less perfected matter, and against an higher degree of material developement -- via a lower degree of material developement. But whereas one can oppose a lofty and free spirit against the enslaving force of technical developement, it is impossible to oppose it with a technology more backward and elemental. Material backwardness ans elementalness do not constitute power of spirit.

It is impossible, for example, to transform a natural economy into an high spiritualness, to idealise an elementary and primitive economic order, as being more spiritual and free a condition. A backward, elementary, primitive economy is no less material, than a developed capitalist economy. If we happen to go backwards along the line of the material developement of mankind, then we would still not reach a free and integrally whole spirit, we would reach only but moreso elementary and primitive forms of material life. And this material line into the past rests upon a very coarse struggle for existence, in quite the same a material dependence, as governs within nature. We do not find a lost paradise with this movement backwards or in an impeded movement forwards. This -- is a crude self-delusion. The Slavophils, in esteeming the primitive and backward Russian material existence and connecting with it the heights of our spirit, have held back that spirit in a servile dependency upon matter. The abolition of the village peasant-commune and the patriarchal customary way of life seemed for them a terrible misfortune for the Russian spirit and its fate. But can the Russian spirit so very depend on a material backwardness? Does it spell ruin for the Russian spirit, with the disintegration of the old Russian material order? Then this spirit stands for but little. It would be shameful for the spirit to fear material developement and shackle itself to a material backwardness. The spirit ought fearlessly to follow out the path of material developement, seeing in this its own proper objectivisation and manifestation. Material developement, technology, the machine -- are paths of spirit. And I tend to think, that not only would it be a mistake to seek to counter a perfected machine with a machine less perfected, but likewise it would be a mistake to try to counter the machine -- with but spirit. One can but counter a lower and servile spirit with a spirit free and lofty.

II.

The cosmic materiality in its developing moves along from its primordial integral organicity, conjoining spirit and flesh and binding spirit to matter, it moves along to a mechanicalness, the pulling apart of spirit and flesh, destroying the integral wholeness and liberating spirit from its bonds with matter. This path can be discerned in all the spheres of life. Everywhere the primordial integral organicity is pulling apart and breaking up, there is occurring a differentiation and stratification. During a period of disintegration and dissolution it would be a mistake to regard the lost integrality and wholeness as a lost paradise, the loss of almost a divine condition. This primordial organic integral wholeness was neither a divine nor a paradisical condition, but rather a natural and enshackling condition. Within natural organic life the spirit and flesh are still not differentiated, and this signifies not some higher condition of spirit, but the rather its elementary condition, always bound up with the grim struggle for existence and beset by evil. The spirit remains still drowsing in its primitive organicity, it still has not risen up over the vegetative and animal aspects, it is still all wrapped up in nature. Splinterings and divisions -- are inevitable stages upon the paths of the developing of spirit, which it experiences amidst torments and not uncommonly is accompanied by a sense of death. In accepting this path of developement we become subject to an aesthetic illusion. We indeed very readily mistake our creative aesthetic perception of nature to be the life in nature itself and it is only with difficulty that we glimpse the evil and constraint, lodged within natural life. Everything organically natural seems to us prettier, than everything artificially mechanical. Beautiful is the majestic oak but monstrous is the machine, ugly in our eyes, ears and nose, causing no little woe. We love the oak and might want, that it should become eternal so that in eternal life we could sit beneathe the majestic branches of the oak. To love the machine we cannot, to espy it in eternity we want not, and at best we but admit its utility. And how tempting is the wish to quit the fateful path of life, leading from the majestic oak to the ugly and stinking machine.

But all this transition from the organicity of the village, from the fragrant vegetation to the mechanicalness of the machine, to its artificial deadness, has to be experienced and lived religiously. In order to resurrect, it is necessary to die, to undergo sacrifice. And the transition from organicity and integral wholeness over to the mechanical and to fragmentation is a suffering and sacrificial path of spirit. And this sacrifice has to be consciously accepted. Through it only is reachable the freedom of the spirit. The machine is a crucifixion of the flesh of the world, a raising up upon the cross the fragrant flowers and singing birds. This -- is the Golgotha of nature. In the irresistible process of the artificial mechanisation of nature is redeemed as it were the sin of inward shackling and discord. The natural organism has to die, in order to resurrect to new life. And here the machine-monstrosities put to death the natural organic wholeness while indirectly, by tortutous paths they set free the spirit from the grips of nature. It has become a commonplace in religious thought, the view that the machine deadens the spirit. But deeper is this truth, that the machine deadens matter and in contrast enables a liberation of spirit. Beyond the materialisation lies concealed a dematerialisation. With the advent of the machine what is deadened in human life is not spirit, but rather flesh, the old synthesis of fleshly life. The heaviness and chaining together of the material world as it were works itself out and passes over into the machine. And from this the world receives relief.

III.

Reactionary romantics, in anguish and fear grasping at a fleetly passing and decaying old organicity, in dread as regards the irreversible processes of life, -- such have no desire to pass through sacrifice, they are incapable of foreswearing the stable and comfortable life of the flesh, they are fearful of the unknown to come. They want to safeguard the old organicity, the old flesh, they strive to hold back the material world from disintegration and dissolution. And how little these people believe in spirit, in its immortality and indestructibility, in its invincibility against the dark powers. The fate of spirit is entrusted by them to antiquated and elementary material forms, from which they fear that spirit will be sundered off. How of little faith are all those that would see the ruination of spirit in the disintegration of the old organic matter. The sons and grandsons of the Slavophils have proven themself suchlike of little faith. Fear in the facing of a new life -- is what has defined their motives.What a pitiful self-delusion it is to see the utmost and best in the backward forms of material life in comparison with forms moreso developed, what a materialism there is to be sensed in this! The religious, the Christian attitude towards life ought sacrificially to accept the death of old Russia, the death of its old flesh, in the name of the resurrection of Russia to new life. The profound depths of Christianity consist in this, to accept and perceive inwardly the whole of life as the mystery of Golgotha and the Resurrection. And all the flesh of the world has to pass through a crucifixion, through the scourging and death. This is death -- for life. But here they tend to say, that a St. Francis is impossible amidst a developed manufacturing industry, amidst the machines and capitalist economy. A St. Francis was possible only amidst a natural and primitive economy, and therefore indeed healthy are the elementary forms of material life, and let there be no developement! But if this be so, then I shall be like the Marxists and draw the following fatal conclusion: St. Francis -- represents the blossoming of a natural economy, and the spirit is but dependent upon economic factours. Wherefore the religious attitude towards life is something ruinous, and concerning the saints it is best altogether not to speak. Or else -- one mustneeds set out alone a different path and admit, that spirit is not dependent upon matter and that the functional connection of spirit and matter on the surface of life, signifies something altogether otherwise inwardly and from the depths. This independence and freedom of spirit has to be discovered by the tortuous path of mechanisation, the machinising of material life. This -- is the path of freedom, of the free living out of all the potentials.

IV.

Initially, everything of the organically fleshly was consecrated and sacred. The religious consecration of fleshly life and its elementary material tools is characteristic to all naturalistic religions, and to Christianity itself in its naturalistic period. Sacred was the plough, by which was broken open the earth. The ground itself was sacred together with the plants and animals and everything in the natural economy. In the initial phase of its developement, mankind could not forge out the economic tools of the struggle for life without a religious sanction. The sense of the sanctity of material life accompanied man everywhere. This consecration of fleshly life and the sense of its divine organicity has not fully forsaken man even in our time. But at the higher stages of historical developement the whole of material life has ceased in fatal a manner to be sacred. Everything has become open to speculation. The machine is not sacred, nor is modern industrialism sacred. It is considered unnecessary to consecrate the machine. Only the organic is felt to be sacred, the mechanical is never sensed as sacred. The secularisation of the entirety of outward life is bound up with the fragmentation and division, with the loss of the primordial organic integral wholeness. The conscious consent to the secularisation of life is a consent to sacrifice, to the renouncing of pretty and lofty illusions. Everything sacred enters inward, into spirit. The reverse side of this de-religious and de-perfuming aspects of life is manifest as a deepening of religiosity and greater an inspiration. Religion ceases to be merely of the fleshly way of life and becomes more spiritual, deeper. Secularisation, just like the machine, kills not the spirit, but rather matter. The process of the machine represents a sundering and working off of material heaviness from spirit, a lightening of spirit. But this lightening up is attainable by those, that survive the nightmare and deadly anguish involved with the machine.

THE FATE OF RUSSIA

That, which was eternal in the oak, in the flowers and the thorns, becomes transformed and dwells in spirit, it preserves its own binding form, freed of material heaviness and enshacklings. But it is impossible to idealise organic nature and its natural order, in which everything is based upon the struggle for existence and dependent upon destruction and devouring. It is impossible to confuse one's own creative insights into the beauty of nature with rather its own natural order. The naturo-organic is not the yet so precious, is not that utmost, which it is necessary to preserve. True life -- is a life created, and not the age-old givenness of life, not the organically elemental, the animal-plant life in nature and in society. Even in the physical organism, struggling for existence in the natural order, there is not an ultimately greater truth, than in the machine. From rather deeper a perspective, both the oak and the machine -- run along the same line. Developement in the material plane happens in the elementary natural organism all the way up to the complexly crafted machine. This -- is the path of the stratification of matter, of its artificial complexification, which leads to a liberation from matter, from the heavy gravity of its organic functions. Humankind has to fearlessly, with a full faith in the indestructibility of its spirit, to pass its way on through material developement, through the machine and technology, and cease seeking its salvation exclusively in the past. Fear and fright concerning the machine represents materialism and a weakness of spirit. The orientation towards the organically elemental past, the idealisation of it, the fear of suffering developement, is cravenness and a love for calm, a laziness of spirit. Only that one attains to freedom of spirit, who obtains it by way of the precious price of a fearless and suffering developement, by the torment of passing through fragmentation and dissolution of the organism, which seemed eternal and so consolingly comfortable. To the old paradise under the old oak there is no return. One cannot return to the more elemental and less tormenting past. The tremendous significance of the appearance of the machine -- consists in this, that it helps ultimately to break with the naturalism in religion. The machine as it were claws out spirit from the loins of natural matter. This process is very tortuous and difficult, much of the joys in life perish in it. And a great faith in the power of spirit is necessary, in order to stand up under this process. Initially it is perceived, as a triumph of matter and ruination of spirit. And only at great depths does this process reach otherwise.

Nicholas Berdyaev

Russia at present is living through a very responsible moment, it stands at a crossroads. What faces it is a sacrificial forsaking of its material organic past, its old form of economy, its old manner of state, which to many still seems organic, but which already has gone to rot at its roots and is decaying. The Russian mindset has to renounce the Slavophil and Populist utopianism and boldly pass onwards to complex developement and to the machine. In Russia there is a mixture of two styles -- of the ascetic and the imperialistic, of the monastic and the mercantile, of forsaking the goods of the world and that of indulging worldly matters and affairs. Such a medley cannot for long continue. If Russia wants to be a great empire and play a role within history, this then incurs upon it the obligation to enter upon the path of material technical developement. Without this resolution Russia will fall into an inescapable position. Only upon this path will the spirit of Russia be set free and reveal its depths.

Translator Postscript

There is particular an irony of fate surrounding N. A. Berdyaev's book, "The Fate of Russia": the peculiar irony of being an untimely book at the immediate moment of its appearance -- no longer relevant, yet timely in its untimely timelessness of insights even for today, for the present, not just for Russia, but for the wider world at large.

Berdyaev's "The Fate of Russia" was published at some point in the year 1918 by the Moscow publisher, G. A. Leman & S. I. Sakharov (Г. А. Леман и С. И. Сахаров) under the Russian title, "Sud'ba Rossii" ("Судьба России"), 240 pages. This work was assigned as № 15 by T. Klepinina in her 1978 IMKA Press "Berdiaev Bibliographie". Some recent years Russian reprints have been 1997 by the Moscow publisher "Сварог и К", 2002 by Moscow publisher "Аст" (1998 Khar'kov publisher "Фолио"), and 2007 by Moscow publisher "Эксмо", among the earlier.

It is helpful here to have a grasp on the backdrop of chronological timelines of the historical dates and events of the period, so easily and readily confusing. The "Great War", WWI, officially ended 11 November in 1918. But Russia dropped out nearly a year earlier. In 1917, Russia suffered two revolutions. The first, the "February Revolution" (22 February O.S.), saw the collapse of the Russian autocracy with the abdication of Tsar Nicholas II, followed by the formation of the Kerensky "Provisional Government" which vowed to continue the war effort. The second 1917 revolution in Russia was the Bolshevik Marxist-Leninist "Great October Revolution" (7 November 1917, N.S.), promising to end Russia's involvement in the world war, officially fulfilled in March 1918 with the "Treaty of Bretsk-Litovsk". And thus, it was only after the 1917 Communist Revolution that Berdyaev's 1918 "The Fate of Russia" book came out in print; apparently at some point before all the free presses were confiscated and closed. It was also in the early months of this same year, 1918, that Berdyaev set about writing his impassioned and fiery tome, -- "The Philosophy of Inequality" (Klepinina № 20), which was published only several years later abroad, i.e. the year after his banishment from Russia. And indeed, "The Philosophy of Inequality" is far different in tone and in scope from our present tome, and well worth reading.

Nicholas Berdyaev

Berdyaev was prolific a writer, a regular contributor of articles to some several journals and literary gazettes of the time, on a range of matters cultural and intellectual. And a number of Berdyaev's books comprise as it were a recycled collection or sbornik of such previously published journal articles. Our present text, "The Fate of Russia", is suchlike a book. It represents a selection of Berdyaev articles previously published in the "war years" 1914-1916, along with several never previously published articles, presumably written also during this period. In our present English edition, the "recycled" articles are footnoted with the info of initial publication along with the relevant "Kl. №".

Why did Berdyaev select the particular articles that he did for inclusion in "The Fate of Russia", -- considering all that he had written during this period.[1] We can imagine that Berdyaev set about his work on compiling "The Fate of Russia" sometime during the turbulent year 1917, during the period of the "Provisional Government", as it attempted to morph into cohesively viable a form amidst fluid a situation.

Berdyaev divides his work into a series of five segments, -- preceded by an introductory warning of a "World Imperiled", with the haunting insight that the war would result in no victors ultimately. Indeed, it led to the turbulent collapse of all the empires involved: the Russian, the German, the Austro-Hungarian, the French, the Turkish, and with the British empire tottering along awhile longer into a replay of the war, leaving it a pale semblance of its former self. A graveyard of empires! And subsequent history has been littered with the bloody horror of its legacy.

The opening article, "The Soul of Russia", originally a pamphlet, serves as an anchor and core to the entire book. It is a profoundly beautiful and moving work, of love for one's native land and its people, all those organic to it, tearfully bewailing its failings, and daring to believe in its stature of potential greatness both within history, and in the eyes of God. In the accompanying articles of this first segment Berdyaev addresses some aspects and issues facing this "Russian Soul". The bitingly satirical

---

[1] For Russian language readers, the massive and comprehensive anthology of Berdyaev 1914-1922 articles became available in 2007 under the book title, -- "Падение священного русского царства: Публицистика 1914-1922" (1179 с.), by Moscow publisher "Издательство Астрель", compiler V. V. Sapov. Our completed English translation of this needs but typing of manuscript to appear in the near future...

"Eternal Baba" article about Rozanov, mocking the placid tea-sipping and gazing out a little window, hits at a certain lack of initiative and irresponsibility, a feminine passivity and lack of masculinity in the Russian character, which Berdyaev oft criticises, leaving matters up to others to worry about (the historical precedent of inviting the Varangians back at the dawn of Russian history). And then too there is the alienation of the intelligentsia stratum from the Russian people, concerned only with its own ideological purview, detached from reality. Russia, in its vast landmass and history comprises a great East-West, in its soul transpires the clash and dichotomy between that of the Mongol Asiatic legacy and that of the Graeco-Roman European, the challenge as Vl. Solov'ev expressed it, to be in the image of Xerxes or of Christ... This vastness of the Russian land, unthinkable to the peoples of the West, was the selfsame endless vastness which so disoriented the armies of Napoleon and Hitler and lured them to their doom. And this selfsame vastness in its backwardness was held together by the Russian autocracy, and later by the Soviet commissars. How accurate Berdyaev's gibe, that it is easier to be a saint than honourable a man, -- indeed, if we are honest, not just for "Russian man", but even moreso for "Christian man" and Christianity in general, humankind in general. Integrity and concepts like honour have been relegated to the meaninglessly obsolete. Dostoevsky's "Grand Inquisitor" has become more sophisticated with time, manipulating "dead souls" at devilish a price. But this is all a volatile subject best left for another time and another place, -- regarding whether one can truly become a saint without being honest with oneself, and with God. An obsolete saying of former times was that, "A man's word was his bond, his surety", but modern rascals have proved them wrong...

The third segment contrasts the souls of several other Western peoples to that of the Russian. The French, the German, the Polish -- a kindred Slavic people yet disparate to the Russian, in its soul and in its messianism...

The second section explores the now touchy subject of nation, of nationalism, which under Hitler assumed rabid a form. Yet the question remains, -- dare one love one's country, one's native land, or is patriotism an obsolete emotion? The events of our modern world increasingly situate us betwixt a sort of Scylla and Charybdis on this: on the one hand, a narrow-minded provincialism of outlook that at its extreme can border on smug xenophobic hatred, and on the other hand, a smugly insipid cosmopolitanism that at its extreme stands for nothing and respects nothing, in its vapid hollowness. The concept of nation is thus at present an indelicate subject. In Russian, two different words typically get translated as "nation": "*natsiya*" -- which seems a Western loan-word directly borrowed, and "*narod*", -- which also tends to mean "the people" (in contrast to the word "*liudi*", meaning just "people"). Berdyaev, along with the Slavophils, holds to an organic concept of "the people", the "narod". The Russian root-word "*rod*" indicates kinship or affinity, and thus "*rodina*" indicates one's native-land, the affinity with "one's people" and its culture (in pervasive a sense). Contrary to the rabid form assumed under Hitler, wherein a people's culture (and soul) are determined "by blood", the culture of a given people would seem to reflect a range of consciousness, largely affected by the dynamics within the language that coheres that given culture. Too little attention has been given to the affective dynamics of various languages that contribute to the uniqueness of their cultures, the linguistic quirks, the nuances and idiomatic forms and inner grammatic rules primordially derived, entering into a national temperament and conceptual vocabulary. Orwell's "Newspeak" represents a frightful example of this in reverse, -- by eliminating "dangerous words" society is cleansed of "dangerous ideas". One experiences this dynamism characteristic to language by exposure to "foreign languages". Philology has become a neglected discipline. A personal example: to deliver the Paschal Liturgy Gospel (Jn.1:1-17) in intrepidly and triumphantly a manner -- in German, is an oratorical delight, since the German tongue lends itself especially well for this; in Church Slavonic, it is a profound spiritual delight; in churchly Latin and Greek it is a vivid conceptual delight; in English, well, a decent translation helps... A nation, sharing a common language, may comprise a number of compatible sub-cultures that happily co-exist as part of a larger culture and consciousness. And people do emigrate and assimilate into a different culture and its consciousness via the benefit of the common language, as was classically the case with the United States.

Our English word "nation" currently is rather oblique as regards its root-word meaning, but seems to be derived from the Latin, suggestive of "*nasci*: to be born of", and hence seems correlative to Russian "narod", as implicitly the place and people of one's birth. In ancient Greece, this was localised in the city-state, although our modern world has become much more mobile and extensive in this regard. Similarly, our much abused word "patriotism" also derives from Latin a root, that of "*pater*", meaning "*father*". It was nowise a mere matter of caprice, of mere chance, that Christ, in His Sermon on the Mount, opened the words of the most famous prayer in all Christendom with the profound words, "*Pater Noster*", i.e. "Our Father". Christian social thought has largely missed the extreme relevance of this, the great significance of this, which has contributed to the increasing irrelevance of Christianity within society.

As previously mentioned, Berdyaev, in sharing Slavophil insights, holds to an "*organic*" view of society and "the people". The word "organic" nowadays is much in vogue and is considered indicative of an healthy "lifestyle", one reliant upon the "natural". But for Berdyaev and the Slavophils, what marks "organic" a perception of "the people", as nation? It is not limited to the myopic view of merely the currently living generation of the Russian people, the French people, the American people. Rather, it involves a responsible consciousness of the generations past, of their historical legacy to the current generation, as well as to the future generations yet to come, to whom, like it or not, we bequeathe some sort of legacy in turn, hopefully decent and good. Thus, all the generations of a nation and a people are involved in common a task, common an endeavour -- as suggested by N. F. Fedorov's "Philosophy of the Common Task". By sharing in a society, we are part of that society, even if individually we choose to "cop-out". There is a genetic sort of parallel to the organic inheritance of legacy between generations, just as there is for the individual. None of us is instantaneously self-begotten, and few likely are begotten of a "test-tube" without parentage and the culture that finds its voice in the underlying psyche of its language.

Strange, is it not, that the Russian word for responsibility, "otvetstvennost'", should have as its root the word "otvet'", -- meaning "answer", signifying "responsibility" as "answerability". How quaint, and how different from the modern practice of "passing the buck", and blaming others and other factours, one's formative environment, whatever...

Implicit in Berdyaev's organic view of the "narod", the nation as a people, is the aspect of answerable responsibility, of integrity and integrality, not merely to the currently living generation, but also generations past and future. There is a curious thread, too little noted, that runs through many of Berdyaev's writings, that calls for an active sense of shared responsibility, so modernly untypical, of our own guilt and culpability, our own sin, and the need to repent thereof, in attempting to heal the past. In the Gethsemane Passion and Cross of Christ were redeemed all the sins of the world; in bearing our own personal cross we share in that salvific deed of Our Lord, when like Simon of Cyrenia, we show responsibility in assisting others to bear their cross, both as regards the past, the present and the future.

If the opening words of Christ's famous prayer, the "Our Father", are not empty words, an hollow intonation, then what does that impute of us, what does that imply of us? We are enjoined to seek our perfection as sons and daughters of the "MostHigh". This perception of the Lord God as "Our Father" is the fundamental connective theme throughout Christ's "Sermon on the Mount" (Mt. 5-7). The responsibility is incumbent upon us to act accordingly, as would any proper son or daughter of nobly high a lineage, -- jealous of and zealous for the dignity of one's ancestry and good name. History of course is replete with examples of degeneracy in offspring, but we are speaking here not of privileged decline and foppery, rather instead of a "proper" son or daughter of their father, seeking glory in the eyes of one's father and forefathers, in their eternal memory and good name. And from religious and linguistic a perspective, "Orthodoxy" in context of "Pravoslavie" connotes a meaning of "Rightful Glory". On human a level, we love our parents, not because they shower us with toys, but because of the natal bond: we rejoice with them at their successes, and weep with them at failings, and conversely, in "normal" a world. The devotion of a free-born proper son or daughter is quite different from that of the hired-hand, the mercenary, the craven slave (too often exhibiting the resentissement discerned by Nietzsche). Christ provides us a notorious example of this in a Vineyard Parable (Mt. 21:33ff.), where wicked hirelings first abuse and murder the servants sent out by the master and finally also his son, in their desire to steal for themself the inheritance. For modern a world, this parable should serve moreso as an admonition for Christian sobriety of mind, rather than an Anti-Semitic calumny of deicide against the Jews, since the first generation of Christians was exclusively of Jewish stock...

The fidelity of hired-hands and mercenaries extends basically only to observance of the contractual laws and rules agreed upon, in anticipation of their contracted due. Of course, employees may develop a sense of loyalty to an employer that follows a "smart business practice" of rewarding and retaining them as "valued employees", a trend too rapidly disappearing. But the basic bottom line is still the bottom line for both ends. There is truth to the old saying, "blood is thicker than water"". For both bad and good, since the enmity that sometimes arises in families has its archetype in Cain and Abel. In the Orthodox Church there is a distinct rank of Saints, commemorated as "UnMercenaries", too little noticed or commented upon. But which begs the question, -- is it possible to have an unmercenary attitude and love towards God? Even perhaps also a dangerous question...

But Berdyaev's patrological fidelity to former generations crashes up against the modern societal reality, a reality that disdains any bond with the past and in especially the popular culture is too often "fatherless". How can a would-be dutiful son or daughter attain to such, in the absence of the role-model love of a "proper father", instead being shown no parental commitment by abandoning them. This is increasingly a societal problem, leading to an increase of social pathologies. The family and marriage have always been on the "endangered list", all the way back to Adam and Eve, but modernly moreso, in a self-perpetuating and growing cycle. There are of course marriages that deserve to be ended, especially in abusive relationships. Even so-called "successful marriages" can be stressful on everyone involved, hopefully towards the building of character. But in failed relationships everyone is left emotionally scarred, with subconscious psychological traumas; it is as though viewing the aftermath of a battlefield, strewn with the wounded, left neglected. What held marriages and families together in the past was moreso a passive observance of religious and civil laws amidst societal frowns, the weight of which has largely dissipated. Berdyaev's perspective, on the contrary, is not passive, but rather pro-active, "responsible", doing what is right because it is right, not merely some capricious law. A torrent of capricious laws engulfs everyone, seeking to shame everyone into an acquiescent attitude as though scripted by Dostoevsky's Shigalev. Berdyaev's pro-active stance underlies all his "new religious consciousness", his unmercenary sense of decorous modesty proper to a knightly-chivalrant "spiritual aristocratism", which without adequate perception must seem merely quaint. Again, unless there is initially a father present to bestow an example of paternal love to begin with, it is almost nigh impossible for a son to reciprocate with filial a love; it must start with the "father" (this could stand as an argument also in support of the Orthodox position on the "filioque" controversy). And indeed, there is something truly heroic with parents "who soldier through to the end" to sustain their families, preserving a true spark of mutual love

Nicholas Berdyaev

for each the other, amidst the "empty nest" (likewise also a troubling societal challenge).

The conscious blindness towards kindred generations past and future, in the mad scramble by a current generation to secure its "daily bread", is caught up in a sociological world-view and its ideologies, in contrast to an approach motivated by cosmic and historical an horizon. In Berdyaev's perspective, a people and its nation may possess a messianic awareness, evidenced by a great culture to be shared amidst the mix of nations, with its vocation and purpose in the eyes of God, although this can become corrupted and perverted, demonically so. This differs however from imperialism, a word modernly gone out of favour, but continuing nonetheless under different expressions. WWI proved to be a graveyard of empires, as mentioned previously, but out of the ashes arose new empires, ideological and economic powers, as with the United States and the Far East and elsewhere. An empire represents an amalgam of nations, held together by conquest either by sword or by monied interests, for which it provides the benefit of a common language and the relative stability and peace of a "Pax Romanorum". The economic colonialism underlying imperialism, draining the spoils of conquest to provide for the surfeit of the centre, over long years plants the seeds that will sap the vigour and prove to the ultimate demise of the empire, and the rise of something different. Thus it was when the Roman Republic imploded into the Roman Empire, and over the course of centuries collapsed into the Dark Ages, under the torrent of successive waves of barbarian peoples, superficially having become assimilated into becoming Latins of a sort in tongue and name, but not in soul, in the spirit of a deeper antiquity. In recent centuries all of Europe has briefly come under tyrannical a grip, the first time under Napoleon, the second under Hitler, with Britain the outlier both times. And at present, Germany by its economic might seems to have succeeded where previously it failed in two world wars; yet there remain tensions whether European nation-states have truly become obsolete. Added to this is a massive influx of barbarian peoples from destabilised places across the world, a barbarism characterised by a primitively degrading view on woman and hesitant to assimilate into Western cultural concepts of tolerance. Added to the rot from within, all this seems to spell the veritable "End of Europe" and its cultural legacy, -- a pessimistic premonition shared by both Spengler and Berdyaev.

242

Which brings us to the fourth section of our present book, -- regarding war. It is maddening to try to justify war from Christian a perspective, it seems sacrilegious that so-called Christian peoples should war upon each other, a blasphemy against the God of Love. For civilised men, the shedding of the blood of one's fellow man is incongruous and unthinkable, save in direst extremity of self-defense, or at least in the defense of hapless others. Moderns recoil even from the bloody business of killing the chicken that will grace their dinner table, leaving the dirty work to unseen others. And this is increasingly the same with modern warfare, at times profitable a "blood-money" business, where the enemy is killed distantly with the push of a button as in a computer game, and it is only the unseen others as soldiers at the front who directly see the carnage and mayhem wreaked, directly facing an enemy that seeks to maim and murder them. In modern parlance there has arisen the demonically inspired phrase, "collateral damage", as though to dehumanise these victims and casualties of war.

Yet despite all the horrors in war and all the pyrrhic victories achieved by war, mankind continues to indulge in war, even a nominally Christian mankind. Obviously, there is the valid element of self-defense, defending one's near and dear against rapine and pillage, against those that threaten death by murder. But what is it that sets in motion these escalating cycles of violence, that erupts into the blood-lust for war? It seems as though a devilish game, manipulated by unseen grinning demons, played out towards inevitability. And yet it is one of the mechanisms by which nations survive, or fall. We too often see an hint of this grimace of the demonic in the distorted faces of the angry mob, convulsed with impending a blood-lust.

The fear of untimely death, the submerged trauma over the finality to life, when thus laid bare, as though shocks us awake from the fog and tedium of the everyday pursuit of "daily bread", plunges us howsoever briefly onto different a plane of consciousness, projects the individual onto the plane of the meta-individual. Berdyaev notes this aspect.

Berdyaev quite validly points out the incongruity of Christianity, of Christ's teachings in the Gospel, to resolve this. Berdyaev notes that Christ's teachings about the Kingdom of God relate to different a plane, to the sphere of the absolute, which has not yet come to full fruition, is impossible of full fruition in our world as it is, as though tangled in a web, and all transpiring upon the plane of the relative. Indeed, we might point out, were the Kingdom of God conformable to our present world, there would be no further need of Caesar, no need for proscriptive laws and coercion and force...

This insight of Berdyaev into the absolute character of the morality preached by Christ, in contrast to the difficulty of applying it within the relative character and context of our world, is an important point. And of course, the morality of Christ is normative, as is ultimately the absolute plane. And yet, at times it seems as though Christ seeks deliberately to muddle matters, with His absolute inner dialectic of perception. Sometimes, just like with the "Miraculous Draught of Fishes", it is needful to "go deep", to wrestle with the enigmatic, rather than scratching but superficial the surface. Consider, by way of example: every scoundrel and his cousin knows well the Gospel adage, "Judge not, lest ye be judged" (Mt. 7: 1-2); yet how few seem ever to have heard or been cognizant of its seeming contrary admonition, its apparent antinomy: "Judge not by appearances, but judge righteous a judgement" (Jn. 7: 24). Most everyone has heard some variant of the Beatitude, "Blessed are the peacemakers (Latin "*pacifici*"), for they shall be called the sons of God" (Mt. 5: 9); yet how does this square with Christ's assertion, that "I have come to bring *not peace, but the sword*" (Mt. 10: 34; "*не мир, но меч*"). Or consider the seeming inner contradiction of "suffering the soul's perishing in order to save it" (Mt. 10: 39; Mk. 8: 35), when properly translated (the Latin/Greek "anima/ψυχη" means "soul", but most English translations incorrectly provide more superficial a rendering as "life"). This example reflects a dialectical convergence of seeming antinomies, in that the Cross, the symbol of death and suffering, bearing one's cross, becomes rather the source of life eternal beyond death, just as more clearly Christ's parable of the example of the seed that perishes to sprout forth more abundantly with life (Jn. 12: 24)...

Far more enigmatic is Christ's admonition in the Sermon on the Mount: "*non resistere malo*; resist not evil" (Mt. 5: 39). This was once a widely known saying, unlike the present. It inspired Thoreau and Gandhi in the concept of "Civil Disobedience", although quite the tragedy is that often yesterday's oppressed become tomorrow's oppressors... In context, it is difficult enough to forego the desire for revenge, to turn the other cheek, *to love one's enemies*... On the one hand, those resisting and fighting evil in the name of the good often themself resort to evil and tend to become evil in the final end, which Berdyaev discusses at greater length in his later book, "The Destiny of Man". Yet great saints in their ascetic exploits would seem to be contending against evil, fighting and resisting evil, or else the manner of their asceticism is different from what it seems, on the surface. On deep a level, at the uttermost spiritual depths of our soul, struggling at times with periods of "God-forsakenness", if we "resist not evil", how then do we not surrender to evil, give in to evil, become ourself evil? It is a verymost profound and serious question, that no one nowadays seems bothered to try to answer. Perhaps a key rests in Christ's Prayer on the Cross: "My God, My God, wherefore hast Thou forsaken Me?". Perhaps it reflects the fact, contrary to appearances, that it is not we that save our soul, else Christ would have died on the Cross in vain, as St Paul alludes. Perhaps, in the beclouded mystical dynamics involved, we are called not to mere goodness, but rather to the perfection that is of God Our Father (Mt. 5: 48)...

The fifth and final segment of Berdyaev's "Fate of Russia" centres round the issue of "Democracy and the Person", amidst the flux of politics and the conventional lie, in its variant forms. As with everything in life, "the devil is always in the details". Democracy, howsoever noble the ideal, can readily degenerate into a tyranny of the majority, the mob, a tyranny of the many in place of the tyranny of one. Indeed, democracy may be moreso a tyranny of the loudest, of monied special interests, rather than the actual majority, busy pursuing the "daily bread". In mass society, the person drowns in an ocean of conformity, becomes an isolated atom cast about aimlessly within the societal flux, an economic statistic, a nameless number, a readily replaceable cog bereft of uniqueness, with no place to truly fit in. We live increasingly in a "throw-away" society, yet how vile it is to regard the human person as mere trash...

In summation, the musings of old men, such as the present translator, may seem at times to meander and ramble about far afield from what Berdyaev discusses. The best remedy for this is to read the book, Berdyaev's own words, and let Berdyaev speak for himself -- directly to the reader. Our continuing effort at translation of "primary works" by Berdyaev and other significant figures of Russian religio-philosophic thought reflects clearly this desire. However, aspects of points and issues that Berdyaev discusses may be more obvious to some, and yet not so obvious to quite many others. We each apperceive Berdyaev through the refractive prism of our own formative history, which of course differs from that of Berdyaev's own intellectual and spiritual "formation", whether as regards span of major historical events, language, religion, societal approach, etc. Moreover, a reading of Berdyaev's early works provides insights into the maturation of his significant motifs -- in our present text that of "Russia", immediately prior to Soviet Communism, and very significant now for a "post-Communist" Russia charting new paths of its vocation within the world: anew the choice between Christ or Xerxes. We in the West, increasingly ashamed of Christ, face also this dangerous choice. Our present text reflects as though the waning precious light of day, just before the onset of the nightmare darkness of a long convulsed night. It is during the early hours of this nightmare that Berdyaev pens his fiery book, "The Philosophy of Inequality", so radically different in tone and thought from his present "Fate of Russia". We invite the reader to peruse both, which remain significant of insight, not only as regards Russia past and present, but for all our modern world. Our choice too is that of Christ or Xerxes...

21 September 2016

Fr. S. Janos

frsj Publications

1.) **N. A. BERDYAEV** "*The Philosophy of Inequality*"
   1st English Translation of Berdyaev's 1918/1923 book,
   "*Filosofia neravenstva*" (Kl. № 20).
   (ISBN-13: 9780996399203 / ISBN-10: 0996399208)
   406 pages (6/4/15)

2.) **N. A. BERDYAEV** "*The Spiritual Crisis of the Intelligentsia*"
   1st English Translation of Berdyaev's 1910 book,
   "*Dukhovnyi krizis intelligentsii*" (Kl. № 4).
   (ISBN-13: 9780996399210 / ISBN-10: 0996399216)
   346 pages (6/19/15)

3.) **FR. ALEKSANDR MEN'** "*Russian Religious Philosophy:*
   1989-1990 Lectures" -- 1st English Translation
   Published in 25th Year Commemoration of Fr Men' Memory
   (ISBN-13: 9780996399227 / ISBN-10: 0996399224)
   214 pages   (7/14/15)

4.) **E. SKOBTSOVA (MOTHER MARIA)**
   "*The Crucible of Doubts: Khomyakov, Dostoevsky, Solov'ev,*
   In Search of Synthesis -- Four 1929 Works".
   (ISBN-13: 9780996399234 / ISBN-10: 0996399232)
   166 pages (5/20/16) 1st English Translation

5.) **N. A. BERDYAEV** "*The Fate of Russia*"
   1st English Translation of Berdyaev's 1918 book,
   "*Sud'ba Rossii*". (Kl. № 15).
   (ISBN-13: 9780996399241 / ISBN-10: 0996399240)
   250 pages (10/1/16)

Nicholas Berdyaev

*   *   *

Forthcoming Works in Preparation:

N. A. BERDYAEV "*Aleksei Stepanovich Khomyakov*"
1st English Translation of Berdyaev's 1912 book,
"*Алексей Степанович Хомяков*" (Kl. № 6).

**N. A. BERDYAEV "*Sub Specie Aeternitatis:*
Essays Philosophic, Social and Literary (1900-1906)".**
1st English Translation of Berdyaev's 1907 book,
"*Sub specie aeternitatis. Опыты философские, социальные
и литературные (1900-1906 гг.)*". (Kl. № 3).

www.ingramcontent.com/pod-product-compliance
Lightning Source LLC
Chambersburg PA
CBHW071856090426
42811CB00004B/631